THE HISTORY OF
LAST NIGHT'S
DREAM

THE HISTORY OF LAST NIGHT'S DREAM

Discovering the Hidden Path to the Soul

RODGER KAMENETZ

HarperOne
An Imprint of HarperCollinsPublishers

HarperOne

Jacob's Dream by Jusepe de Ribera is reproduced by permission of Scala/Art Resource, NY.
Vitruvian Man by Leonardo da Vinci is reproduced by permission of Alinari/
Art Resource, NY.

HarperCollins books may be purchased for educational, business, or sales promotional
use. For information please write: Special Markets Department, HarperCollins Publishers,
10 East 53rd Street, New York, NY 10022.

HarperCollins Web site: http://www.harpercollins.com

HarperCollins®, 📖 ®, and HarperOne™ are
trademarks of HarperCollins Publishers.

FIRST HARPERCOLLINS PAPERBACK EDITION PUBLISHED IN 2008

Library of Congress Cataloging-in-Publication Data is available.
ISBN: 978–0–06–123794–2

08 09 10 11 12   RRD(H)   10 9 8 7 6 5 4 3 2 1

IN MEMORY OF MY FATHER

Lately, I've been re-reading psychology books and I have felt singularly defrauded. All of them discuss the mechanisms of dreams or the subjects of dreams, but they do not mention, as I had hoped, that which is so astonishing, so strange— the fact of dreaming.

—JORGE LUIS BORGES

Contents

PART 1   IMAGES

1   The Descent into Dreams   3
New Orleans, January 2007

2   The Gate of Heaven in Newton, Massachusetts   15
Newton, November 1995

3   Colette and the Waking Dream   27
Jerusalem, Summer 1995

4   Kitchen Kabbalah and the Vault of Images   37

5   The Little Shocks   42

6   The Case of the Disappearing Dream   50

7   A Convention of Dreamers   54
Berkeley, June 2003

PART 2   INTERPRETATIONS

8   Marc Bregman and a Punch in the Gut   63
Morrisville, Vermont, June 2001

9   The Book of K de G   73

10   You Are a Dead Man   80
Dumuzi and Abimelech

11   Jacob, the Hero of the Revelation Dream   86

12   Joseph the Dreamer and Joseph the Interpreter   92

13   The Untimely Disappearance of the Dream   98
Numbers and Deuteronomy

14   The Rabbis Ameliorate the Dream   102

15   Peter Sees a Dream, and Jews and Christians Part Ways   108

16   The Gnostic Heresy and the Mystical Dream Journey   114

17   Sigmund and Irma   122
      The Secret of Dreams Revealed

18   The Two Belly Buttons   129

19   Blind Spots Removed While You Wait, and
      the Book of K de G Speaks   139

20   How Dreams Abolish Time, and
      the Secret of K de G at Last   148

PART 3   DREAMS

21   The Three Gifts of the Dream   157

22   Lost and Wandering Dreams   161
      The Predicament

23   The Opposition: Gravel Grandma   166

24   The Opposition: Freud's Staircase Dream   174

25   The Orphanage Dream   182
      The Situation of the Soul

26   Becoming the Boy   189
      The Pins and the Desert

27   A Very Important Person   198

28   The Male VIP   205
      The Second Gift of the Dream

29   Jung's Descent into the World of Dreams   211

30   Marc Bregman Meets the Animus   220

31   Return of the Orphanage Dream   225
      The Father Archetype

32   North of Eden   230

Acknowledgments   241
Notes   245
Bibliography   253
Index   257
PLUS   263

1

IMAGES

Of You my heart said, Seek My face;
Your face, O Lord, will I seek!

—PSALM 27:8

Chapter 1

THE DESCENT INTO DREAMS

New Orleans, January 2007

Awhole world inside us is asleep. We wake to it but rarely.

We glimpse and barely remember. Or we don't understand what we've seen.

A third of our time on earth we've spent sleeping, with little to show: an image, a face. Only rarely does a dream come that wakes us to ourselves.

Will our lives someday be forgotten as we have forgotten our dreams?

I know there is a conscious mind and an unconscious. But I don't always think about what that implies—that more than half of who I am and what I am is completely unknown to me, except in fragments and glimpses, images and dreams.

Is it possible that all we don't know about ourselves includes also the most important thing? That our self-knowledge is trivial by comparison, and yet we use only our conscious awareness to guide our lives? And so we miss receiving great gifts that have been waiting for us all along.

To receive these gifts, we must learn how to dream, which sounds easy enough. But I mean dreaming with a purpose, learning to use dreaming as a way to depth. That proved difficult, at least for me.

I had to make a wayward pilgrim's progress to the dream because I had so much to unlearn—and I am a slow unlearner. The progress falls into three parts, which I've titled "Images," "Interpretations," and "Dreams."

First I had to learn the true power of images. Then I had to unlearn the ancient reflexes of interpretation. Only then could I explore the world of dreams.

In part one of this book I introduce my first teacher, an eighty-seven-year-old Algerian-born mystic living in Jerusalem whom we students called Colette.

My encounter with this powerful personality was a once-in-a-lifetime adventure full of strange, hilarious, and sometimes harrowing incidents, like the time she tried to lengthen my arms an extra inch. But she taught me the valuable ancient practice of directed waking dreams. This practice reverses the flow of ordinary thought, taking words back to images. By this reversing, I understood for myself, as she often said, that "images are sovereign in the mind."

Part one, then, deals with one obstacle to dreams, which is the habit of thinking in words; part two concerns the habit of interpretation, which is another barrier. I introduce Marc Bregman, my teacher of dreams as Colette was my teacher of images. We struggled together over a puzzling dream about reading a book, a huge blue book that seemed to be a commentary on Genesis. Before I could fully enter the realm of dreams, it seems, I had to unlearn the habit of interpretation. This habit is so thickly and deeply rooted in ancient history and religion and modern psychology that it feels like the only and natural response to dreams. But there is another approach to dreams, and this is what I needed to learn.

So in part two of my wayward progress, I dig up the roots of interpretation in Genesis and follow them where they lead: to the influential dream theories of the rabbinic sages and Church Fathers, all the way to Freud. I learned for myself how in every age, interpretation has repressed the power of the dream.

Only then could Marc Bregman teach me to undo interpretation and enter directly into the world of dreams, the journey explored in the third part of this book. Here he proved as shamanic a master as a contemporary American can be who wears red flannel shirts and hunts moose and drives a Chevy Avalanche.

What I experienced in dreams became not only real for me, but the touchstone for what is real.

But to explain that paradox more clearly, I have to back up and give a brief spiritual and personal history of who I was when I met him.

To all appearances I was awake the summer afternoon I first met Marc Bregman. But I was also unconscious in important ways. I had no awareness of my true predicament in life, though my dreams would soon demonstrate it vividly.

All I knew was, I needed a fresh start. Three frustrating years of work on a book project had ended in failure. It was a book about religion, and a major impasse was that I no longer felt sure in the truths I was writing about. The gap between what I wanted to believe and what I felt inside was wide; the empty space between belief and feeling troubled me.

I am very comfortable with words and metaphors, with books and ideas. I enjoy explicating religious doctrine. I love the stories and the stories about the stories, the commentaries and the traditions. But in the back of my mind, disquiet whispered: What if all this talk is about nothing? What if it isn't real?

I was not raised in a religious home. My extended family were good people; we loved our roots and tradition. The rituals we did were all about family, and warmth, and being together. Our grandparents had traded the Old World for the New, and they'd brought with them the warmth and the family closeness but had left the piety behind.

My family did not pray in a crisis; we worried. Our faith was in ourselves: in what we could see with our eyes and touch with our hands, in hard work, and, for the children, in school. Education was everything: with education you could become a doctor, a lawyer; you could be somebody. We were striving to fulfill the American promise: it was a story our grandparents began by immigrating, and we were completing it with our little triumphs. It was all very practical and obvious. This was how we lived.

I don't recall God being taken seriously in anyone's mouth.

I wasn't gifted with a simple faith, like the man my father told me about once who never prayed in the community: while others worshipped, he walked in the park and talked to God.

My interest in religious consciousness came in my adult life, and it was an anomaly among my family and most of my friends. It came through certain teachers I'd met, and those I've written about. A lot of it came from books.

I once had a very pious friend. He observed all the rules; he prayed every day. One morning, while praying, he realized he was talking to a wall. That was the end of the religious life for him.

If God isn't real to you, then the rest—the rituals, the traditions, the beliefs—are empty.

And how can you personally know that God is real? The books can't help with that one. How can you make the connection?

Up in the sky, down on the earth, in a human face . . . where exactly do we look for God? I admired simple faith, but I was low on it. After so many years of schooling, my mind was too restless to stop at a simple truth. For me, it had to be a complicated truth, the kind I found in religious books and commentaries and commentaries on commentaries, where too often I got lost in words.

· · ·

When I met the dream teacher, Marc Bregman, in his home in northern Vermont, I didn't know what I was doing. I was just poking around looking at dreams because dreams had inspired me in the past, and I felt in need of inspiration.

I thought maybe if I spoke to Bregman about dreams, eventually this gruff, astounding character might become a curious footnote to my erudite history of dreams. I had no idea where dreams themselves would lead me.

Five years later I'm still making the descent into dreams that I began with him that day. I call it a descent because that is where dreams take me, down and in. Deeper and inward. I am still going down into my dreams, still learning new lessons every morning from last night's revelation.

The very first steps are difficult, for once you accustom yourself to their language, dreams reveal you to yourself with a sure and deadly accuracy.

In my dreams, I saw my life stripped of its defenses and its pretensions. I saw my tangled emotions and assumptions, where I was blocked, and, most powerfully, where I did harm. My education in dreams radically reopened all my most intimate relationships.

In time, dreams took me deeper, below the layer of conscious and subconscious emotions and feelings, to another place. I had to change profoundly to go where the dreams wanted to take me. But as this new dreamscape opened up, I had experiences that live at the core of all religions.

Before this descent into dreams, I'd read about religion in books. Now I knew where the books came from.

In dreams all the old religious quests and dramas are vividly real, including that most ancient and impossible mystical quest, to see the face of God. A quest, more than any other, where the image and the word collide.

Even as a child I never dreamed of seeing God. But my friend David, the stockbroker, did.

"It was just like I was talking to a friend in my living room," he told me.

Unfortunately there was one catch: David couldn't remember anything God said to him. He told me, though, "God is a good listener."

—Did you see God's face?

No, it was weird, David said. I was looking at myself talking to God, but all I could see from where I was, was God's back.

—And your face?

Right.

—You saw yourself talking to God?

Yeah.

—But you couldn't see his face?

Nope.

Why was David's dream so odd? Why two Davids? One David talks to God, while the second David looks on at the scene. The David who talks to God—we don't know what he sees. The second David sees the first David's face—but from where he's standing, he can only see God's back.

A dream of two Davids! Bizarre, yet it captures perfectly all our contemporary ambivalence about God. We yearn and we doubt.

We yearn to talk to God as a friend—but the God we can actually believe in is too vague or abstract to talk to. We want to see God as a loving father or a generous mother—but the God of our belief has no gender. We want to see God's face, but our God has no face; we want to be seen, but our God has no eyes. God has become so remote and absent, so theoretical and vague, there's nothing human left.

The pioneering psychologist of religion J. B. Pratt tells the story of a prayer meeting in a small New England village. The pastor asked those present to describe their idea of God. One deacon piped up: "I see a kind of oblong blur."[1]

How do you open your heart to an oblong blur?

Every Western tradition, Jewish, Christian, or Muslim, teaches us about this perfect God of "the oblong blur"—the Unknowable, the Invisible, the Infinite, the Absolute. This is the God of philosophy and reason, a God that answers our intellectual requirements. Aristotle named it the "Prime Mover" and St. Thomas Aquinas, the "First Cause." In the *Star Wars* movies, it's "the Force." A long tradition of heartfelt prayer has come down to this: "May the Force be with you."

Distilled from sacred books, commentaries, doctrine, and logic, our religions of the word have given us a perfect abstract God of the word. No wonder David dreamed of talking to a God whose face he can never see.

Whenever we think of getting "close to God"—a common phrase full of paradox and ironies—we encounter a detour. Instead of struggling with ourselves, we struggle with our beliefs and traditions.

That's because for most of us, revelation is history. It's something in the past that happened to someone else; it's never last night's dream. We don't know how to look inward, so we look up to religious authority, or into sacred books.

That's how I reacted to David's dream. It recalled a story in Exodus, and I wondered if he knew it. But David told me he'd never read it.

Exodus tells its tale on an epic scale: an entire people are freed from slavery, wander in the desert, and receive revelation at Sinai. Cecil B. DeMille had it right in *The Ten Commandments:* a cast of thousands, huge miracles, the shores of the Red Sea, a vast wilderness, and awesome mountain peaks.

But in the midst of this grand epic comes a very poignant spiritual encounter after the noisy debacle of the Golden Calf. The people have failed Moses, and now in a moment of anguish he returns alone to Sinai and asks for one reassurance: to see God's face. But he is told, No, you can only see my back.

David's dream and Moses' story suggest how the desire for intimacy with God runs up against an intrinsic limitation. You can talk to God, but you can't see God's face.

David's dream resolves this dilemma neatly by splitting the dreamer into two Davids: one who talks to God but doesn't see God; and one who sees, but only God's back.

In the same way, the biblical text splits in contradictions as the narrative approaches this paradox of seeing the invisible.

So we read in this same episode of Exodus that "the Lord spoke to Moses face to face, as a man speaks to his friend." Nine verses later, though, the Lord tells Moses, "You can not see my face; for no man shall see me and live" (Exod. 33:11, 20).

Which is it? Can you or can't you speak to God face-to-face? Of course the tradition supplies many interpretations to explain this difficulty away, but such a blatant contradiction still feels like a rough seam in the text. The desire is very human: to know God face-to-face means to know ultimate reality as a "you" and not an "it."

But then the word, the dogma, the theology intervenes and says: no. *No one can see my face.* The final word comes in Deuteronomy when the story of Sinai is retold. Here it is emphasized that at the grand revelation at Sinai, you "saw no form, you only heard a voice" (Deut. 4:12).

Deuteronomy speaks here on behalf of a religion of the word—which is the direction Judaism took. Except in the eyes of certain mystics, the image of God's face became an impossibility, and this appeals to reason: God, whatever God is, must be ultimately unknowable, invisible, beyond all human imagining. Certainly beyond all seeing.

But why is the voice favored over the form? If the problem is that God is beyond the human, then isn't imagining a God who speaks just as anthropomorphic as imagining a God with a face? This decided favoritism of word over image runs very deep in Western thinking. The image must be very powerful to require so much repression.

That's why, instead of speaking strictly about "religions of the word" in the West, it makes more sense to speak of *religions of the struggle between the image and the word.*

This same struggle underlies the history of dream and interpretation right up to last night's dream.

The struggle between word and image begins in Genesis, and smolders in the seams of the biblical text. It flares up regularly in all three monotheistic traditions with violent intensity.

For millennia, in the name of the word, book-wielding fanatics of all three faiths have smashed holy statues, destroyed ancient icons, and killed the people who worship them. It's Jews versus pagans, Muslims versus Hindus, Christians versus Christians. From the Hebrew invasion of Canaan in the tenth century B.C.E. to the Muslim invasion of India in the tenth century C.E., from the struggles in the Byzantine Church of the eighth century to the Thirty Years' War of the sixteenth, this violence erupts periodically. Something about the image drives people of the word mad. As recently as 2006, cartoon images of the Prophet Muhammad sparked riots all over the Muslim world, the torching of embassies, and multiple deaths. Closer to home, we also see it in the jostling of symbols in the public square, where crèches battle giant menorahs in our annual December dilemma. The battle between the word and the image is still going strong.

It's a struggle within each individual mind as well. There it affects the core of how we think and feel. Artists and writers know this struggle well. George Orwell, in his powerful essay "Politics and the English Language," warns that if a writer "is not seeing a mental image of the objects he is naming . . . he is not really thinking."

Yet unless we pay special attention, as Colette taught me to do, words so dominate our thoughts that we lose awareness of the life of images within us, churning like a mighty fountain just below the surface of waking consciousness.

The religious significance of the dominance of the word over the image comes down to this: the God I can imagine, I can't believe in; the God

I can believe in, I can't imagine. For, as the etymology suggests, *to imagine* means, at root, "to see an image."

What does it mean to have no acceptable images of God? Let me put it slightly differently: What does it mean to lose all imagination of God?

One group of people who wrestled seriously with this question were the earliest teachers of rabbinic Judaism, who came to prominence in Babylon and the land of Israel in the first three centuries of the common era. They are known sometimes as "the rabbis," and sometimes as "the rabbinic sages," or simply "the sages."

In the period that followed the fall of the Second Temple at the hands of the Romans in 70 c.e., the sages felt that all was lost. Jerusalem was laid waste; the people were scattered into exile. Worst of all, the Temple was destroyed, the place that in Hebrew is called "where God dwells." God was, in effect, homeless, and the world was bereft and desolate of meaning. In bitter defeat, the rabbinic sages called this era by a terrible name: "the hiding of God's face."*

A certain biblical curse had now come true. For in Deuteronomy, God spoke of a time when "my anger shall be kindled against [the people] . . . . And I will hide my face from them."[2]

And today? At the dawn of the Enlightenment, when modern ideas challenged faith everywhere in Europe, the Hasidic master Rabbi Nachman of Bratzlav gave a far-reaching diagnosis of our current spiritual condition, reading deeply this same curse in Deuteronomy.[3] Nachman said we live in second-degree hiding. Not only is God's face hidden from us; it is also hidden from us that God's face is hidden from us.[4]

We live in a time of the hiding of God's face, but we don't even know it anymore. We are unable to feel deeply how much we have lost. We are doubly unconscious, for we have forgotten that we have forgotten.

Except perhaps in our dreams.

I n awakening us to a deeper and more imaginative dimension of experience, our dreams have a difficult job precisely because they come to remind us not only of what we have forgotten, but of what we have forgotten we have forgotten. Rabbi Nachman's second-degree hiding recalls Sigmund Freud's concept of repression, which arose from his study of dreams.

---

*In Hebrew, the "hiding of the face" is "*nistar ha panim*."

But I have found that repression of dreams does not end in sleep. Even when we don't consciously choose to forget or ignore our dreams, we may do something even more harmful—interpret them.

How we interpret last night's dream is a cultural reflex that joins a long history of cultural repression of dreams going back to the ancient world.

In the second part of this book I explore this history, to undo its effect. For from Genesis to Freud, interpretation always writes over the dream. Thus dream interpretation is often enlisted in the larger struggle between the word and the image—on the side of the word.

To reverse interpretation is to return dreams to their deep past. Long before there was writing, or even language, human beings must have been dreaming. We can only speculate on how that massive routine visionary experience shaped primordial consciousness. It's conceivable that every great invention, from fire to the wheel to language to writing itself, originated in dreams, along with the songs, the dances, and the stories of prehistoric culture. There's no doubt that dreams powerfully shaped the religious imagination. As the first Latin dream authority, Tertullian, states plainly, "The majority of people get their knowledge of God from dreams."

The earliest written records going back to Sumer and the Near East indicate the huge religious influence of the dream. In ancient tales and stories we see that dreams play a crucial role in the lives of the early heroes Dumuzi and Gilgamesh.

But our more familiar and influential dream texts are in the book of Genesis. There, almost from the start, the struggle between the image and the word takes place in stories about dreams.

There are two main types of dream stories in Genesis. One is about the revelation dream, such as Jacob's dream of the ladder.

The other type concerns interpretation, and all these stories involve Jacob's son Joseph.

Just as the Bible is ambivalent about the question of seeing God's face, so biblical religions are greatly ambivalent about dream revelation.

Can dreams directly show us heavenly realms, as Jacob's dream does, or even the face of God? Do dreams mean something in and of themselves?

Or, as the interpretations of Joseph stories suggest, are dreams basically tricky puzzles to be solved? Does the real power of dreams come only through an interpreter and interpretation?

The usual emphasis on interpretation overshadows the possibility of direct revelation. The rabbinic sages and the Church Fathers wrestled with this issue, and we do, too, whenever a dream seems real enough to make us wonder: Is the revelation dream still possible in our time?

Two modern dream explorers, Freud and Jung, resumed the argument that began in Genesis. Freud took the part of interpretation, and in his masterpiece, *The Interpretation of Dreams,* he presents himself as a new Joseph. Jung's approach is much more in the spirit of Jacob's dream of the ladder and its manifest revelations.

Yet each partook of the other side. Freud did not come to his "secret" of interpretation without first taking a personally difficult plunge into the world of his own dreams. About that intense period of discovery Freud later wrote, "Insights such as this come but once in a lifetime." Despite his "firm" atheism and skepticism, the very of fact of his plunging so unrelentingly into his dreams joined him to ancient traditions of mystical dream exploration.

Jung, like Freud, made a direct descent into the world of dreams, and he, too, felt that this was the experience of a lifetime. He wrote that he spent the next forty-five years of his life sorting out the treasures he first discovered in his intense three-year exploration of his own dreams.

But Jung and later Jungians soon developed fixed interpretive schemes of their own. And Jung consciously abandoned the spirit of his original experiment because he viewed it as far too risky for most people. Today followers of Jung take a highly intellectual approach to dreams, just like their Freudian counterparts. They rely on "amplification" and draw on libraries of symbols to find likenesses to the images they see.

Among the neo-Jungians, James Hillman has brilliantly "re-visioned" psychology as a study of the soul, though in a decidedly polytheistic context. I might have been captivated by his brilliant erudition, but for whatever reason I found myself in the hands of a very different kind of teacher, one who lives the risky spirit of Jung's original dream expedition.

Marc Bregman is not a doctor, either of medicine or of psychology. He has worked as a postman and as a street astrologer, though now he devotes his life to dreams. In a small town in northern Vermont, he lives far removed in every sense from the world of academia. But he has a direct and strongly intuitive way of working with dreams. He is mostly self-taught through thirty-five years of direct experience. He is blunt honest. To the state of Vermont, he is an officially licensed "non-licensed" psychotherapist. To me, he is a folk botanist in the backwoods of consciousness who knows how to gather the rare wild plant of the dream.

. . .

In four years working with Marc Bregman I would record more than eight hundred pages of dreams, sometimes three or four a night, and averaging twelve to fifteen a week. I learned that the images in dreams are wildly powerful, which is why taming them with words has been perennially appealing.

Dreams reveal, but often just what we don't want to see. I had to do hard work on myself, work that changed me. But that change allowed me inner experiences I could not have imagined otherwise.

Bregman's method is direct and simple, but also subtle and arduous. One main roadblock I've mentioned already is the long history of dream interpretation, which is also the long history of how our culture forgot all the revelatory gifts of the dream. Whether we know it or not, we believe that the only proper response to a dream is to interpret. That's an immediate reflex I can't undo in a few words.

As a man of words, a bookman, it was especially difficult for me to give up the interpretation reflex. I struggled with Bregman, and when I finally stopped struggling with him, I struggled with the truth I was seeing. It was too hard to be with dreams on their own terms. It seemed too incredible to accept that dreams directly reveal the truth about our lives.

But dreams are true. They reveal us to ourselves. That became clearer and clearer to me in working with Bregman, but it was no linear process. I had to repeat the struggle again and again, dream by dream. I had to reenact in the timescale of my own life the larger historical sweep of the ongoing struggle between the word and the image, the interpretation and the dream.

The reason is simple.

To make the dream descent, you have to deal with your predicament in life, which is often pictured in very vivid terms, and to do that involves facing painful truth and truthful pain. Everyone wants a revelation, but no one wants to be revealed.

But if you can face the pain, you can learn how to change by changing how you behave in your dreams.

The beauty of Bregman's work is to show a definite path for going deeper, seeing how dreams fit together over time into a larger pattern, feeling the story they tell about your predicament in life, and, deeper, the situation of your soul. In time, a whole new world opens up—this world of sleep, image, dream, the unconscious.

It's like being alive twice.

. . .

My curiosity about dreams goes a long way back in my life. Certain dreams left permanent marks on me. Everyone, I believe, has such dreams, which feel like powerful messages. Sometimes they come in times of crisis to show a new direction. Even if we dismiss dreams in general, there's always that one exception that feels intensely meaningful.

True, for many years I didn't think much about dreams. My curiosity gained impetus because of my encounter with the highly visual tradition of Tibetan Buddhism, which was so different from my concept of an entirely abstract and invisible God.

I began to ask about the power of images in a religion of the word.

I sought out a teacher of healing imagery in Jerusalem, in the summer of 1995. This was Colette Aboulker-Muscat—though everyone called this eighty-seven-year-old mystical lady with the piercing eyes and the scalpel tongue "Colette."

On her front porch in Jerusalem, she taught her students how to access the images that are constantly rising within us, though we are mostly unconscious of them.

My work with Colette's waking dreams first built a bridge for me from words back to images. I had a chance to pass on some of what she taught me at the bedside of a dying man in Newton, Massachusetts.

Chapter 2

THE GATE OF HEAVEN IN
NEWTON, MASSACHUSETTS

Newton, November 1995

A man was dying in Newton.

A friend said he wished to meet me.

But before the two of us could actually visit him, we had to go to the grocery store and buy his favorite items.

I don't remember now precisely what they were. Since he was a Jewish man of my father's generation, I would have thought "a slice pastrami," a tongue of pink lox, a good hunk of black rye bread. But more likely we brought vegetarian delights: a pint of hummus, a bag of baby carrots, apples, juice. The foods were sacred offerings to a local saint, who had drawn thousands to him simply by dying while still awake. His name was Morrie Schwartz, and he would become famous after his death because of Mitch Albom's book *Tuesdays with Morrie*.

I could not imagine his courage: to lie on a bed, watching paralysis creep up his body. Or could I imagine it only too well?

Paralysis is the stuff of our nightmares. A huge man with a knife comes to stab me, but I cannot move, I cannot open my mouth to scream. I have awakened with this muffled scream pushing out of my throat, locked by my lips. It is a physiological fact that in the sleep stage of dream, the limbs become completely paralyzed. This must mean something truly profound about our bodies, about sleep, about dreaming.

The old sociology professor looked at his death square on. He'd cried, too, on national television, and was not ashamed to cry. But because he was open to whatever the moment was, he was also open to joy. Death was coming for him, slowly, painstakingly, the kind of death anyone would fear the most, and yet he was not morbid or self-pitying. He preferred to live, but he knew that the only way he could live with dignity was by accepting his death boldly.

He had long ago turned away from any outward sign of religious practice, and he wasn't going to change it now for the sort of consolation that comes from stumbling through prayers left unsaid for decades, or adopting a ritual late in life that has been rejected in adolescence. Consolation, if it came, could arise only in the present moment. As for the future, he had asked to be cremated, plain and simple, and—"please, not overcooked."

Laurel Chiten and I came to his door. She is a documentary filmmaker and had been visiting this home for months. The professor lived in a nice solid stone home in Newton, a leafy suburb of Boston. I felt absurd clutching our offering. His wife, Charlotte, let us in. I saw how weary she was. It is hard enough to watch your beloved die, and now, thanks to a national television program, his death was a public event. Strangers like me showed up at all hours. I didn't know anything about their relationship, but I liked her for putting up with all this, for not shutting it down. Being married to a saint can't be easy. She seemed to me a sensible woman, and our coming to her door certainly could not have filled her with pleasure, but she let us in, and she was polite. She pointed to the small kitchen just off the hallway. I was carrying our bag of groceries—ridiculous, really, when I saw him, for at this late stage of his illness there was no way he could be eating solid food. We opened the refrigerator, and it was stuffed already with identical foods—vegetarian delights, because Morrie had studied with a local meditation teacher and become something of a Buddhist.

As we fumbled in the refrigerator, trying to make space for our newest pilgrimage offering, I glanced down the hall and saw the dying man's attendant, who helped with the most basic functions; then we waited on the couch as he prepared Morrie to meet us. All of this took a very long time.

It was expensive to have that kind of care at home, but by staying there he was able to live for what he lived for, which was, in part, us, the rest of us, the world that he remained so curious about. Laurel said she used to come and just hang out with him. Lots of people were hanging out with him at that time, drawn by his spirit, his sweet presence. He'd talk to Laurel about her film project in India, which was based on my book *The Jew in the Lotus*. Was he curious about India? I asked her. "No, he was just curious about whatever you were interested in." He was that way.

He was doing all this for us, but also for himself, because this openness, which was not so much a spectacle as a witness, was how he had chosen to live out his dying. The Buddhists talk about the essence of reality as openness, as open space. That's its essential nature. We visitors were all part of the opening. Because we came, he had to prepare for us, and I think the preparation gave him his days. He understood that self-pity would kill him quicker than poison. Only in joy—and curiosity—could he live.

Laurel Chiten had last seen him five weeks before. She'd gone off to India to research the film, and that good-bye had been difficult because she wasn't sure she'd see him again. All that time in India she'd dreamed about him, and somehow the dreaming meant he was still alive. And so he was—but quite withered, she thought, when we were ushered into his bedroom.

Morrie was lying flat on the bed, with his head propped by a pillow. His body, completely immobile under the sheet, was hardly a body at all. Laurel recalled later, "His eyes were bright; he was smiling. He was wasted away, but his eyes took up the whole room."

All the animation, all the soul in him, had traveled to his face. He was all face. His eyes danced, bright and shining; he moved his lips and spoke softly; he smiled with enormous, benign warmth. There was so much joy and sweetness in that face that I did not at all feel I was with a man who was dying. That had to be a myth. I had been more dead, many days in my life, than this man was now. I had lived grim and sad, hung my head, shuffled around, lost interest, phased out, lived as though asleep.

Against the white of his hair, the rosy pink of his forehead glowed. He'd sipped an extra spurt of oxygen just before we saw him.

He made us comfortable; he had us sit down on either side of him. He said to Laurel, because he was exquisitely conscious, "I'll hear about India later."

Morrie told me that he'd read *The Jew in the Lotus* and liked it very much. I saw it on his shelf beside the bed. I said, "Do you want to ask me anything about it?"

"What have you learned since then? What are you thinking about *now*?"

I got it. The book was from the past. In his circumstance, the word *now* was magical.

I told him that because of my contact with Tibetan Buddhism, I'd gotten very curious about visualizations. More than most Buddhists, the Tibetans use inner visions, or waking dreams, to produce transformations of consciousness.

My fascination also raised a question. I have a crazy theory that wisdom is wisdom, and that whatever is profound or wise in one religion could be found somewhere in another. That's why I began looking for work with images in what I believed at the time to be essentially a religion of the word. Even though the Judaism I knew is usually understood as an aniconic—anti-image—tradition, perhaps somewhere in its vast store of practices there might be in a hidden corner a Jewish form of visualization. I was just back from my summer with Colette, so I started to describe her waking dream technique to Morrie.

Then he said, "Could we do one?"

I wasn't prepared. Most of the visualizations I'd learned from Colette I had written down in a marble composition notebook, copied meticulously word by word on the old woman's porch in sunny Jerusalem. I didn't have the notebook with me. But I had an idea.

"We'll do it together, the three of us. It's better that way. And it's very simple. We are going to close our eyes. I'll say some words and the images will come, maybe very quickly, maybe just a glimpse."

I decided I was going to take him on a journey to heaven.

Before my work with Colette I had always associated deliberately induced visionary experiences with the obscure practices of a mystical elite that I had read about in books. They are the chariot riders, or, in Hebrew, "those who descend to the chariot"—the *yordei merkabah*.

These "descenders to the chariot" are also known as throne mystics because they journeyed to paradise in order to see the heavenly throne. Some went even further: their quest was to see the body and the face of God.

In his magisterial work *Major Trends in Jewish Mysticism*, the great scholar Gershom Scholem traces the authoritative history of Jewish mysticism. He begins with the merkabah mystics who practiced over a period of a thousand years. He identifies them as "the oldest organized movement of Jewish mysticism in late Talmudic and post-Talmudic times." They are at the genesis of the whole story, the ancient originals of the kabbalah, the first, writes Scholem, "to invest Judaism with the glory of mystical splendor."[1]

Using waking dream meditations, they descended to the chariot, which meant they ascended to heaven through seeing images, leaving behind vivid accounts of their journeys in texts such as the Greater Palace, the Lesser Palace, and the Hebrew Apocalypse of Enoch. Most of these accounts are written in the name of famous Talmudic sages. Enoch, for instance, "purports to be an account by Rabbi Ishmael of how he journeyed into heaven, saw

God's throne and chariot, received revelations from the archangel Metatron and viewed the wonders of the upper world."[2] Though the attribution to the great Rabbi Ishmael in this case is fictional, it's believed that certain of the merkabah mystics were in fact rabbinic sages. Scholem, for instance, mentions Raba, a fourth-century Babylonian sage who championed the revelation dream, as among those who studied the secrets of merkabah.[3]

Although we don't have an exact record of their meditative technique, we do at least know their posture. The meditator sat with his head between his knees like the prophet Elijah on Mount Carmel. (After all, Elijah was a chariot rider, too: he never died but was taken on a chariot full-body up to heaven.) On either side of him, note takers recorded what was uttered in the dream trance, "writing down his ecstatic description of the throne and its occupants." That the mystic in his rapture succeeded in penetrating even beyond the sphere of the angels is suggested in a passage that speaks of "God who is beyond the sight of His creatures and hidden to the angels who serve Him, but who has revealed Himself to Rabbi Akiba in the vision of the Merkabah."[4] It seems that some of the merkabah meditators achieved what was denied Moses: to see the face of God. Others, however, ventured only so far as to see God's throne.

The meditations were arduous and complex. The merkabah meditator recited long mantras; a few of these prayers ended up in the standard prayer book. He—we only know about "he"s doing this—went into a trance. His soul voyaged upward, yet the journey was mysteriously called the "*descent* to the chariot"; there are many explanations of that verbal puzzle. The visionary came to the entrance gates of the palaces of heaven. At each gate he met fierce angels with unusual names.

These angels served as doorkeepers, gatekeepers—the bouncers of heaven. They demanded passwords—"seals"—from the heavenly travelers. Errors were punished swiftly. We read in the Talmud of iron bars applied to the heads of impudent mystics, of their being tossed whole-body out of heaven. These vivid encounters at various gates represent the struggle to free oneself psychologically from earthly concepts and attachments. They analogize the struggle with moral impurities that separate even the righteous from God.

Even after gaining admittance to the heavenly palaces, there were always dangers of projection. "When you see the shining floor, do not say, 'Water, water' "; we read this travel advice in the Talmud, which suggests in a glimpse a whole scene of mystical experience. Having entered the sixth celestial palace, after many tests, the would-be traveler, if he mistook the gleaming marble floors at his feet for water, would instantly fall from the heights into burning lava.* You cannot see heaven with earthly eyes.

But in the end, despite all the dangers to health, sanity, and faith, some meditators passed from palace to palace, gate to gate, and arrived at a vision of the heavenly chambers. They saw a throne and "the appearance of the likeness" of a man on that throne. They saw the Shekhinah, the divine presence. They saw the angel Metatron, who acted as a heavenly scribe. They saw the Messiah as he waited for the future. They learned new revelations and understandings of the Torah. But the main prize of the journey was a powerful affirmation of the awesome and utterly glorious nature of God. Through a conscious meditative practice they climbed Jacob's ladder, and renewed the promise of the revelation dream.

The specific traveling secrets of the original merkabah mystics were lost in time, but the practice of visionary ascent continued in small elite mystical groups where techniques and secrets were passed on orally, from teacher to student. "I have it as a tradition—a 'kabbalah,'" the teacher would say before instructing his student. A "kabbalah" meant originally simply "that which is received"; later the word came to indicate the entire esoteric tradition.

These meditative journeys to other worlds fueled the mystical prayer of the German Jewish pietists of the twelfth and thirteenth centuries, and inspired the imaginative midrash of the greatest masterpiece of Spanish kabbalah, the Zohar or "Book of Splendor."

The Zohar recounts several tales of heavenly journeys. Though they are works of imagination, they must have had some basis in the meditative experience or the dreams—or both—of the author, Moses de León.

In one Zoharic story, as retold by Aryeh Wineman in his *Mystic Tales from the Zohar*, Rabbi Hiyya weeps at the grave of his departed master, Rabbi Simeon. "Dust, dust, be not proud," he cries, because Rabbi Simeon, "the very light of light," has perished in the dust. We have to understand this weeping as a profound pouring out of sadness, an extraordinary humbling that paradoxically leads to an ascent. It's as if you can't possibly get to heaven until you lose all your pride and lower yourself into the dust. Rabbi Hiyya fasts for forty days and forty days more. "Then, in a vision, he saw Rabbi Simeon" and is himself welcomed to the "celestial academy of the heavenly firmament."[5]

---

*In the same way, not seeing in the immediate moment what is going on in a dream leads to a crucial error. Bregman spoke of this as the dreamer's blind spot.

The heavenly ascent is one half of kabbalah. It began with the chariot but was later practiced through dreams. (The other half of kabbalah, based on mystical readings of the book of Genesis, concerns the secrets of creation.)

Closer to our own era, the Hasidic tradition absorbed the kabbalah and popularized its teachings among the oppressed and poor in the eighteenth-century Jewish settlements of the Ukraine. The local rabbi became a rebbe, a beloved leader and teacher, and in the Hasidic literature we read legends of rebbes who ascend to heaven.

In some cases these rebbes ascended through complex kabbalistic meditations. Or, they simply prayed intently with a full and burdened heart. The practices varied, but all involved seeing images of other worlds. In some cases they had visions in a dream.

In the Hasidic movement, the rebbe carries the pains and suffering of all his followers, his Hasidim, and especially at the Jewish New Year, the time of divine judgment, he is moved to plead to heaven for mercy on their behalf. It's as if the rebbe needs to make a personal appearance for his clients in the trial courts of heaven. The Baal Shem Tov, the founder of Hasidism, describes such an ascent in a letter to his brother-in-law.

It was the Jewish New Year of 1746. He learned "three special charms and three holy names and these are easy to grasp and to expound so that I thought to myself, it is possible by this means for all my colleagues to attain to the stages and categories to which I have attained, that is to say, they, too, will be able to engage in ascents of the soul and learn to comprehend as I have done." Unfortunately for his brother-in-law, and for us as well, "no permission was given to me to reveal this secret for the rest of my life."[6]

Which brings me to Newton, Massachusetts, 250 years later.

"Close your eyes," I said, and Morrie closed his eyes, and Laurel Chiten closed hers, and I closed mine so I could do it along with them. "Breathe out slowly—" Colette always gave that instruction, to breathe out—to focus on the breath leaving the body. It was very effective, very relaxing. "See and feel that you are standing in front of a huge wall." I saw a vast wall, of enormous stones piled up. It was the Western Wall of the Temple in Jerusalem, only the scene was completely bare—no men in black hats praying, no soldiers standing guard with machine guns. Just a wall, with its huge ashlar blocks. "Now," I said, "walk up to the wall and you will see a door."

I don't know what Morrie or Laurel saw. The door I saw was very small, wooden, like the door to a wine cellar or coal cellar, not full-size. I said, "Now breathe out again, and you will find a way to open the door." I had to crouch down to pass through the door, and then I saw. Afterward I opened my eyes and glimpsed Morrie's face. He had a big smile; he was seeing it all, in his own way—a different wall, a different door. Each of us would see something different in its details. The images came from within, built from bits of memory, chips of recollection, reading, personal history, and something else—some deep substance of the self. In my vision, I saw the high Western Wall of the Temple in Jerusalem. Perhaps Morrie saw a brick wall from his gritty childhood, or Laurel saw a cinder-block wall with graffiti from the back streets of Somerville.

Now, "Breathe out," I said. "See yourself on the other side wearing new, clean clothes and hearing a new name. Breathe out. Sense the essence of this day, of this moment, of this instant before you have been named." These were Colette's instructions as well as I could remember them. We'd reached the goal of our own journey to paradise; we were passing through the gates to the other side.

I asked him to open his eyes and describe his vision. Morrie told me that he passed through the door, and that now he was dressed all in white. On the other side an angel was singing. They were in a green park, leafy trees, dappled sunshine—and yes the angel gave him a new name.

—What was it?

Moshe.

I guessed that Moshe is his Hebrew name. It was a name given by his parents shortly after his birth, to be used ceremonially, a name with a certain ancientness in his life, a name he might not have used or thought about for many years.

Laurel had also heard a new name, one she never heard before. As for me, I heard the name of an angel.

The real magic of Colette's work was in how she created her scripts. I never spoke with her about that process, but she often drew on phrases from the Bible or the prayer book. While a philosopher like Maimonides sought to extract the poetic image from the language of the Bible, and make the Bible safe for philosophy, Colette moved in the opposite direction. She found the poetry in the language and brought it to life as images. Dissolved in the chemistry of a waking dream, her words and phrases magically flowered into images that engendered more images.

So we heard the words *door, wall, angel,* and inwardly dreamed. I believe, too, that this particular visualization—whether by Colette's design or her intuition—re-creates in part the voyage of the chariot riders.

The descent to the chariot was necessarily more complicated than any of Colette's scripts. But the purpose was the same: to have what Scholem calls a "private religious experience."[7]

Such experiences were sought by certain of the sages in the era of "the hiding of the face." With the Temple destroyed, it seems natural that they would seek reassurance by experiencing with their own eyes a vision of the heavenly realm, of the throne, and, in some cases, of the face of God.

Some scholars believe that the first merkabah meditators took the topography of their journey from the living memory of the architecture of the lost Temple. The visionary ascent of the merkabah retraces the footsteps of those who "ascend to the mountain of the Lord" (Ps. 24:3). The Temple in Jerusalem was in effect a giant three-dimensional architectural mandala, where concentric gates surrounded precincts of increasing holiness, and where at the center, one found a building called "The Holy," and, within it, the most sacred place "the Holy of Holies." There one saw two cherubs with outstretched wings, and in the space between them rested the Shekhinah, or presence of God.

Today, except for its outermost wall, the Temple stands no more, but as an inner architecture it is eternal and belongs to all of humanity. Eternal is the ascent, eternal the wall, and the door, and eternal the meaning of passing through, whether the meditator is Jew or Christian, Tibetan or Hindu.

Our journey to heaven in Newton was quick and simple, but it touched on an ancient significance. Not ancient in the sense of history, but ancient in depth—for there is a part of us older than our bodies, and that part is called, in Greek, *psyche*; in Hebrew, *neshamah*; in English, soul.

We each saw the wall, which evoked for me the Temple wall in Jerusalem, and we passed through a gate, which indicates the many gates of the Temple and the chariot rider's voyage. In the end Morrie met one of heaven's angels.

Did he really meet an angel? It depends on what you mean by real.

I know this: our hearts were wide-open. And we had gotten very high.

At the time I met Morrie, I had not yet done any dream work. I didn't know that there was a way to use dreams to repeat the experience once arrived at through the complex meditations of the merkabah.

Colette's waking dream was as close as I could get. It offered me a temporary visitor's pass to a world that I could not really enter fully until my dreams changed me. In order to really pass through the door in the wall, I had to become someone else. I couldn't have such a big head, nor could I be quite as big an ass as I was. There was work on myself to do before I could squeeze through that little door.

Yet her exercise was very valuable. It gave me a definite image of where I was going, my own gate to join all the other heavenly gates of Jewish literature, from the glorious gates of the merkabah mystics to the sad, frustrating gate in Kafka's *The Trial*, which a man stands before all his life but never passes through.[8] There are the gates of prayer in the liturgy of the Day of Atonement that close as the sun sets, and the gates of repentance that never close. But the first "gate of heaven" is found in Genesis, and it is a gate of dreams, where Jacob lay down " . . . and behold a ladder set up on the earth, and the top of it reached to heaven; and behold the angels of God ascending and descending on it" (Gen. 28: 12).

Jacob's situation is desperate. He is on the run, sleeping out in the wild, his head on a rock. He has deceived his father and cheated his brother, and now he's on his own. In this dire circumstance comes this strange and fabulous dream. He sees a ladder to heaven. Angels climb up and down. Jacob looks up and sees God standing at the top of the ladder. (Some translate it as God standing *beside* the ladder; the wording is ambiguous.) We are not told, though, precisely what Jacob sees. Does he see the "face of God" in his dream? He seems to, but we get no description of it.

He also hears a voice. The Lord makes very powerful promises to Jacob and his descendants, promises some people are still living out today.

The Lord promises Jacob that wherever he goes, "Behold, I am with you, and will keep you in all places where you go, and will bring you back to this land; for I will not leave you, until I have done that about which I have spoken to you." The story tells us that "Jacob awoke from his sleep, and he said, Surely the Lord is in this place; and I, I did not know it.* He was afraid, and said, How awesome is this place! This is no other but the house of God, and this is the gate of heaven" (Gen. 28:16–17).

Why does Jacob call the place where he dreams the gate of heaven and at the same time the house of God?

The rabbis believe that this dreaming place of Jacob's was the site of the Temple in Jerusalem. However, today's scholars tell us that it was a shrine site

---

*The Hebrew text uses a special version of the word "I," *anochi,* which translates into an emphasis. Hence, "I, I."

in northern Israel, a place of pilgrimage. (All the stories about dreams in the five books of Moses come from the northern or "E" strand of the text.)

But what about the gate of heaven?

I would say: not the site, but the dream, is the gate of heaven.

That is: through dreams, if we learn how to use them, we can pass from one world of consciousness to another.

The ladder in the dream has been interpreted in many other ways throughout the millennia. But for me, the ladder is the dream and the dream is a ladder. The dream rests on the ground of our experience but permits us to climb into a numinous realm. But I could never have climbed the ladder by myself. I needed a teacher to show me the way.

Morrie told me he liked the visualization very much. It made him feel expansive, renewed. But he said he was also feeling tired, and now I saw that the color was not quite so rosy on his face anymore. (Often, in my experience, doing visualizations leads to fatigue. The effort to turn words into visions can be exhausting.)

We'd made a quick trip to heaven. We had been together for only fifteen or twenty minutes. But images, Colette had insisted, don't take place in ordinary time—and there's a mystery to that, but it's true. They appear in an instant, but touch on great depth. They come from a place before logic, a great seedbed of time.

Morrie told me to unpin one of his photographs from the bulletin board for a souvenir. A snapshot of him in his college classroom, teaching with animation.

Now he was very quiet, very still. It was time to leave. I came to his bedside and thought about how to say good-bye. I knew I would not see him again, and I was full of that feeling, and yet I, a onetime visitor, didn't want to trouble him with my sadness. Really, his eyes did not allow it. There was nothing to do but lean over and kiss him on his rosy forehead. It didn't seem bold at all; it seemed just right. It wasn't as if we were strangers. We had traveled to heaven together and opened the same door. I pulled back and whispered, "Shalom, Moshe." My eyes brimmed with tears. He smiled and said, "Shalom, Raphael." That was my angel name. He had the gentlest voice.

Laurel and I left, and we sat in her car for a long time at the curb. It didn't seem right to move back out into the world; we weren't ready to go anywhere or do anything. We looked out the windshield. It was November; the street was splattered with wet yellow leaves. She knew she would never have that conversation with Morrie about India.

After a long silence I said, "That name you came up with, Nechama. Do you know what it means?"

She shook her head. It was a bit mysterious.

"Consolation."

Morrie died three days later.

Colette's visualization had been just right. To go to the wall, to find a door through it, to come to the other side, to hear your new name—this was being born again, passing through death to life, from the death of our material existence with all its boundaries and walls to an eternal life.

And we'd heard our secret names. The inner name that lives below the outer, the spiritual identity thriving under the outer coat of practical life, the Moshe under the Morris, the angel riding under the Rodger, and the consolation riding under us all.

In our waking dream visualization we went to a place that was beautiful and deep—we traveled, all three of us, in a movie-trailer version of the grand heavenly ascent—to a world behind the wall, a world where names have not yet taken place, a world of great possibility and pleasure and freshness, which is also paradise, and which is also beyond life and, somehow, hidden in life.

And we'd done it in Newton, Massachusetts, a place that is also "awesome" as Jacob says of his dreaming spot—and I, I did not know it.

Chapter 3

COLETTE AND THE
WAKING DREAM

Jerusalem, Summer 1995

I called Madame Colette not long after I arrived in Jerusalem, on a July morning. She answered the phone, "*Allô* . . ." I told her my name and that I would like to meet her. She answered exactly as follows. "I am eighty-seven years old. I don't take any more students. I only work with terminal cases. You can see me this afternoon at 5:30." Then she hung up.

I held the receiver in the air and laughed. Was I a terminal case? Her first words to me were fair warning of the abrupt, prickly, and penetrating treatment I would receive from her.

I wasn't alone. I'd heard stories of other students who'd been dismissed abruptly by Madame Colette. One woman journeyed all the way from the United States to her home. Colette stood behind her gate like those fierce angels in the merkabah and asked her, "What do you want from me?" When the would-be student couldn't come up with a clear answer, Colette told her to leave.

So I was nervous circling the road to Colette's house around a cliff that overlooks an overgrown park. Her neighborhood at the southwestern edge of Jerusalem is about a mile and half from the Old City. Many of the residents are French-speaking Jews who emigrated from North Africa in the 1950s. I got out of my car, but I had trouble finding her apartment and rang several doorbells on the block. Stopping before a modest two-floor stucco building, I heard enchanting wind chimes sounding in the upper story and thought this must be hers.

I walked toward the house down a pathway to a blue gate. I saw a woman on the porch in a red and gray housecoat, her white hair piled up in a neat chignon. She signaled me to come in. I fumbled with the gate, blue as the summer sky in Jerusalem.

She asked me to sit in the chair facing her so that she could hear me clearly. Because of the beauty of her garden, lush with bougainvillea and jasmine, she liked to sit outside. But the noise gave her earaches. Jerusalem's familiar *Egged* buses roared through her sentences, leaving clouds of dust and diesel, obliterating whole words and phrases. She spoke English with a strong French accent. I was instantly charmed. She had a dignified, aristocratic bearing and little balls of white cotton in her ears.

She asked me again to state who sent me and who I was. I explained that five years earlier I had joined her friend Rabbi Zalman Schachter for a trip to meet the Dalai Lama. I said we had heard from the Dalai Lama about the power of visualization in Buddhism and now I wanted to learn from her about the use of images in Jewish spirituality. She said, "Your answer is very clear and succinct, but the word *spirituality* is not used in my house."

That gave me pause. I had passed through the blue gate, but was she about to kick me out of heaven? This frail old lady in a lawn chair was a fiery angel. I would have to mind my p's and q's in her presence—and all the other letters of the alphabet.

However, I spoke her natal language, French, and that was a charm. When I mentioned my work as a poet, she rose and opened the door, inviting me inside her home. She had just published her own book of poems, *Alone with the One.* I had passed through a gate and a door, and maybe, just maybe, I wouldn't get driven out by any angels with iron bars.

Her home did seem another world. The foyer exploded with images: the smiling faces of hundreds of people who had passed through her life were crowded together, looking out at her from snapshots pasted on the wall. They were her former students and their children, and the many seriously ill patients she'd helped with her healing imagery.

At the end of the hall, a gorgeous Chinese porcelain caught my eye. We stopped to admire it. She said, "This is a Taoist figure of longevity. He is holding a certain peach, which promises a life of three thousand years. It is the peach of perenniality. The Chinese don't speak of eternity; they speak of three thousand years."

I said, "That is probably more realistic."

She told me that the perennial peach was one of only two in the world; the other was in a museum in Paris.

"My grandmother gave it to me because I loved it. Objects will come to us if we love them."

"And people?" I asked.

"People are not objects," she said firmly.

I would have reason to think about that perennial peach later on.

In the next chamber, a sitting room with low Oriental couches of red and green velvet, smothered with embroidered pillows, she told me that the perennial peach as well as the decorations in her bedroom were gifts to her grandmother from a lovesick French general who'd been posted to China after she refused him. The two were forbidden to marry because he was not Jewish. China and Taoism led naturally back to Buddhism, and she asked me about my experiences with Buddhist meditation.

I told her that after many hours of sitting in simple meditation, I was able to perceive anger in itself. Not my righteous indignation, or my just cause, or my other justifications for being angry, but pure anger with no excuses. I saw anger rise like a flame, saw it intensify to white heat, and saw it gradually die down and disappear like the black smoke after a candle is put out. As I watched this combustion take place within the private laboratory of my meditation, it came to me how many times in my life I'd taken a ride on that flame, making others angry in turn and thus building up future occasions for more anger. In meditation, in calm, a certain distance grew between me and "anger." It was no longer my anger, it was just "anger." That distance—an inch—had changed my life profoundly.

"This is very good for improving relationships," she said. "Because meditation produces calm. But it is not spirituality, though *spirituality* is not a word I use. I speak of the truth."

I was disappointed to learn that conquering anger had nothing to do with spirituality. I had thought of it as a great inner achievement, the gift of many hours of Buddhist meditative practice.

"If you don't use *spirituality,* what word would you use?"

"Leaping into the unknown."

Colette had a rare self-assurance that came through in her firm dicta. She presided over every occasion like the genuine Jewish aristocrat she was, for she descended from two ancient prominent families. On her mother's side, the Sheshets could boast two very great Torah scholars, known as Ribash and Rashba.* They in turn descended from King David himself.

---

*"Ribash" was Rabbi Isaac Ben Sheshet Barfat, a fourteenth-century Talmudic authority born in Valencia, who died in Algiers. "Rashba," Rabbi Shlomo ben Aderet, was a thirteenth-century Talmudic authority from Barcelona.

Her father's side was also illustrious. His great ancestor was Rabbi Machir ben Judah, who had been invited by Charlemagne to found a dynasty of Jewish kings. The Machir family later became known as Aboulker, and after the Spanish expulsion they had become leaders and teachers in Algiers. Among them were rabbis bearing traditions from the old kabbalah of Gerona, as well as the later kabbalah of Rabbi Isaac Luria of Safed.

Colette's father, Dr. Henri Aboulker, a distinguished neurosurgeon, was an important community leader in Algiers. In the 1930s he united Muslims and Jews against French racist politicians. During World War II, Colette's brother, José Aboulker, led the Resistance in Algiers and, through a brilliant coup de grâce, took control of the entire city ahead of the Allied invasion. Without a shot fired, he handed Algiers over to the Allied forces in November 1942. Thanks to the Aboulkers, the Jews of North Africa were saved from the Nazis. For their work, both José and Colette were recognized with the Croix de Guerre and the Croix de Résistance.[1]

But in the late 1950s, the bloody struggle for independence forced out most of Algeria's ancient Jewish population. Like many of them, Colette made her way to Israel.

Over time word about her special work with images had spread around the world. Students had come to her home from Europe, the United States, and Canada, to learn her practice of healing visualizations. Her longtime student Dr. Gerald Epstein has published several popular books on the subject, including *Healing Visualizations.* Other teachers trained by her include Catherine Shainberg[2] of New York, Carol Rose of Manitoba, and Eve Ilsen of Boulder, Rabbi Zalman Schachter's wife.

In Jerusalem, Colette had a large local following. Tirzah Moussaief had left New York and her modeling career to study with Colette. She had also come by way of a practice in Tibetan Buddhism. The link was already clear in my mind: Tibetans used visualizations to program the mind through the contemplation of wholesome images. Colette discovered something similar in kabbalah and Jewish folk wisdom. I thought if anyone could give me insight into the battle lines between the image and the word in Western religion, it would be a woman who seemed to care passionately about both.

Colette first discovered the power of visualization on her own as a child in Algiers. She later explained how it arose from a traumatic situation when she was a little girl.

She'd learned more from the kabbalistic tradition of Gerona—a "kabbalah of light" taught in the family by her maternal grandmother. As a young woman, she refined her techniques in Paris, working with a French psychologist, Robert Desoille. In 1925 Desoille invented—or rediscovered—a method for exploring the unconscious that he called "directed waking dream" ("*rêve éveillée dirigé*").

Desoille placed the client in the best physical conditions to concentrate "on the interior universe of his images": lying down, relaxed, silent, and in half-light. He suggested a starting image, which the subject described in as much detail as possible: shape, color, feeling. Right from the beginning, Desoille writes, there is "a considerable element of active collaboration with the treatment."

"One asks him to see himself moving in this space, preferably in the direction of an exit, a door or window, from which he can go out to the exterior. Here the space enlarges and one asks him by degrees first to follow a road, then to climb a mountain path, to accede finally to a path in the clouds on which one invites him to enter. Or even to try to rise on the wings of a powerful bird. . . . Calm, serenity, hope, peacefulness, should accompany the movements of ascension which will lead later to images of light."[3]

From the elaborate heavenly ascent of the merkabah mystics, Desoille preserved only the upward motion. Yet this imaginary ascent, Desoille maintained, cured neurotic symptoms and inhibitions. Climbing and flying in the waking dream restored contact with parts of "the imaginary" (*l'imaginaire*) that had been lost, and led to a healthier outlook. A blocked indecisive person who learned to move more freely in a waking dream became more decisive and freer in personal life. The work with images led to changes in disposition and then behavior, from the inside out.

The great French phenomenologist Gaston Bachelard, a distinguished professor of philosophy at the Sorbonne, became fascinated with Desoille's work after he turned his attention from the philosophy of science to the philosophy of poetry.* Bachelard's numerous studies of poetic imagery, such as *The Poetics of Space* and *The Psychoanalysis of Fire*, are highly influential works having a revival these days. In *Air and Dreams* he writes an appreciation of the work of Robert Desoille.

Bachelard argues in *Air and Dreams* that an ordinary psychiatrist tells a patient, in effect, "Get rid of your cares." But, he says, Desoille avoids the "abstract formula. . . . Instead he will replace this very simple abstraction with a very simple image: sweep away your cares. But don't limit yourself to words. Feel the gestures; visualize the images; pursue the life of the image.

---

*Interestingly, Bachelard, like Marc Bregman, was once a postman.

To do this, we must give the imagination 'control over the broom.' This very small, image-filled psychoanalysis delegates to images the task of the terrible psychoanalyst. Let 'Everyone sweep his area' and we will no longer need indiscreet help. Anonymous images are here given the responsibility of curing our personal images."[4]

Tibetan masters use "anonymous images" in the same way. Geshe Sonam Rinchen is a learned exiled Tibetan who teaches Buddhism at the Library of Tibetan Works and Archives. I first met him in 1990, and whenever I've been in Dharamsala since, I've visited his classes.

Geshe Sonam taught me that before meditation practice, a monk carefully sweeps the meditation room and imagines with each stroke of the broom that he is also sweeping away the poisons of the mind: ignorance, aversion, and clinging.

Likewise, Colette explained that when working with cancer patients, it's necessary not only to cleanse any immediate resentments or angers (such as quarrels with family) but also to revisit childhood (to the age of four and a half, she said).

The way to do this, she explained, is to return very quickly to the traumatic incident where there are hurt feelings, see it, then clean it, literally wash the whole scene clean, scrubbing with brush and soap—always to the left. The cleaning, she insisted, is in this order: first clean the feelings, then clean the place, then clean the persons involved. And very fast. I asked her, "Why fast?" Because, she said, otherwise one will think too much, and when one is thinking, one is not making images.

For the phenomenologist Bachelard, such cleansing had healing power because "the imagination dominates emotional life." Moreover, he wrote, "I believe that emotional life is really hungry for images. . . . It is always a good thing to offer 'images' to an impoverished heart."[5] To Bachelard, "Only the image can heal the image, only reverie can heal memory."

Arriving in Israel in the 1950s, Colette became well known for her using images to supplement medical treatment of serious illness—which is why she'd told me when I first called that she sees only "terminal patients." But I was mainly drawn to her version of Desoille's "directed waking dreams," which she called "imaginal exercises." Perhaps she could reconnect me to some of the lost secrets of the merkabah that Reb Zalman spoke about, for she clearly recognized the power of the image in a religion of the word.

From the outside, to the passerby on David Shimoni Street, we must have looked strange, this little band of students gathered on Colette's porch in the heat of a July morning. Colette read to us in her high, thin voice, from a script she'd handwritten in a notebook—a script in English, with French and Hebrew phrases sometimes thrown in. We breathed out, closed our eyes, and dreamed. We opened our eyes and told her what we saw. We closed them, and she read more. We dreamed a little more and opened our eyes again.

Sometimes we would have problems. People would get stuck and see nothing or encounter painful, difficult images. Her interventions then were poetic, mysterious, and beautiful.

She asked us to open our eyes during the session and describe what we'd seen. She then responded to problems as they arose by making new suggestions. She spoke directly in dream language, in images. This was very intense work, empathic and marvelous. She created images in you and repaired your painful, broken images as well.

Someone would visualize the "book of life" but report that the letters were too small to read. Colette would intervene and do a repair: "Now you have glasses and can read what the words say. Close your eyes and breathe." The dreamer could now return to her dream and complete it. For another student who was battling a wild bear, Colette invented a magical white turban that allowed her to fly out of the scene.

The first few times I worked with her, I had trouble seeing anything at all. But after some practice, Colette's words strongly stimulated the imagination. I could see more and more the more I tried. The images would sometimes flicker by rapidly. But I was seeing.

One time she asked us to begin by seeing ourselves raking leaves.

I closed my eyes, and, following her words, I raked a big pile. Then at her instruction, I picked up a brown leaf. I held the leaf in my left hand and clasped it with my right. When I opened my hands, the leaf was green, alive, with pulsing veins. I passed it through my body—this was no problem at all—and touched it directly to my beating heart. The leaf clung tightly. The fresh green filled my heart with its energy. At the end of the visualization she instructed us to sweep the leaves into a pile and then carefully put the rake away in the toolshed.

Colette told us that this exercise was useful for healing any internal organ. You could apply the magic leaf to the liver or the kidneys, lungs or heart. But the whole visualization was designed to be helpful from beginning to end. Seeing yourself sweeping up leaves gathers the scattered forces of the mind. Even putting the rake away gives a feeling of completeness and satisfaction.

In everyday experience we know how powerful such images are. Sitting in a cold room, you imagine a sunny day and feel warmer. Or perhaps you are feeling rattled. You close your eyes and visualize for a moment the face of your child, and instantly your heart opens and expands. In such circumstances, my wife visualizes a flower opening in her heart.

Images powerfully enlist sensations and feelings. At a very simple level, when we are hungry we visualize food, when we are thirsty we visualize drink, and when we are lonely we visualize love. Some religious cultures have cultivated this power of images to a very high degree. For instance, highly trained Tibetan Buddhist monks can raise their body temperature significantly through "*tum mo*," or "inner heat" meditations in which they visualize a flame burning in the imaginal body. Dr. Herbert Benson of the Harvard Medical School, a pioneer in mind-body medicine, applied the meditative practices of these monks to help cultivate the "relaxation response" in patients suffering from the effects of stress.[6]

Why are images so powerful when it comes to influencing the body and mind?

Desoille theorized that "the waking dream, being intermediate and nuanced between the state of waking and the state of sleep, between the physiological and the psychic," enabled the patient to draw on a deep reservoir of feelings. Augustine, the fourth-century Church Father whose dream theories I'll return to in part two of this book, had a similar idea. He wrote that "spiritual vision"—we would call it imagination—"can be reasonably and naturally said to occupy a kind of middle ground between intellectual and corporeal vision. For I suppose that a thing which is not really a body but like a body can be appropriately said to be in the middle between that which is surely a body and that which is neither a body nor like a body."[7]

Placing a green leaf against my heart, I feel the physical sensation vividly while at the same time my spirit is uplifted. From a middle space between the soul and the body, the imagination activates both.

Over the years, Colette created specific exercises for a wide variety of psychological, physical, and spiritual conditions, from asthma and headaches and broken bones to heart disease and cancer. Borrowing a term from the great French Sufi scholar Henry Corbin, Colette called her exercises "imaginal." Her point was to avoid the term "imaginary," which always implies something unreal. The imaginal is very powerful and very real.[8]

For the problem of simple anxiety, a simple image might do.

Breathe out; see yourself drink a glass of water. Sense what is being released.

For a patient with "too many questions," Colette offered the following:

"See yourself holding a rope in your hands horizontally with four knots. Untie the knots that bind you."

In his book *Healing Visualizations,* Colette's student Dr. Gerald Epstein has recorded her repertoire of images for specific diseases.[9] She never claimed that visualizations alone could heal a disease. She always referred ill people to medical specialists. What she promised was a supplement, to enlist the healing power of the image on behalf of the body. A person receiving chemotherapy, for instance, might actively visualize the chemical destroying cancer cells. This bolstered the patient mentally and spiritually during the struggle to be cured.

However, images do not always go according to plan. A patient's response to images may reflect disturbing feelings that need to be dealt with in the very moment.

Colette was training a wonderful woman from Jerusalem's Sephardic *haredi* community* who did volunteer work with the terminally ill. One morning she reported difficulties in using a Colette exercise with a cancer patient. The patient visualizes a large tree, with lopsided growth of branches. She is to see herself trim the tree, working from side to side, until it is symmetrical. This balance would give her a sense that the tumor growth could also be brought into control.

Initially, the patient visualized the lopsided tree. But suddenly, she saw the tree violently uproot itself from the ground.

"What did you do?" Colette asked her student.

"Nothing."

"That is wrong. You must tell her to replant the tree; it is vital she puts the tree back in the ground."

Here I understood the principle of repair—in Hebrew, *tikkun.* Colette insisted on intervening forcefully when necessary with the images people produced.

She was in effect the guide and the gatekeeper of our visualizations, and the author of the scripts we followed. This degree of control eventually became a problem for me, but at the time I was happy to follow her lead. She was teaching us the power of images to heal or to harm. She showed us how she could speak back to them in their language.

Haredi means "pious" and is the self-designation for those Jews whom others label "ultra-Orthodox."

We students were learning the language of images together, dreaming in company, our eyes closed, sitting on a small concrete bench while she guided us and the light came through the purple bougainvillea or the smell of white jasmine filled the air. We were dreaming in Jerusalem, where, two thousand years before, merkabah mystics had first closed their eyes and dreamed their way into heaven.

Chapter 4

KITCHEN KABBALAH AND
THE VAULT OF IMAGES

Colette gathered people from all over Jerusalem to her home on Saturday evenings, after sundown, a lovely Sephardic custom from her youth in Algiers, a way to linger, enjoying "the perfume of the Sabbath." At this weekly salon she presided formally, like a *grande dame*, as people gave talks and read poetry, and the rest of us sipped herbal tea.

One night she asked me to speak about the Dalai Lama's request for "the secret of Jewish spiritual survival in exile." Colette said that, had she been there, she would have answered, "'Next year in Jerusalem' repeated every year."

She meant the words proclaimed by young and old at the end of the Passover seder.

Someone else said, "The secret is the first commandment. Remember that I am the Lord your God that led you out of Egypt to be your God."

But Colette wouldn't budge. "No, that is not something a child can understand."

Colette had learned Judaism at the knees of her maternal grandmother, and had taught her own children. Religion doesn't start with a book: it must be grounded in sights, sounds, tastes, and smells to touch a child deeply.

For children, religion is always more than lip service. Sensual experiences are the ground of feeling and connection, in which all the later words and teachings are rooted.

Colette's work touched on that ground because certain childhood images live perennially in the imagination, like her porcelain Chinese peach.

Colette's took a firm position on the relative power of words and images. She often said, "Images are sovereign in the mind."

Her imaginal exercises increased our awareness of this sovereign life. At first I had difficulty seeing anything, but she encouraged me by saying that it might be no more than a quick glimpse. After a few sessions, the images poured out: I'd tapped into a deep source. The spontaneous way images bubbled up in response to her words indicated their fervid hidden life below the surface of conscious thought.

We are dreaming all the time and don't know it.

One of her long-term students, Eve Ilsen, told me, "She offered a key to the vault of my own rich imagery, and the only way to keep that door open is not to censor it."

But the question arises: Why is it that for most of us, images are locked up in a vault? Why do they require a key?

Before working with Madame, I, like most people, thought of dreaming as a uniquely nighttime activity. But Madame demonstrated with her exercises that dreaming happens as much awake as asleep, that there is an undercurrent of dreaming going on all the time. We don't focus so much on the images streaming constantly in our minds because we pay so much more attention to the words that float on top.

The Tibetans call this typical word-oriented consciousness "conceptual mind." Conceptual mind is isolated and divided from reality by the words that isolate, separate, and divide up our world. In conceptual mind we don't deal directly with sensual reality; we touch the world wearing gloves of words.

When I met him in Denmark, the late Tibetan dream yoga master Tarab Tulku confirmed Colette's views. Not only is there conceptual mind; there's also "dream mind," as he called it, which is always active. Working directly with dreams is a way to experience how "dream mind" functions in its pure state so you can be better aware of it when awake. For "dream mind" continuously projects images on the people and things around us. We mistake waking perception for actuality when very often that "perception" is a waking dream. Colette made me aware of it, Tarab Tulku named it, and finally Bregman taught me how to withdraw projections, first in dreams and then in life.

Images are sovereign in the mind. Therefore, Colette said that "to choose one's freedom is to choose one's images."

Her imaginal exercises were specific training in such choice. Likewise, Tibetan visualization looks—at least to a nonexpert like me—to be a training in how to dwell on extremely powerful transformative teachings, immersing oneself in images that reprogram the mind toward higher states of consciousness and away from the delusions implanted by the material world.

In the same way, the merkabah meditations offered images of ascent to the throne of a high palace, deep images that had the effect Desoille spoke of and Bachelard had praised, which is to heal the imagination itself, to replace troubled images with wholesome ones, to use "anonymous images" to sweep away broken personal images.

In today's world we are bombarded with a huge number of manufactured images from morning to night. The proportion of artificial to natural images in our consciousness must be very much higher than at any time in history. Many of these artificial images are markedly violent. For instance, according to a worldwide study conducted by UNESCO, in many countries, children watch an average of five to ten aggressive acts per hour of television. These powerful "anonymous images" have no deep purpose. They are created purely to entertain and to sell something.

Much pleasure and entertainment comes our way through film and television and the Internet; the visual richness of our lives can be a splendor. But these commercial images aren't produced to liberate us. By contrast, the visualizations of the Tibetan *kalachakra* and the merkabah seem to represent a profound use of images to heal.

The spiritual potential of images is realized in great works of art. A visit to a museum or gallery becomes a pilgrimage, and the refreshment we find there a solace. There would not have been a great history of painting in the West without an implicit understanding of the spiritual potential of images.

Of the three monotheistic traditions, Christianity is by far the most friendly to images and icons. Great Christian artists have given us indelible images of God, such as Michelangelo's painting on the Sistine Chapel ceiling of a muscular old man with a white beard flying through the clouds reaching out to Adam with his finger. However, Christianity has also had to struggle with the extremes these images evoke: either excessive devotion amounting to idolatry, or the total literalization and banality of mass-produced stereotypes such as the familiar image of a Jesus in sandals, with blue eyes and a brown pageboy.

There have been serious forms of visualization in Western spiritual practice, such as the meditations of place in the Jesuit tradition. But for most people these days, religion is primarily lip service, reciting prayers, reading and interpreting books. Deuteronomy still reverberates: "You saw no form, you only heard a voice." The recitation of prayer is often so perfunctory that even the verbal images in the text are rarely seen as such because people don't pause to visualize them.

In general, visions and dreams are referred to in sacred books, not experienced. Our religion is sometimes about them, no longer of them.

All of this is true enough for mainstream religion, but a mystic is someone who dreams a path to heaven. However, it would be hard to find practical guidance in working with dreams in contemporary Jewish mystical groups.

For instance, most kabbalah taught today is concerned not with direct experiences, but with the study of other people's experiences. It is text-based and somewhat dry and abstract. Colette's direct engagement with our personal images therefore represented the exception to the rule.

One of her favorite students, Carol Rose, told me that when a *haredi* asked her why she was in Jerusalem, she said, "To study with the city's greatest living kabbalist."

"What is his name?" the *haredi* asked.

"Colette."

He was astonished that a woman might teach any form of kabbalah, because in traditional circles, and certainly among the Jews of eastern and central Europe known as Ashkenazim, kabbalah is a matter of text study, and text study is for men.

But in the Sephardic world—the world of the Jews of Spain and North Africa—kabbalah has a more domestic side. The men, Colette said, had not been able to pass the teachings on because, in Spain, they were under pressure of the Inquisition, and many had to hide their Jewish lives behind the walls of their homes. So it became the role of the women to pass on deep spiritual teachings.

I had not heard about this secret tradition, but it seems imaginable because very often the contributions of women have not been recorded or written down. Much of the kabbalah we hear about in the West is from the Ashkenazi tradition and comes from male authors in the form of commentary on books of kabbalah. Some call such commentary "kabbalah-ology." But a woman's kabbalah would be very different. Taught informally, in the course of raising children, the mothers of Judaism brought down and applied ancient mystical wisdom to everyday matters, and everyday life.

Colette claimed that she drew on such a lineage of Jewish women teachers who taught a "kitchen kabbalah," a practical form of kabbalah useful in medicine and healing.

This kitchen kabbalah would be taught the way a mother teaches a child. Colette often taught us that way, cutting to the core and to the quick. For instance, the first day we met, she told me there are only two sins in Judaism: sadness and humiliating others. I felt the whole tradition condensed into a simple phrase.

At moments in our encounter, though, I wondered if she really believed the part about "humiliating others." Especially when she discharged one of her "little shocks."

Chapter 5

THE LITTLE SHOCKS

Although she was often sweet and tender, and she was adored by her students, Colette could be austere and magisterial in her pronouncements. She had a strongly theatrical streak, and used it, along with her verbal wit, to keep her students in her thrall. One morning, Colette decided to teach us a special visualization, to be used, she said dramatically, only in the most extreme cases, when a person is on the verge of death.

You see yourself walking down a very long road toward the vanishing point, and then turn around and walk back. It was spooky. The image I saw of myself was much larger when it came walking back to me. She said, "Naturally, because at the end of your life you will be so much bigger than the way you know yourself to be now."

She was extremely sharp with words. One afternoon I was sitting on her porch with a French visitor. He decried the lack of metaphor in contemporary poetry. I replied that often today, the preferred figure of speech is metonymy.

The term was unfamiliar to the visitor, so I explained to him that in metonymy a single detail stands for a greater whole: "The pen is mightier than the sword"; "The White House announced today . . ." Colette listened carefully and interjected, "My students must be more precise. Metonymy is when the unique becomes the One."

This was brilliant. Every person, every event, every unique experience is a metonymy for God, a pathway to the One. She was eighty-seven years old and sharper than sharp. She delighted me even as I felt abashed at being labeled imprecise.

But that was Colette's way: she liked to inject drama into every situation and give her students what she called "*petits chocs*." Little shocks. It seemed cruel sometimes, but she felt that this was the way to teach. I once watched a student break down in tears while Madame clinically handed her one tissue after another.

Because she was raised in a traditional family in Algiers with a long lineage, Madame's roots went deep into the premodern era, the era of late-nineteenth-century phrenology and spiritualism that was also background for the psychology of Freud and Jung.* She taught something she called "*morphologie*" or "*physiognomie*," an old nineteenth-century idea, now pretty much discredited, that physical body type determines psychology.

For Madame, it was all tied up with the teaching of the shattering of the vessels in Lurianic kabbalah. The primordial imperfections are necessary and built into the nature of the universe. Every being, body, and form emerges somewhat damaged from its ideal development. However, for this shattering there is a repair, known as *tikkun*. Thus she was always interested in shattering and repair, repair and shattering. She was constantly awake to even minor imperfection, because she believed so much in the goal of perfection.

One morning I sat on the porch behind the blue gate with a man in his twenties from the United States who'd come to ask for advice. She remarked that his ears were very bad, whereas my ears were quite good. "That's why," she said to me, "you are a very good listener."

I was feeling proud of my perfect ears, and a little sorry for the young man, when Colette added, "Your mouth is very bad."

She touched my lip and said, "You often speak from the side of your mouth because of a trauma you sustained when you were young." But she had a special exercise I could do that might help. She demonstrated immediately by jamming my upper lip into my teeth.

Another time she pointed out to me, in public, that my arms were too short. I'd somehow gotten through life so far without that information, but she insisted on it.

In the ideal man, the "wingspan" of the arms is the same as the height from head to toe. (That's what Leonardo shows us in the well-known Vitruvian drawing of a man, his arms and legs stretched out to touch the circumference of a circle and the sides of a square.) Apparently my body is far from

---

*Freud studied hypnotism (or "mesmerism") in his early years; Jung investigated séances; Desoille first studied images as an aid to ESP, believing that two people concentrating on the same image could communicate telepathically.

ideal, though how Colette had observed this I have no idea. I had to measure to figure out that my arm span is a few inches shorter than my height.

Colette had nailed me as a short-armed guy. The next day she told me she had an "*exercice*" to cure that. It combined visualization and calisthenics.

"Stand," she said, "close your eyes, stretch your arms. Now, see yourself touching opposite walls of the room with your palms, while stretching a bit farther." I did as she said. Then she added, "Push the windows open."

I heard something crack.

"See yourself touching the leaves of the trees . . . Grab a handful of leaves." I did. Something snapped inside my armpits; they ached for hours. Colette commented that I could gain at least a centimeter if I kept the exercise up.

But what was the point?

She said, "You have used the word *anxiety* four times in this house."

"Yes," I said, still wondering what the connection was.

"You see," Colette said, "you've had a little success in life—but you are afraid of losing hold of it—*because your arms are too short.*"

She had me there. I can laugh about it now, but at the time it felt true and there was no escaping it.

Colette was a remarkable teacher because of her precise awareness of defect and her passion for perfection. She was equally passionate about images and words. This was a powerful tension in her personality. She lived the battle between the image and the word, and, as I learned one day, she had battle scars.

She was teaching us a new visualization. We were supposed to imagine a "*stratégie*" from childhood. What is a "*stratégie*"? someone asked.

She explained that a *stratégie* is an adaptive behavior you learned as a child to respond to a difficult situation. In adult life it remains a habit when perhaps it is no longer useful. When I worked with Bregman, I'd come to see clearly how these childhood "*stratégies*" show up in our dreams, though he used a harsher word for them—pathology.

To explain "*stratégie*" further that morning, Colette told us a revealing story.

As a child she was very talkative and precocious. At age five, her father, Dr. Aboulker, had her mouth taped up during the day so she could not speak. (The tape was removed at meals and at night.)

She explained that the tape was to correct a malformation of her trachea. This was an example of a *tikkun*, she said.

When her father went away to fight in World War I, he instructed the family that the tape should remain in his absence. Colette added that even now, in her eighty-seventh year, she still could feel the pain in her face because the tape had to be ripped off several times a day.

Colette admitted that the experience of silence "was very difficult."

She recalled a time in particular when she was just bursting to speak out. "I sat with my grandmother and my cousin. And my grandmother said to her, 'You are my peach.' The peach is very special in my family. It blooms once every three thousand years. (You have seen the sculpture of it—the Taoist figure holding the peach of 'perenniality'). So I am sitting with my mouth taped shut. Later my grandmother takes the tape off, and the first thing that I say to her is, 'What sort of fruit am I?' She said, 'You are an apple, an apple of paradise. You must always be refreshing because you are at the source of life.'

"I am not so happy, then, to be an apple. But that is what she told me. But you see, later she gave me the peach as an inheritance."

Colette insisted she valued the whole ordeal because, she said, with her mouth taped, she discovered the work she would do for the rest of her life.

"That is why I developed my *stratégie* of making images. So you see that a *stratégie* can be very useful."

As the father of two daughters, I couldn't accept her father's *tikkun*. It sounded like abuse. The quest for perfection can cause more pain and suffering than the evils it seeks to correct.

I guessed that the rough treatment her father had given her explained Colette's penchant for teaching us with little shocks.

Not that I regretted any shocks I received, because overall I had to take her as she was. Whatever her flaws, Colette's greatest teaching was herself. She was a poet of Judaism, and Judaism needs her poets. I loved her for her quirks, her strange theories, her "*physiognomie.*" I even loved her imperious ways, which made it possible for us to trust her as a guide when we closed our eyes.

I especially admired her sensitivity to language. She had the kabbalist's understanding of words as shattered fragments of the primordial creative word. As her imaginal work showed us, words have a power to enlist images in the unconscious. Therefore, what you say commands what you are. She believed that to constantly voice certain words like *anxiety* and *problems* creates anxiety and problems for you.

The first time we met, I was taken aback by the first of her little shocks when she said, bluntly, "*Spirituality* is not a word we use in our house."

But I think now that she said this because the word *spirituality* has become a bland catchphrase for a self-indulgent dabbling, not a real "leap into the unknown," with real risks.

Including the risks of solitude. That same day she showed me her book of poems, *Alone with the One*. The title indicates that she knew that at the deepest level the spiritual quest is lonely and has to be.

Her inner experience supplied creative words that helped others discover beautiful images in themselves.

Still, I wondered if those images truly belonged to me. What images would come to me spontaneously when I, too, was "alone with the One"?

For a few years after meeting her, I practiced working with images. The visualization I did with Morrie Schwartz was one of several. Once a friend with breast cancer asked for help—and I did the "green leaf" exercise with her. Another time I created a group visualization at a retreat center based on the powerful New Year's prayer that describes God as a shepherd looking at each of his sheep as they pass by. People visualized themselves as the shepherd and saw the sheep. The effects were powerful—maybe too powerful. One woman told me in tears that one of the sheep she saw had a tumor on its head. She was devastated—because she herself had stage-four breast cancer—but she looked again at the lamb and the tumor turned to a dry leaf, which she brushed off. She had made her own spontaneous *tikkun* or repair of the image. But her account shook me because I realized that the unconscious forces I was playing with could touch people more deeply than I knew how to respond to.

It sounds foolish to admit now, but I did not think of asking Colette about working with dreams. Much later, I found out that she did this work, which she called "waking dream" or "waking the dream," with certain special students. Dr. Catherine Shainberg described it to me. It was one-on-one. Catherine brought Colette a dream; Colette would make a few comments; then quickly, using images fresh from the dream, she created an imaginal exercise. In some cases this was to repair the images in the night dream; in other cases, to extend the movement begun in the dream to its conclusion. I am sorry I never did that private work with her, but Catherine Shainberg has kept it alive in her own teaching through her School of Images and in her book on the subject.[1]

I often thought about coming back to see her. For many reasons, I never did. Just as Colette had warned me once, not long after we met, the spiritual quest is best done when you are free of obligations. I had young children to raise and responsibilities that made it hard to return to Jerusalem and devote myself to a leap into the unknown.

Over the next five years, I explored other areas in my writing, including Jewish meditation. Over time, as I reflected on the experience of working with Colette, I became convinced my journey in images had to become more unconditional, totally open, not tied to any received ideas, even hers.

This desire to be free of any teacher I thought of as very admirable at the time. I see it differently now. I have trouble being a student. Yet my very desire to be free of teachers led me to an experience in dreams that helped me become a much better student. But that jumps ahead of the story.

No doubt I was rebellious. No doubt I was still caught up in ambition, my short arms grasping for what they could not hold. But then again, hadn't Colette said, "To choose one's image is to choose one's freedom"? Eventually I took that to heart. I wanted to make sure that the images were mine. I needed the unconditioned. And dreams are unconditioned, as far as I could tell. Dreams in and of themselves come as they wish and leave as they wish, and in their wild anarchy and strange roughness and exquisite beauty, they touch on currents deeper than any guided visualization.

It was a risky journey I would take, riskier than I knew, because I didn't know myself deeply enough. The unknown world of dreams really can be dark and dangerous, and at times it was more than I could bear. Dreams can take you to heaven, but first they take you to hell.

When things got rough in my dream work with Marc Bregman, I did take courage from what Colette told us one morning: "I am going to die soon, and you must learn not to depend on me; you must depend on yourself. You do not really need me, for you have the source within yourself."

Colette opened for me the immense power of images. She gave me an insight into what the chariot was all about, and how we might find, for ourselves, revelation through images. And she encouraged me to look in my dreams for "the source within" myself—the source within all of us, I believe—which is a primordial light.

The night I spoke at her Sabbath-evening gathering, I had asked Colette, "Can you tell me something about the connection between your work and the kabbalah as it is traditionally taught?"

She answered, "Light is the connection. You spoke about Buddhist enlightenment, but there is no such thing as a permanent state of enlightenment. We can have only a glance at the light."

She drew on her heritage, the early kabbalah of Gerona, a Jewish center north of Barcelona. Colette's ancestor Rabbi Jacob ben Sheshet was a prominent teacher and author in the group of mystical rabbis there. He writes of God's glory appearing as "images formed in the heart."

Did not Colette teach us how to form images in the heart? There is something called spiritual light. It is the light of the first day of creation, the light that existed before the sun, moon, and stars. This spiritual light manifests as images in dreams.

In dreams, then, if one knew how to look, and how to overcome those "strategies" that block us, one could find the ladder of the revelation dream. And open a blue gate to the palaces of the night.

Chapter 6

THE CASE OF THE
DISAPPEARING DREAM

I t was a shame I hadn't asked Colette about dreams, because I had a very hard time finding teachings about the use of dreams elsewhere in the Jewish world. This puzzled me—surprised me—and then it led me to investigate the case of the disappearing dream.

People on a spiritual search speak of "seeking God." Yet somehow no one these days talked about seeing God's face. The psalms are unafraid to speak that way of this powerful inner prompting to see: "Of you my heart said, Seek My face; Your face, O Lord, will I seek!" (Ps. 27:8).

Rabbi and professor Arthur Green quotes that verse in the title of his own book of personal search, *Seek My Face, Speak My Name.*

Green writes, "Seeing God. The Torah itself seems to be conflicted on the question of whether such a thing can happen.... [T]he conflict among ... Biblical sources may indicate that there was a debate among our most ancient thinkers over the question of God's visibility. This is a debate that accompanies Judaism throughout its history. Philosophers, sages, mystics and visionaries through the ages have all had their say.... To be a religious Jew is to walk the tightrope between knowing the invisibility of God and seeing the face of God everywhere."[1]

To see God's face is a quest in imaginal reality. Dreams are a natural way to taste visionary experience. My friend David dreamed of seeing God's back just as others report their own powerful spiritual dreams and experiences.

In Dharamsala I saw how Tibet's traditional culture is a profusion of icons and mandalas that support the practice of visualization.

But we also live in a highly visual culture. We stare at screens full of lively graphics: computer screens, video games, DVDs, television, film, pictures on cell phones: the image is ubiquitous and alive. The tension between a religion of the word and the visual imagination is higher, more electric, in our time than it has been since the beginnings of biblical history, when idolaters and monotheists, iconophils and iconoclasts, first contended for supremacy.

We think with images, but we seek God exclusively in words. Have we lost something vital?

Since in the Jewish world the more Orthodox communities preserve more traditional practices, I thought I would look there for traces of the lost revelation dream.

I spoke to a friendly Orthodox rabbi from Boro Park, an enclave of traditional, or Torah Judaism in Brooklyn. Rabbi Meir Fund is a very learned man open to speaking to all sorts of Jews. I'd heard that he had done some work with dreams in his community.

He told me, "Basically there are two kinds of dreams: those that are our personal conversations with ourselves, and those with divine messages." The first, he emphasized, have no prophetic significance.

However, from time to time he has consulted with people who felt that they were receiving a prophetic message, and he had helped them sort this out.

He told a story of a European cousin who had a dream during the years of the Holocaust. His grandmother appeared and told him to get off a train he was on. Everyone who remained on board died; his life was saved. Rabbi Fund said this anecdote confirmed a saying among the rabbis—that a dream is one-sixtieth prophecy, meaning a certain small but definite amount of prophetic power still endures in ordinary dreams.

However, he added, that's not the emphasis or takeaway from Talmud. The main practice, as specified in the prayer book, is a ceremony to ward off the anxiety of bad dreams. In contemporary practice this does not involve discussing the dream's content.

I knew I was getting a traditional Torah view and respected that, but I was surprised at the overall approach. If the main focus of the tradition is to ward off bad dreams, that didn't sound very promising to me. The ceremony Rabbi Fund mentioned, known as "amelioration of the dream," loomed ever larger in my thought because it exemplifies our reflex response to dreams in the West.

After talking to Rabbi Fund, I wondered if perhaps in the more mystically oriented Hasidic world more was going on with dreams.

I turned once more to Reb Zalman, speaking to him at his home in Colorado. Since his roots are in Chabad, the largest Hasidic group today, I wondered about the current Hasidic take on dreams.

"They didn't make a deal out of it. Because I once wrote to the [Lubavitcher] rebbe that I had a dream about him and he said, 'It's all right. Dreams are only dreams.'"

"So there's skepticism?"

"It was like, 'Don't make more of it than they are.'"

In the same vein, when I asked him for a Hasidic story about dreams, he told me this one:

A man goes to the Kotzker Rebbe and says, "I should be a rebbe. My father came to me in a dream." The Kotzker laughed, "If your father would have come to three hundred people and told them you were to be a rebbe, it's a different story. If he came to you it's nothing."

Reb Zalman added, "So you see, there is a discounting of dreams."

Sensing I was disappointed, he said, "But there's another wonderful story about the Hasid who comes to the Rebbe Tzemach Tzedek. He comes to him and says, 'Rebbe, give me a blessing that I should grow in Hasidic learning.' The rebbe says to him, 'When does a person grow? When he sleeps. When he sleeps, he dreams. Study each one of my teachings at least sixty times; then you will think about it during the day and you will dream about it during the night.' This guy then became a Hasidic dreamer."

I could add from Arthur Green's superb biography, *Tormented Master*,[2] that Rabbi Nachman of Bratzlav wrote down many of his dreams and based tales and teachings on them.

Reb Zalman said, "Then there's the story of Rabbi Isaac Luria. On a shabbas afternoon he had a dream. In twenty minutes, he said, I saw more than it would take me eighty years to preach about."

Luria's most important disciple, the kabbalistic master Chaim Vital, is probably the most prolific recorder of Jewish mystical dreams.

They are collected in *The Book of Dreams and Visions*. In one dream, Vital is led to "a beautiful garden with large rivers flowing through it" by Elijah the Prophet.

His dream seems like a plain vanilla version of the heavenly ascent. At "the center of the garden . . . he saw a tall attic." Vital climbs a ladder, and goes through the door.

"There he saw God sitting on a chair. He looked like the Ancient of Ancients, with a beard white as snow, sitting in infinite splendor."[3]

Chaim Vital's dream is humble, homely compared to the elaborate visions of the ancient merkabah mystics. Instead of an ascent through seven heavenly palaces, there's a climb up a ladder into an attic. Instead of Ezekiel's "appearance of a likeness of a man" there's "God sitting on a chair."

Very few dream accounts like this are found in Jewish mystical literature because most Jewish mystics are extremely reticent about recording their personal experiences. If there are any contemporary Jewish mystics practicing such dream journeys, they have kept it to themselves.

However, Reb Zalman told me that his wife, Eve Ilsen, who was Colette's student, has always kept an extensive dream journal.

"And for yourself?"

"Me? Very seldom a special dream comes up. Most of the dreams I have are about not knowing where I left my car . . ."

After my talk with Reb Zalman I felt overall discouraged. Yes, in the Jewish esoteric realm there were the prophetic dreamers Vital, Luria, and, most important, Nachman of Bratzlav, who I sensed was going to be more and more important to this story.

But in general, there wasn't a huge interest in cultivating the prophetic dream among the people of the dream. There weren't specific practices designed to help a person use dreams for religious experience.

I'd go further. The main response to dreams I felt from various authorities was shadowed with skepticism, caution, and fear.

Joel Covitz, a rabbi and Jungian psychotherapist, confirmed that fear for me. His *Visions of the Night* is a thorough study of Jewish dream interpretation based on the work of the most important kabbalistic Jewish dream interpreter, Rabbi Shlomo Almoli. Reviewing all the relevant texts, Covitz discovered "a monumental Jewish ambivalence" about dreams.

"The resistance to dream material in Judaism—I would even go so far as to call it a phobic reaction—is significant because to a great extent it persists even to this day and explains why [Jewish] religious leaders have never universally accepted the dream as a source of insight and knowledge." He traces this phobia to a passage in Deuteronomy that prescribes death to dreamers and finds it "even among nonreligious Jews who are largely assimilated into American culture."

In general, Rabbi Covitz concludes, "dreams have no religious significance at all in mainstream Judaism."[4]

I was searching for the revelation dream in contemporary religion, but Jacob's ladder had long been put away.

Chapter 7

A CONVENTION
OF DREAMERS

Berkeley, June 2003

I met my dream teacher, Marc Bregman, in the summer of 2001, and leapt into the unknown exactly as Colette prescribed.

A couple of years later—and for the sake of this narrative—I decided to check out the competition. I attended the twentieth conference of the Association for the Study of Dreams. Founded in 1983, the ASD is a totally diverse group of people, all drawn by the magnetic fascination of the dream.

Most academic conferences bring scholars from the same discipline: the dream brought together scholars and nonscholars from every discipline and nondiscipline to a hotel by the bay in Berkeley.

There were brain physiologists and crackpots; people doing PET scans of the brain, and people dreaming together to stop the war in Iraq. There were artists and poets, painters and musicians: they dressed in monster costumes at the dreamer's ball. Anthropologists studied the dreams of female Swedes and Japanese truckers. Sociologists surveyed dreamers with questionnaires. There were Freudians and post-Freudians, Jungians, and post-Jungians. There were lucid dreamers from the research laboratories at Stanford, and lucid scientists from the Harvard Medical School.

We were addressed in full plenary by Dr. William Dement. In the 1950s at the Stanford University sleep lab, he put dream study on a scientific basis with his study of REM sleep.

His research showed that sleep has a definite architecture, moving through stages of EEG activity night after night, in a shape that looks on a graph like a staircase moving up and down. On our way up from the deepest sleep, our eyeballs move rapidly—rapid eye movement, or REM, sleep—and we repeatedly dream, about every ninety minutes for most adults, and four to six times a night.[1]

By studying the architecture of sleep, and where dreams fit in, scientists could move beyond some of Freud's theories and create new theories of their own.

I heard a lecture by Dr. David Kahn from the Harvard Medical School, who works on the research team of Dr. Alan Hobson of MIT. Hobson's research took advantage of advances in our understanding of brain physiology and brain chemistry and the instruments available to measure how the brain changes electrically and chemically during dream states.

Hobson's *The Dreaming Brain* (1980) put forward to the general public the result of his research: his "activation-synthesis" theory of dreams. The brain stem activates the dream; the cerebrum synthesizes. Random firings of neurons activate images and feelings in the lower brain; the higher brain takes these random data and does what it always tries to do with chaos—organize a coherent story out of it. The result is the dream.

In his presentation Dr. Kahn summarized the profound changes that take place in the dreaming brain. These changes helped me understand why dreams could have so marked an influence on consciousness.

To begin with, the brain does not turn off in sleep like you turn off a TV. Overall, the brain in REM sleep is actually more active than when we are awake. It's just that certain parts receive more stimulation than normally, while others receive less.

The lower-activity parts of the brain, Kahn explained, are said to be "unlinked" or "disconnected"; the term is metaphorical, but it gives the idea. One area, the dorsal-lateral prefrontal cortex, or DLPFC for short, "is dedicated to the where and the what. Where am I and what am I doing?" But in dream sleep, this part of the brain is disconnected. Therefore, the brain "assumes that internally generated stimuli have an external origin"; that is why a dream can feel so real.

The DLPFC is the brain area of conscious decision making. When I asked Dr. Kahn if this corresponded, in a sloppy way, to the ego, he answered slyly, "If that makes you feel more comfortable."

Let's say it does make me comfortable. In REM sleep, the ego is loosened. Also unhooked is the precuneus, which governs scratch-pad memory, the brief moment-to-moment recall. For instance, while I'm looking for a pen,

I have it stored there that I'm looking for a pen. When I find it, the scratch pad empties.

The precuneus is also activated when you recall an autobiographical memory; in other words, it's how you remember who you are. "It is also aware of spatial orientation." Another part of the brain "disconnected" in REM sleep governs the sense of the body being in a particular location.

Thus altogether, what's disconnected in REM sleep is ego, identity, and the location of the body in space and time. This already suggests why dreams can feel so powerful.

But as some areas are disconnected, other areas of the brain are more highly activated. Among them are the various organs of the limbic system, such as the amygdala and hypothalamus, which govern emotions and feelings, and which receive auditory and visual stimulation. In dream sleep, conscious control goes down; feelings and sensations are amped up.

This effect is further amplified because the brain also changes biochemically. "We are on drugs every night, our own drugs," said Dr. Kahn. (Another scientist said REM sleep is like being on LSD.) There are changes in neurotransmitters, changes that in waking brains are responsible for hallucinations. Serotonin levels go down to zero.

Then there's the body: it also goes through a very peculiar change in REM sleep. With the exception of the diaphragm and eyeball muscles—and an occasional twitch—our larger muscle groups, such as arms and legs, are completely paralyzed.[2] This seems to account for those strange dreams where we are terrified by an attacker and cannot move, or we are scared witless but cannot muster a scream.

It's as if our bodies are being restrained and we must concentrate only on those sensations the dream shows us.

In REM sleep the body is paralyzed but the mind is liberated from all ordinary constraints—the constraints of morality and of self-interest, the ego that drives us by day, the constraints even of time and space and of life itself.

This dramatic change in the electrical and chemical brain of billions of sleeping people, night after night—what is all this for? Does it have any purpose or meaning?

A biologist asks this question in one way, a spiritual seeker in another. A biologist would ask how dreaming is "adaptive behavior," how it contributes to the survival of the species. Scientists don't yet know the answer to this question.

One proposed explanation for dreaming is "memory consolidation." Some research shows that deprivation of REM sleep makes new learning harder. However, more recent studies have called this finding into serious question.

The late Sir Francis Crick, who won the Nobel Prize for codiscovering the structure of DNA, drew a lot of attention to his theory that dreams clean out redundant associations in the "neural nets" of the brain. He claimed that dreams are a form of "reverse learning." Therefore, Crick suggested, it's best to forget dreams. They have no possible meaning and are essentially the recycling of neuronal garbage.[3]

Crick's skeptical theory has skeptical critics. However, for me it is somewhat beside the point. Crick could be right about the biological function but wrong about the cultural function. There is an objective dimension measurable by instruments and a subjective dimension of vast depth that is measureless. As I worked with Bregman on my dreams, it just became obvious to me how much dreams can mean.

I'm eager to learn more from science about the dreaming brain, but understanding the biological necessity of dreams is very different from understanding their cultural use. There's probably no biological necessity for singing, either, but what would it mean to be a human being in a world without music?

Dreaming is clearly a built-in capacity of the brain-mind, and it's for us to explore and discover what can be done with it. In our culture it is a neglected capacity, perhaps because of our lack of skepticism about skepticism, our certainty that only the objective external is real, even though subjective internal experience of images governs more of our behavior than we know. For millennia, before the invention of writing, before the invention of language, human beings underwent this nightly brain transformation called dreaming, which was like a powerful psychotropic drug administered en masse. Isn't it likely that this shared experience shaped much of how humans think and feel?

At the ASD convention, I learned that brain physiology is not the only scientific approach to the dream. There's also social science. This was University of California professor Dr. William Domhoff's contribution to the discussion.

Researchers collect thousands of dreams and analyze their content. The data helped Domhoff critique many current and past theories of the dream, from Freud and Jung to Hobson. Domhoff was a ubiquitous presence at the

ASD meeting. I called him "the undertaker of dreams" because he'd laid so many other people's theories to rest.

Domhoff's mentor, Professor Calvin Hall, had in the course of a long career beginning in the 1940s carefully collected dream "reports from children, older adults, people in other parts of the world, and those who kept dream diaries. He had over 50,000 dream reports when he died." Hall "developed a quantitative coding system that divided dream content into settings, objects, characters, interactions, emotions, misfortunes."[4]

Following in his mentor's footsteps, Domhoff developed a theory of dream interpretation based on an empirical correlation between dreams and personality.

From this vantage point, he concluded, "[The] judgment could be changed tomorrow by new and original studies by a new generation of young dream researchers, but right now the preponderance of the evidence weighs against any physiological or psychological function for dreaming and dreams.

"This doesn't mean that dreams have no 'meaning,' that they make no sense. To the contrary, dreams correlate with age, gender, culture, and personal preoccupations.

" . . . We have shown that 75 to 100 dreams from a person give us a very good psychological portrait of that individual. Give us 1000 dreams over a couple of decades and we can give you a profile of the person's mind that is almost as individualized and accurate as her or his fingerprints."[5]

Domhoff writes, "Even if dreams have no physiological or psychological functions, human beings gradually invented uses for them. In more technical terms, dreams have an 'emergent' function that develops through culture."

In certain cultures, for instance, shamans use dreams "to diagnose illness . . . and to enter the spiritual world. In that sense, shamans were the first psychoanalysts, and Freud and Jung are modern-day shamans."[6]

He probably meant to use *shaman* as a put-down of Freud and Jung, but having worked with Colette and Bregman, I found the quality of a dream shaman not at all foreign.

Even though much of his psychoanalytic theory is in shambles, in the popular mind Freud remains our most potent authority on dreams. He's an iconic figure with a beard, a Viennese accent, and a couch: his ideas have thoroughly penetrated popular culture and still influence the nonexpert thinking about dreams in the West. Everyone knows Freud's famous metaphor: dreams are "the royal road to the unconscious."

In actual practice, however, working therapists long ago abandoned the royal road. Dr. Paul Lippmann, a training psychoanalyst, told the conference that the relationship between dreams and psychoanalysis could best be described now as a "love affair turned sour."[7]

Lippmann described the early psychoanalysts as "a dream addled bunch, possessed by dreams. By the time Jung joined the party, dreams and psychoanalysis were joined at the hip.

"The current situation is this; for reasons both internal and external psychoanalysis has turned from dreams. . . . In danger of being replaced by drugs and fast cures in a nervous population with an increasingly short attention span, no longer interested in taking the time and the money for prolonged personal exploration, psychoanalytic therapy is competed with by every variety of new age promise, harassed by HMO clerks, reduced by its own failure to deliver on its grand promise of cure and transformation. Thus, psychoanalysis is hardly in the mood to take the time to hang out in dreamy dreamland."[8]

We can blame patient impatience or medical-insurance protocols, but perhaps the trouble with dreams in psychotherapy began at the beginning. By current standards of social science, Freud spoiled his own data. He not only insisted dreams were wishes; he insisted to his patients that dreams were wishes, and argued with them when they didn't agree, and called that disagreement "resistance." He didn't recognize he was cooking the evidence and affecting the dreams his patients reported.

The more empirical research Domhoff espouses—that is, just plain looking at lots and lots of dreams—shows that a number of Freud's scientific hypotheses don't pan out. For instance, Freud believes that almost every dream arises from memory of the previous day's events; but Domhoff writes that "five detailed studies demonstrate that only about half of dreams contain even the slightest 'day residue.' "[9]

Still, without Freud there'd probably be no Domhoff, no Lippmann, and possibly no Dement. We might not be thinking about dreams at all.

If we lose Freud the scientist, there's still Freud the poet and Freud the shaman. He showed the modern world that dreams can change people profoundly. Unfortunately, dreams are rarely used that way anymore. The dream has been left to fend for itself.

That's a shame, because Freud was onto something. It is a precious knowledge and rare: how to use dreams, not only to describe the personality or reveal the unconscious—but to transform a person, to heal, to change and repair what's broken inside.

As the conference ended, and I thought over the different approaches to the dream, I realized again how exciting a discovery Marc Bregman was for me.

I always figured a shaman would have feathers in his hair and live in the jungle of Brazil or sleep in a cave. Or that he would talk in mysterious apothegms like Don Juan in the Castañeda books. It just never occurred to me that I would find a genuine shaman wearing a flannel shirt and blue jeans in a farmhouse in northern Vermont.

2

INTERPRETATIONS

*He dreamed, and behold a ladder set up on the
earth, and the top of it reached to heaven*

—Genesis 28:12

*Happy the mortal, said R. Hoshaya,
who beheld such a thing!*

—Numbers Rabba 4:1

Chapter 8

MARC BREGMAN AND
A PUNCH IN THE GUT

Morrisville, Vermont, June 2001

I drove Route 15 east out of Johnson, Vermont, in a deeply shadowed valley of the Green Mountains. The road keeps climbing, and along the way I saw big open fields, and the beautiful flowing Lamoille. The French named the river for the seagulls—*les mouettes*—that glide over on their way west to Lake Champlain. But some old mapmaker crimped the vowels and uncrossed the t's, and rewrote "La Mouette" as "Lamoïlle," which in French means nothing. Another defeat for the image (seagull) by the word (misspelled).

I passed a cemetery just outside Johnson. In the side of a grassy hill is a bricked-up wall with a door.

But the door in that wall doesn't take you to an angel. It takes you to a cold vault. They stack dead bodies in there in wintertime because the ground is too frozen to bury them.

I love the greenness of the Vermont summer, especially when the gray clouds threaten and the grass gleams with a strange light. But Vermont in the summer deceives you. Everything you see—the roots of dandelions, the peeling hardware sign, the dogs and cows—has survived mountains of snow, tons of ice, and acres of frozen air. The ground is soft with tufts of green, but tougher than it looks. So was Marc Bregman, whom I was on my way to see about my dreams.

I stumbled onto Bregman by accident. All that spring and summer I'd kept busy tracing the lost revelation dream. I saw it as a detective story. *The case of the disappearing dream.*

What is the case? Simply, today we no longer believe in revelation dreams. We lost that, really, a long time ago. Yet there's a contradiction. Privately, individually, dreams still change many lives. Even though we might think it embarrassing to say so out loud, many cherish the memory of a special dream, a dream that carries a message, or makes a promise.

Why and how did we lose the ability to incubate such dreams and use them to grow and to heal? How could a tradition that gave us the dream of the ladder end up essentially "phobic" about the revelation dream? By day, I was investigating these questions when I met Bregman, with piles of books on my desk and stacks at my feet.

But by night I was on a personal search. I was writing down my dreams.

I wrote down dozens that June. I was living at the Vermont Studio Center, an art colony in Johnson, Vermont. I had time to dream.

At first I had trouble remembering. Many mornings I woke with the faint sense I had dreamed, but little more. The memory trace slipped out of my hands and finned off into dark waters. With practice, I fished up fragments: an old boot, a rusty hook with line wound round it. Then, more practice and whole dreams swam into recollection, live, lithe, with sharp teeth, and shiny sharp scales from head to tail.

The more attention I paid, the more dreams repaid my attention. Recollection improved, though not the content. My dreams were gruesome catfish, muddy bottom feeders. They weren't keepers. In content, they were pointless wanderings in cars, meaningless treks on foot through strange cities. These were not the beautiful visualizations of Colette. I was compiling these dreams for a book, but they were embarrassing. I wouldn't show them to my dog.

Dreams carry accusations you don't like to hear, plunge you into embarrassing circumstances. You might show up in your underwear, or worse, in your hypocrisy.

I see a famous politician. In waking life, I despise him. But in the dream, I walk up to him like a fatuous ass and shake his hand, just because he's famous.

I see an ex-husband of an old friend of mine. He's slipped and fallen on the ice. I don't really care, but I run over to him and express concern because "it's the right thing to do."

I see some folks in wheelchairs. I feel sorry for them and invite them for tea. But I know I don't really mean it. When they say yes, I weasel out of it.

I'm lost in a train station, frustrated by clerks who won't answer. I get furious at them, but when I wake I realize I didn't really know my destination.

Where was the ladder? Where the door? I had read all the spiritual books, Jewish and Buddhist. I had the privilege of meeting high lamas and brilliant rabbis. I had lectured on religion, taught high ideals and concepts. I had practiced meditation and prayer. I even thought I'd been "close to God" a few times. I may not be the holiest guy on the block, but I'd gotten somewhere. Except in my dreams.

In dreams, policemen stopped me and asked for my ID. That was a good question: Who was "I" in these dreams? Because the "I" that I was seeing couldn't be me. The person who regularly starred as me nightly was dishonest, a hypocrite and worse. He was far from kind, though he always wanted to look kind. He sure wasn't enlightened.

I wondered about this huge gap between who I thought I was in waking life and how I showed up in my dreams.

Thanks to Colette, I'd seen the door in the wall; I'd passed through and heard an angel sing my new name. But that was just a temporary visit. Where was that angel now? My dreams accused me of spiritual fraud. They were all parking lot and no angel, all wall and no door. These dreams stung more than Colette saying my arms are too short.

My reaction was, The hell with these dreams.

I was beginning to understand for myself the long-standing "phobia" about the dream that Joel Covitz describes.

As the bad news of my dreams swam in night after night, I disposed of them conveniently by the usual method: trivialization. Oh well, I said to myself, they are *only* dreams. Why should I judge myself based on my behavior in my dreams?

My dreams exposed a gap I'd been reading about between personal psychology and spiritual teaching. Our spiritual teachings address in a general way the highest aspirations of humanity: equanimity, enlightenment, goodness, kindness, the desire to know God. They provide practices for reaching these goals: study, prayer, meditation, chanting, yoga. But individuals have personal issues that get in the way: traumas, phobias, anxieties, rage, sexual urges, egotism. They come into spiritual groups and are told: Meditation is the answer. Prayer is the answer. Yoga is the answer. But their personal questions never get answered. All the answers are supposed to come from the teachings, but psychological problems are sometimes papered over. The prescription doesn't match the sickness.

Soul healing has to be one-on-one, heart-to-heart, and many spiritual teachers don't go there anymore. It was a priestly function in Temple times and through confession in the Catholic Church. The great rabbis of Hasidism also practiced it. The *yihud,* or personal one-on-one relationship with their followers, is what made these rabbis "rebbes." Nachman of Bratzlav, for instance, demanded a personal confession from his *Hasidim,* a complete baring of the soul. From that place he could begin the work of spiritual elevation.

But few spiritual groups work that way today. The great divorce between "psychology" and "soul healing" began over a hundred years ago with the rise of psychotherapy. In the Jewish Buddhist dialogue in Dharamsala, Rabbi Jonathan Omer-Man told the Dalai Lama, "We have a very big problem in the West. The work of transformation has been stolen from us by the psychiatrists. The work of transformation, for us, is a holy path. But more and more people who seek transformation, and who are stopped, don't go to a rabbi or a priest. They go to a psychiatrist who will teach them, not enlightenment, but self-satisfaction."[1]

The divorce between psychotherapy and soul-healing has left many spiritually hungry and emotionally incomplete, a result lamented by a number of authors in recent years.

Dr. Mark Epstein, a psychotherapist and vipassana meditator, addresses the failings of Buddhist meditation in *Thoughts Without a Thinker.* He cites a paper by psychologists who "found, to their surprise, that meditators were just as anxious as anyone else. . . . Meditation on its own is not particularly effective in solving people's emotional problems."[2]

It seems equally true to many experts that psychotherapy is incomplete when it fails to address spiritual growth. *Psychology* at root means "the study of the soul." Dr. James Hillman, a prolific neo-Jungian thinker, has led the charge for a restoration of "soul" to psychology.

In *Insearch: Psychology and Religion,* Hillman addresses the role of religious counseling in the task of "reclaiming the lost area of the soul."

"The religious moment," he writes, "is an experience and that experience takes place in the psyche."[3]

This is why I was looking for a practical teacher who could use my dream as a "religious moment."

Such a teacher could go one-on-one like a therapist, but move past the level of personal problems to the soul.

was living that summer in Johnson, Vermont, at the Vermont Studio Center, a terrific refuge for writers and artists founded by painter and architect

Jon Gregg and his wife, Louise von Wiese. I met Lou Albert there, a painter and Buddhist meditator. One morning at breakfast, I shared with Lou my plan to visit the Tibetan Buddhist dream master Tarab Tulku in Copenhagen.

Lou said, Well I've been seeing a dream teacher.

—Where is he?

Morrisville.

I was surprised. Here I was, flying all the way to Copenhagen, and Morrisville is the next town over from Johnson.

—Is he a psychologist?

No, Lou said, he's a postman.

Lou told me that Bregman was so loaded with clients, morning, noon, and evening, that he took new calls only after 9 P.M. I had no great hopes for him, but thought meeting this postman for an hour would make an amusing chapter in a book on dreams. I called Bregman that night. A gruff voice answered after a couple of rings, with a Philadelphia accent I immediately recognized.

Yes, he could see me. In the first session he would lay out his whole dream theory and then work with my dreams. There was no chitchat; his abrupt phone manner was like Madame Colette's.

He gave me directions to his place. Then he said, When and where were you born?

—What do you mean?

I'm going to cast a chart.

—*Jeez*, I thought after I hung up, *a postman—and an astrologer, too.*

M orrisville is small but not quaint. The road in from the west passes two homely shopping centers and then you twist left over the river and then right uphill toward the main drag, past a single movie theater, the Bijou, and a couple of outdoors shops, and a tae kwon do storefront dojo. Not exactly prospering, not falling apart. Fishing is big in Morrisville; hunting, kayaking, bicycling, shooting animals is very big. Morrisville is sturdy and dowdy, not as poor as some Vermont towns, not as prosperous as others, but hanging in there. I like Morrisville. There are evangelicals among the native folk; there are rednecks but also a few ex-hippies.

Another twist and Route 100 has finished its job as Morrisville's Main Street, and you are in the countryside pointing toward Stowe, a tony ski resort with quaint Alpine lodgings, ski shops, and the big mountain looming above.

I passed a dairy farm, a small airport, a golf course, a giant evangelical church shaped like a barn. I'd heard from Lou that Bregman's wife is a minister there.

I pulled into Bregman's driveway, greeted by a large white barking dog. I opened the car door slowly as the dog—who looked part wolf—glared at me. There didn't seem to be anyone around. I stood with my back against the car and talked to the dog, explaining carefully that I was going inside and meant no harm. He growled. I walked slowly down the drive, then waded through a rich planting of day lilies.

Bregman's house is homey and folksy, a large, solid, sturdy place, a Vermont farmhouse. I stood at the door and knocked, but no one answered. I waited, and the dog eyed me. So I pushed the door open and went inside.

Mail was strewn on a dining-room table, and beyond that I saw the entrance to the kitchen. A wood stove for the long winters, and framed needle-point samplers on the wall. Bregman came through a door and told me to come in.

I sized him up. In his fifties, not too tall, but solid, too, like the house, with a graying beard and hair brushed straight back. His hands are big, and I noticed damage, a knuckle missing. Behind his wire rims were intense blue eyes. He wore a checked flannel shirt and jeans. He led me into his office and sat me down in a leather chair. He sat behind his desk.

The crazy white dog trotted and prowled around. The office is full of cuckoo clocks, and a few strange paintings that I later learned were gifts from his clients. One showed a woman held between the paws of a giant dream-hound. I saw a kitschy pageboy Jesus on the wall and a 3-D *Last Supper* on the coffee table and lots of books: Jung and Hillman, but also, surprisingly, a Zohar, the medieval masterpiece of kabbalah. Bregman can be a Jewish name, but since his wife was a minister, I marked him down with a question mark in the religion category.

Bregman asked why I'd come. I told him I wanted to trace the history of the revelation dream beginning in Genesis and find out why it disappeared. He took that in without much comment. I brought a printout of dreams I'd fished up that week—short dreams, long dreams, fragments. I was curious to see what he would do with them, because they made no sense to me.

He took a half hour to explain his theory in general, and some of his words engaged me intellectually, but I thought, Who is he, anyway? In my mind, he was a postman with a nice farmhouse. Maybe my arms were short, but I figured they were longer than his.

How do you know when you've met the teacher of your dreams? By which I mean the spiritual teacher you trust. It's not an intellectual decision. At that level, as Bregman told me his theory, I reacted to his words with words of my own, those gummed strips that come continuously flying through your mind one after the other: *yeah he's got a good rap, a great rap . . .but he's a postman. And he's got my astrology chart there . . . what's with that?*

Then he stopped the theory talk and went to my dreams, and for a time the chattering stopped, replaced by a shock bigger than any Colette had ever dished out.

There's a difference between information and transformation. Plenty of teachers can give you information, but how many can change you in a deep, electric way? Colette had her formidable gift of making brilliant images that spoke back to your images; she had her poetry and her special powers of close listening and seeing—her keen eye for the tiniest physical malformation, her exquisite sensitivity and precision of language, her memory of every time you used the word *anxiety*. An eighty-seven-year-old woman who could define metonymy on the fly as "the unique becoming the One"; she was simply astonishing, quick and brilliant.

Bregman didn't work like that at all. He sometimes used simple words and phrases incorrectly. Every time he did, the English teacher in me winced, and I heard Madame say, "*My students should be more precise . . .*"

I am a word man, so it took a long time to figure out: what Bregman has isn't about words. At least not the way I am used to thinking about words. His point of view was so much based in dream that he heard language from the dream point of view. He'd take a term like "selfish" and hear it as "the self of the fish"; "complaining and blaming" became "comblaming." He was making up his own language out of dreams. He was so deeply rooted in image that words were molten in his mind, not hard bullets like in mine.

But the first hour, I didn't know that. I just knew what he had to offer when he stopped explaining his theory altogether and started working directly with my dreams.

People have different approaches to recording dreams. Some elaborate and explain; some make drawings. I can't draw, but I recorded every detail precisely, because I didn't know yet what was important.

When Bregman asked me to read one of my precision dream accounts, he didn't exactly seem to be listening at all. His mind was tilted sideways and he was listening to a slant off the words, not the words themselves. He ignored many details. He asked me questions that sounded obvious. Or he'd ask, repeatedly, who is so-and-so in the dream, which I'd already explained, and I'd think, I just told you that. . . . You just asked me. . . .

There'd be long pauses, strange pauses, then boom—. . . He told me later, "In this work, we don't interpret; we let the unconscious guide us."

I didn't understand what he meant. Wasn't I bringing him my dreams so he could interpret?

The way he responded to dreams was from intuition. He'd ask a question, and it was just what you were thinking. He had a way to reach into you, to feel into the reality of another person.

I felt that power and resisted. But then he gave me a shock. It was not "*petit*."

William Domhoff, the sociologist of dreams, wrote that "75 to 100 dreams from a person give us a very good psychological portrait of that individual. Give us 1000 dreams over a couple of decades and we can give you a profile of the person's mind."[4]

But Bregman didn't need one thousand dreams or even seventy-five. Just three, and a glance at my horoscope. It's a trick he's done with others many times.

I was horrified by the astrology part.* I don't know what he was doing with the horoscope on his desk—something to do with Dane Rudhyar and Jung. He's patiently explained it a few times since, and each time I've practically fallen asleep with boredom. But he could nail you with a horoscope and three dreams.

He had a way of weaving the dreams of a session together into a single convincing story. Three quick dreams. One was about crickets, the second a fight in a London bar. The third was about a cop who stops me while I'm riding a bicycle. The cop asks me, "Do you have a license for that thing?" I get angry. Then the cop says, "Is this your lawn mower?"

---

*I'm still uncomfortable with it.

I didn't know what the lawn mower symbolized—or the bicycle, for that matter. I told Bregman I'd been taking up biking lately. I was baffled by that dream; Bregman wasn't.

The cop makes a joke, he said, but you don't have any humor about you because you are pretty scared.

—It was funny.

Right. He makes two jokes. You don't get either. He calls your bike a lawn mower, and he asks for your driver's license.

—Right.

If you could have said to him, *Where do you get off?* you two could have had a good belly laugh.

—Yeah I see that now. But I didn't get it in the dream.

What the cop is trying to do is say: What the hell are you scared about? He's trying to deal with your fear and play with it. To get you to see the idea that maybe it's all right for you to be you. He's making fun of you and you don't get the joke. Because you don't trust that you are all right with him.

It was a curious way he was talking: as if the cop in the dream had a motive, as if I had a choice in responding. As I took all that in, Bregman went for the kill.

Did you have issues with your father about being accepted?

—Both ways. I didn't accept him and he didn't accept me.

Oh. Okay. So basically that tied you to your mother.

—Yes, and that was her strategy also.

Because she wanted you to not be with him. She was competitive.

—Absolutely.

Oh boy.

—She won. . .

And you lost. You lost your father.

Boom. A punch in the gut, a blow to the belly. I'd been opened up like a cheap safe and all my cash was on the table. I couldn't believe he'd gotten to this core issue so quickly. It hurt and stunned, but I knew that what he said was true.

As far back as I could remember—and there was no sponge to wipe it clean—I'd always felt distant from my father. Until Bregman said it, though, I'd never thought of it before as losing him.

What made it powerful was how Bregman hooked his point into that silly dream. He was right. The cop was being funny and just kidding me guy to guy, but I completely missed it.

I realized that the dream was showing me a very familiar scenario. It was something I knew about myself but had never been able to finger before: something missing in how I related to men in authority. It was the story of every male teacher I'd ever subverted, every potential mentor I'd found flaws in, every male acquaintance I'd failed to connect with as a friend. It was a template for all my failures to relate to men, and behind it was this huge loss of a father I hadn't realized was a loss.

So Bregman gave me a big shock. He told me later that he liked to get in quick, the first session, because, he said, "the pathology is listening in," and that way, the pathology knew that he knew.

He hadn't won me over completely.

I felt the blow to the stomach, yes; but the stronger the blow, the more I doubted. I set in on his theory; I seized on his words. What did he mean—emotions versus feelings; aren't they the same? What was all this talk about pathology? I found that term difficult, even offensive. The counteroffensive was already beginning, for Bregman was also a male mentor, and the pattern of opposition didn't quit just because he'd pointed it out.

But when he asked me at the end of the session, "Do you want to come back?" I knew the answer was yes.

The words kept coming. But the blow to the stomach had also happened, and even though I had no idea where it would lead me, the journey in dreams was now happening.

I went back to my stacks of books, to Genesis, to my study of the disappearing dream. I tried to go back to normal, but I was shaken.

Every week after that he'd ask me, "Do you want to come back?" Every week I'd say yes.

One night, two years after that first encounter with Bregman, *I dreamed. . . .*

Chapter 9

THE BOOK OF K de G

. . . it was dark in my study but the computer screen was lit.

So many times in the waking world, I'd come to this room lined with books, sat at my blue chair, typing, sometimes knowing where a sentence was going, other times trusting that the right words would come in the right rhythms.

I came into the study to write. But a large blue book blocked my way, propped against the monitor. Four feet tall, six inches thick. Embossed on the cover in gold were mysterious initials, "K de G."

I'd seen books like this before, books that opened from the back, old Hebrew books of knowledge, the "*seforim*" collected by eager scholars with trembling hands. You feel that excitement bubbling around books in certain ultra-Orthodox enclaves in Jerusalem. Books are sold in small shops but also spill out onto the streets. On a small card table at a street corner, two thin men rummage through a mad pile of books, glance at a few pages, put them down, pick up another. There people fiercely believe that a book—this book, the next book, some book—will contain the word that will set all the other words on fire.

The devout believe that a book can change your life. So do I. It may be one book for me and another for you; it may be poetry or physics, philosophy or history—but we believers in the word are all, one way or another, people of the book. For us, books are holy. They are how souls travel, how the spirit of one person enters another. Who ever says, "My life was changed by a DVD"? We still say, though: a book changed my life.

There's an e-mail from my father. His friends have met the teacher who wrote this book. They say the teacher is entirely "natural, warm, and human."

Intrigued, I open the book from the back. It appears to be a commentary on the book of Genesis.

How nice, because I was writing about the revelation dream in Genesis, and now a dream came to help.

Rabbi K de G is very literate, very modern. He quotes a poem by Shakespeare. He says, "The poem appears twice in the same play. Once in the mouth of Cleopatra. Another time in the mouth of a second character."

In the dream, I thumb through the book of K de G. I'm fascinated by this nonsense about two poems in Shakespeare, which in the dream I believe is true.

When I wake, I get the joke. In the dream, I come into my study to write.

But I am not writing. I am reading.

It is a funny dream, with an exact sense of humor. It fits my brain like a glove fits a hand; it fits my life. A dream is never off-the-rack. A dream is always sewn with your exact dimensions in mind, your humor, your obsessions. A dream fits.

When I began to study my dreams closely, I noticed how exquisitely made many are, how difficult to communicate that exquisite beauty to another because in most dreams the exquisite is idiosyncratic. Each dream invents its own beautiful language, and something always gets lost in translation. My dream was made for me as your dream is made for you.

A dream provides an exact tincture of the soul, a strong whiff—ammonia or perfume—to wake us from a faint-hearted life.

Was the dream really just a joke? I thought about an interpretation: the big blue book, a commentary on Genesis—propped against the screen. This seemed to say, Beginning is hard. Originality is impossible. Writing about dreams is surely impossible. The best you'll ever do is a commentary.

Before every new book stand all the other books. Before every word is the history of all the words ever written or spoken, and the confusing reverberation of how they are read and heard. And the perverse way words are manipulated, twisted away from the world of truth to the world of power and lies. The Jewish mystics say, "The world is wrong names." This is a profound understanding. All the names we use to describe our world are somehow wrong. It's like this: someone has washed all the jars, and the labels slipped off; now the right names can't be read or they've been re-pasted on the wrong jars.

Abstraction is the problem. Every word, even the most abstract, begins life as an image, but as words become mere words, the images die inside them and all we are left with are the shells. The word *is*, for instance, once meant "to breathe." Being is breathing—how lovely.

Once words lose anchor in the sensual world, they drift inevitably toward the world of lies. It's not the fault of words; it's how they come between us and things. The word *abstract* means "to draw away"; our abstractions draw us away from the world. Then we forget their sensual origins. For every word once grew out of the five senses and everyday life. If you brush off the ignorant dirt that covers it, a word is a potato—with deep roots in the soil, and even eyes that grow underground.

If the images in our dreams are "sovereign in the mind," as Colette insisted, then the poor words we bring to them after we wake can be only second-best.

When I try to interpret my own dream, the attempt fails miserably. It's like trying to catch a glimpse of the back of your head in a mirror.

Who is Rabbi K de G?

Why is K de G's book written from back to front?

Why does K de G write about Shakespeare? What does it mean? What does it all, if anything, mean?

All such questions are tendrils of weeds. *But I couldn't help asking them.* They are how the delicate flower of the dream hides itself in prickles and thorns. *But I didn't know that at the time.* I was still struggling against Bregman dream by dream. He spoke of facilitating the dream. But I wanted him to interpret the dream.

In the manner of Freud, I could make my own free associations to the book of K de G. Its mix of wisdom and poetry, Genesis and Shakespeare, recalls the admirable writing of Dr. Avivah Zornberg, a brilliant Orthodox teacher with a Ph.D. in literature whom I heard lecture in Jerusalem the summer I met Colette. Dr. Z. has herself written a commentary on Genesis, which combines traditional reverence for the Bible with a wide range of literary references.[10]

So is Dr. Z. the prototype for the mysterious Rabbi K de G?

She mixes modern literature with respect for the ancient word. That is a very attractive sort of presentation for me, for others—one foot in the contemporary, the other in the ancient world, arms and legs stretched out wide.

But it's also easy to fall in that position.

We so much want the old truth and the new to match that we stretch and stretch, modifying the old words or reframing our new experience until sometimes something—truth—has to give.

This is the problem of all established religion. Old words stiffen into dead dogma. Fresh revelations don't fit old paradigms. We interpret and reinterpret to fit it all together until the words seem stretched out of shape.

Dreams, in particular, can be terribly irreverent. They challenge received wisdom. A dream offers private revelation, not public religion. A dream can offer a glimpse of life from an entirely unknown perspective, a lightning flash—of self-exposure.

Such clear-cut dreams are rare. The more run-of-the-mill dreams, the dreams most of us have—lost in the parking lot, looking for a purse or wallet, desperate to find a bathroom—these common dreams seem easy to dismiss.

But dreams offer a deceptive surface: we have to navigate very carefully to arrive at the true point of view of our dreams and what they are showing us about life. Actually, the more banal the dream, the more powerful a statement it can be.

The boring parking-lot dream conceals its intent because dream thinking is completely alien to waking consciousness. The dream hides its message in the obvious; it recycles images from waking, but the images aren't about waking. You need someone to sort the confusion. Bregman went for what he called the belly button: the cop was making fun of my bicycle—but I couldn't see why.

If understood rightly, a dream has a unique attitude toward our daylight experience—a destructive attitude, one might say.

Once I dreamed I was on my deathbed reciting my résumé. What an absurd image to wake me from the sleep of daily life.

Now, that was a distinct message, and if looked at from the correct angle, the point of view was bitterly ironic. That's clear when you examine how they made the dream, what the materials were they used, how they twisted them with a certain mockery.

If you ask, Who is "they"?—I understand.

Bregman often spoke of THEY when we first met. He'd ask, "Why did THEY send you that dream?" I chalked it up to his outlandish way of talking. It intrigued me, but it also gave my doubts ammunition.

What could he mean, "THEY"? Now that science sticks electrodes into the dream, how could anyone speak of THEY?

But that is how this postman spoke. I decided to humor him.

My research suggested that the ancients were on Bregman's side. The oldest cultures of the Near East that we know of—Sumer, Babylon, Egypt—saw the dream as coming from outside the dreamer. This was the reigning theory almost everywhere you looked for thousands of years in the ancient world—from, say, 3000 B.C.E. in Sumer to the end of the cult of Asclepius in the sixth century C.E.* Before the hiding of God's face, there was no trouble believing dreams came from a divine realm beyond the consciousness of the individual. The dream lived its own mysterious life, independent of the dreamer.

Bregman spoke from that ancient view. If you accept "THEY," even provisionally, then a dream can no longer be dismissed quite so easily as a chance by-product of the undigested egg foo yong I ate last night. Nor as the battlefield report of those two great Freudian antagonists the ego and the id. Nor as the random activation of neurons from an overactive hippocampus, as Hobson theorized.

No, the dream has its own right to exist. Every other theory, modern or ancient, implies that a dream is my product; that, mind or brain, I am the sole creator of my dreams.

That misses something subtle. Certain dreams don't feel that way. They seem too well made, too brilliant; they speak from a knowledge I don't have, of worlds I don't know and of perspectives I can barely grasp in waking consciousness. It is what Freud spoke of as "the uncanny," the strange knowledge dreams can have. They challenge too many of my assumptions to have come only from me.

In the ancient world, it was natural to speak of THEY who send the dream. THEY could be angels or demons, gods or goddesses; Enki or Apollo or Hades; the angel Jibril, who dictated the Koran to Muhammad; or the angel Gabriel, known in Hebrew as the "master of the dream." These supernatural dream masters had many names, but the common belief was that anything this beautifully made, this brilliant, complex, and powerful, must have come from a realm beyond the limits of the personal.

To the Greeks this seemed obvious. "Dreams" are demigods with wings who roost in a tree outside Hades. "Dream" has a body, walks around your house, stands at the head of your bed, reminds you you're asleep. You catch a glimpse of Dream stealing out of your chamber as you wake. The Greeks must have felt at one time that the dream is independently real.

---

*In the temples of the physician-god Asclepius, the healing god appeared to the sick in dreams.

Now we think real only what we can see and touch.

We divide the world: brain versus mind, body versus soul, reality versus dream. We have no THEY.

So, to ask Bregman's question: Why did THEY send me this dream of K de G?

Were THEY trying to help me write? Or chide me for my chutzpah? Did THEY want me to study the great blue book? Or remove it from the monitor and start typing?

THEY are very playful, these masters of the dream, and I couldn't solve this puzzle quickly. I could only live it.

In general, dreams present to the imagination the thorniest of philosophical issues: What is real? That is why Nietzsche traced the origin of all metaphysics to dreaming.[2]

The Chinese philosopher Chuang Tzu asked, Do I dream of a butterfly or does the butterfly dream me? Is a dream real or less real than waking life? Surreal or unreal? The dream questions reality as much as reality questions the dream. I am open to these questions and want to stay open to them.

So I come back to live the images of K de G. These were my images, not Colette's, not anyone else's. I was entitled to my own quandary.

A blue book blocks the computer screen. That's where I do my writing. If the monitor represents my writing, the book gets in the way.

"I think yes the book is all the intellectual stuff that gets in the way. So pick up the fucking book and throw it out the window." My painter friend at the Vermont Studio Center hates books, believes devoutly that words and concepts are useless to him.

"Right," I say to my painter friend. "But I can't. And I don't. In the dream I'm fascinated with the book and also somehow the book comes from my father and there's some connection to my father."

"Or to the fathers," someone else at the table says. "The forefathers."

Yes, to the forefathers, to the ancestors, biblical and literary, Genesis and Shakespeare, the rabbis, the authors, the mentors—all of that. I am drawn to them.

It's not so easy to throw this *fucking* book out the window. It is way heavy. It carries the weight of my whole life.

So, even though I think my painter friend might have a good point, I can't do it. I am just too fascinated with this book of K de G, with books in general. Surely that fascination is good. Surely there must be a reason why THEY sent the giant blue book in a dream. Surely THEY want me to open the book and read it.

In my study, my desk is stacked with books about Genesis. (Sometimes they do block a view of the monitor and I have to shove them aside to type.) I have a tea-stained bookmark in *Visions of the Night,* Joel Covitz's translation and commentary on seventeenth-century Rabbi Shlomo Almoli's kabbalistic work on dreams. I am studying the Talmudic discussion of dreams, the so-called rabbinic dream book. I am digging into the history of the revelation dream. I also want to learn how and why it disappeared.

Before meeting Bregman in our regular session, I landed on a provisional interpretation of "K de G" that I found very pleasing. After so many lousy dreams of cops chasing me, at last THEY have sent me encouragement. THEY are showing me the book I am to write, a commentary on Genesis.

I even began to think I'd cracked the code of K de G. The *G* stood for *Genesis,* and the *K* for *Kamenetz.*

As it turned out, my celebration was premature. I didn't have a clue who THEY were or what THEY wanted to show me.

Chapter 10

YOU ARE A DEAD MAN

Dumuzi and Abimelech

To begin at the beginning of the revelation dream, I should go back further. For Genesis is not our oldest story of dreams.

There are much older stories from southern Iraq, where the Sumerians built their civilization over five thousand years ago, prospering on the agricultural plenty of the flood plain of the Tigris and Euphrates. They learned to build storehouses for grains, and towns and cities. They learned how to build tall towers of brick; the ziggurat of Ur is the prototype for the Tower of Babel. They also invented the wheeled chariot, prototype for Ezekiel's vision. Around 3400 B.C.E., they invented writing, inscribing clay tablets with a stylus—the writing we know as wedge-shape, or cuneiform.

Among the oldest cuneiform writings is the dream of Dumuzi, the shepherd king, culture hero, and god of Sumer.

In ancient times . . . the shepherd lay down, he lay down to dream. He woke up—it was a dream! He shivered—it was sleep! He rubbed his eyes, he was terrified.

Dumuzi tells his terrifying dream to his sister, Geshtin-anna:

"A dream, my sister! A dream! In my dream, rushes were rising up for me. . . . Tall trees in the forest were rising up together over me. Water was poured over my holy coals for me, the cover of my holy churn was being removed, my holy drinking cup was torn down from the peg where it hung, my shepherd's stick disappeared from me. . . . The churns were lying on their side,

*no milk was poured, the drinking cups were lying on their side, Dumuzi was
dead, the sheepfold was haunted.*"[1]

This is one of the world's oldest recorded dreams, and it's a nightmare.
The shepherd stumbles through his former life and sees everything he owned
broken, destroyed, or vanished. It's a dream of being exposed, the ancient
ancestor of our modern nightmares of being stark naked in a classroom or
business meeting.

Except Dumuzi's dream is worse: he sees the world from the point of view
of his own death. No wonder he panics when he wakes. He cries out for his
sister, the dream interpreter:

"Bring, bring, bring my sister! Bring my Geshtin-anna, bring my sister! . . .
Bring my wise woman, who knows the meanings of dreams, bring my sister!
I will relate the dream to her."

But Geshtin-anna offers no comfort:

"My brother, your dream is not favorable, don't tell me any more of it!"
Reluctantly, she tells him that malevolent demons will destroy his life.

The people who inscribed this story on clay knew about dreams and their
corrosive power to strip you of your old life and its pretensions, to show you
the one thing you don't want to imagine, your own death. This is revelation
with a sting: the Sumerians believed that dreams were implacable omens. A
dream like this just can't be interpreted away easily.

Sumerian nobles also practiced dream incubation, deliberately cultivating dreams in sacred settings to receive visions and guidance from their gods
and goddesses.

To incubate a dream, a very pious royal person would sleep in a ritual hut of
reeds. There he could deliberately seek a dream to bring down a message from
the divine realm. That's how the Sumerian Noah (Ziusudra), listening through
the thin walls of his hut, overheard the gods decree a worldwide flood.

"Evidently," writes Dr. Curtiss Hoffman, a student of dreams in the ancient Near East, "the Sumerians made a distinction between clear dreams
which require proper preparation and obscure symbolic dreams which come
to everyone else."[2]

I n my obscure symbolic dream of K de G, every word, every letter, demands
interpretation. I play both parts: dreamer and interpreter, brother and
sister, Dumuzi and Geshtin-anna.

In the one-hundredth year of our Freud, this is the game we love to play with our dreams. We want to solve the dream puzzle on our own. Despite all the debunking of Freud in recent years, he has not been dislodged from my mind. His beard, his cigar, his couch—they still haunt me. He shapes how we think about thinking. He's the interior designer of my mind: here's the unconscious, there's the ego, this is the id. To think about dreams without him is impossible. My whole effort to trace the history of interpretation would lead inevitably to him, but I did not know how I would get past him.

Suppose, though, as Bregman insisted, dreams do come from a THEY. Suppose all the details—the big thick book, the "K de G," Shakespeare, Genesis—are bait to mock the proud intellect.

Yet this clever mouse goes for the cheese every time, because I, like everyone else, buy into a central idea in Western culture about dreams, an idea Freud did so much to revive.

Dreams are meant to be interpreted.

This idea did not begin with Freud, but lodged itself much earlier in the mind of the West, where my dream pointed: the book of Genesis.

For that reason, although the Sumerian dream stories are oldest, and Homer could claim some rivalry in the matter, Genesis remains our primordial dream book in the West.

Not that we read actual dream reports in Genesis, any more than in the clay tablets of Sumer. We read dream stories. But for millennia these stories framed how we think about dreams—and every subsequent theory answers to them.

Genesis gave us the promise of revelation, and initiated the tangled history of our response to dreams.

Genesis also bequeathed us those two great heroes of the dream, father and son, Jacob and Joseph.

Moreover, hidden in Genesis are three very usable patterns for the revelation dream. I call them the warning dream, the essential image dream, and the dream journey. But we have seemingly forgotten these gifts.

In fact, the very first dream in Genesis is one most of us have forgotten.

That may be because the Bible's very first dream implies the outlook I had so much difficulty accepting from Bregman. An outlook that sounds quaint, odd, superstitious, or credulous.

Where does the word "dream" first appear in the Genesis narrative? We read of no dreams in Eden, for Eden is itself a giant dream, where Adam and Eve and God and talking serpents mingle freely; where, with odd surrealism, the voice of God can be heard *walking* in the cool of day.

No dreams enter the biblical story line until human beings have lost all innocence, gone through the flood, and screwed things up again with the Tower of Babel. God communicates to Adam and Eve, to Noah and Abraham, by voice.*

The first dream in Genesis comes as an incident in Abraham's story. He has received his call from God and is on his way to Canaan with his wife, Sarah. In the southern desert, he has a run in with a petty king, Abimelech.

"Sarah is my sister," Abraham tells him. He fears that Abimelech will take his wife, which is exactly what happens. But that night, God appears to Abimelech in a dream and says, "You are a dead man, because of the woman whom you have taken; for she is a man's wife."

Abimelech defends himself: "Didn't he say, She is my sister? And she even she herself said, He is my brother. In integrity of heart and innocence of hands have I done this."

God says, "Yes I know you did this in the integrity of your heart. For I also kept you from sinning against me. Therefore I did not let you touch her. Now therefore restore the man his wife for he is a prophet and shall pray for you, and you will live. If you don't restore her, know that you shall surely die, you and all who are yours" (Gen. 20:1–6).

The story assumes quite casually that God warns people in dreams. That's a belief ancient Israel shared with the entire Near East—with Sumer, Babylon, and Egypt—and with ancient Greece as well. We find this in literary form in the tales of Gilgamesh, the book of Genesis, and the Iliad and Odyssey of Homer. To the skeptical mind it seems all too simple and very unlikely. To the heart it has implications that challenge everything we think is real.

The first hour, Bregman made clear that he is an ancient, too. He told me, "A dream is a net cast by the divine to bring us back to ourselves."

Genesis is a book woven of many strands, with tales from different eras redacted by later hands. Abimelech's tale may belong to an older strand of oral legends.

In the ancient Near East, it seemed obvious that dreams can be divine messages. In the information age, Dr. Crick says dreams are only spam.

---

*In Genesis 15, the Lord speaks to Abram in a "vision" and again after an overpowering sleep, but the word *dream* is not used.

Perhaps our dreams seem like "garbage" because we don't show them the proper respect. Perhaps if we really want to hear God speak to us in dreams, we would have to sleep as the Sumerians did, in a reed hut open to the wind, or at least in a tent in the wilderness, far from the harsh static of civilization. Maybe then we'd get a clear transmission into our busy minds through our thick skulls.

Our dreams are rarely clear warnings like Abimelech's. We aren't easily granted such revelations. Few would claim to hear God speaking directly in sleep. (Even my friend David could not remember what God said to him.)

Those who do believe that God speaks to them in dreams are usually classified in psychiatric categories. It would be crazy to take dreams that seriously, to take them as warning messages from God, as Bregman did.

Wouldn't it?

Even if we wanted to believe it possible, our dreams are commonly muddy and confusing. We tend to dismiss their warnings if we hear them at all, or we forget them easily. If a dream breaks through our indifference or amnesia and scares us to death, then, like Dumuzi, we cry out—for a therapist: Dr. Geshtin-anna. "Bring my sister! Bring my wise woman, who knows the meanings of dreams, bring my sister! I will relate the dream to her."

Suppose, though, the problem isn't with the dream, but with us. Suppose dreams try to scare us because we are so stubborn. Our dreams may know our faults better than we do and try to provoke us until we admit what's wrong, the way the motorcycle cop tried to tease me about the bicycle.

Our dreams tease us and bait us and humble us with their red herrings and their blue cheese, their embellishments, their K de G, their Cleopatra—but we don't get the joke.

If I do not feel that a dream can warn me, I cannot change my life as Abimelech did—before it is too late.

Yet I knew for a fact that dreams had changed me. At two different points in my life, dreams fished me from the waters of oblivion, jerked me up into consciousness sputtering like a man nearly drowned.

True, I did not hear God speak in my dreams as Abimelech did. But they brought me twice to the borderland of life and death. Once I saw my dead grandfather, and he gave me courage; another time I heard from my mother after her death. These were eerie, lucid dreams, where you know that what you are seeing is impossible but you see it anyway. My dead ones spoke to me in the dream as though very much alive, though I also knew very clearly that they were not. I've never forgotten what they told me.[3]

To a scientist looking at the brain level, these dreams may have been, as the Nobel laureate biologist Sir Francis Crick proposed, no more than the "recycling of neuronal garbage." But that's not how they felt in my life.

How did Abimelech feel when he heard, "You are a dead man"?

Certain dreams carry a grain of terror. During the first year of seeing Bregman, I would occasionally have out-and-out nightmares.

My tennis shoe sticks to an icy sidewalk: I leave behind five bleeding toe stumps. A sadist surgeon performs a gruesome operation while I watch in horror. Skinheads in a London bar threaten me and corner me in an alley; I wake screaming. Dangerous criminals chase me through city streets; I'm fearful, I'm in panic. But if these are warnings, I don't yet understand what's being revealed.

Dumuzi lives in a Sumerian realm of implacable and relentless demons; he cannot escape his doom. Abimelech's dream comes in a new moral framework, where the terror is not absolute, where there is hope for justice. It's possible for Abimelech to avoid his fate, but only if he changes his behavior. His dream comes as a warning, not a death sentence.

Bregman, likewise, sought to facilitate the warning . . . so you can change the behavior. To do that, he had to persuade you to face what the dream is trying to show you. You have to face "the fact of the dream."

The first revelation dream in Genesis is a pointed warning, full of fear. The second is a promise: Jacob's ladder is the most important dream story in the West.

Chapter 11

JACOB, THE HERO OF THE
REVELATION DREAM

Jacob's dream of the ladder is loved by mystics, by dreaming children, and by anyone with a dreamer's soul. It makes a promise to us all.

At the top of the ladder, God tells the dreamer something we'd all want to hear if we could only believe it: "I am with you . . . and I will be with you where you go. . . . I will take you where you are going . . . I will not leave you."

If Abimelech's warning dream comes with fear, the promise dream shows the face of love.

Jacob receives a promise rooted in a special knowledge: he sees a whole heavenly world revealed. Yet such knowledge is difficult to live with. Jacob is one of the most human figures in the Bible. We see in the story of the dream and its aftermath how revelation feels, how Jacob struggles with its implications, how he loses grasp of it.

He is on the run from his past. Under the influence of his mother, he has just deceived his father and cheated his brother. He flees the consequences, sleeps out in the wild, alone and frightened, his head on a heap of rocks.

A powerful painting in the Prado by José de Ribera pictures Jacob as a strong young man with a beard, with his eyes shut, sleeping on the ground. Ribera's Jacob is so full of life and youth, vigorous flesh and blood, that you feel you could touch him. But the angels in the dream are limned in a very bright yellow, against a white sky, so they barely can be seen.

Ribera vividly paints two worlds meeting, one substantial and grounded, the other etched in air.

Jacob dreams of a ladder between earth and heaven, angels walking down it. He sees God at the top. What face of God he sees we do not know. The story avoids the issue by emphasizing God's voice. God promises Jacob and his descendants, "I will be with you."

Seeing is believing; seeing is knowing. Isn't this exactly the seeing Moses yearned for when he asked to see God's face, the glory the chariot riders sought in their visualizations? Of all the characters in Genesis, only Jacob seems to see God, and when he wakes from this dream, he looks around in awe. The very rocks he laid his head on, the ground at his feet—all have been transformed. "How awesome is this place," he says, for this is the place of God.

For the moment, the dream has transformed his reality instead of the other way around.

His words capture the uncanny quality of waking from a revelation dream in the light of its truth. The revelation of an entire new reality is a knowledge different from the secondhand knowledge in books. In English we don't make the distinction generally, but in Greek there is a separate word for direct knowledge: *gnosis*.

Jacob's dream gnosis sets him on the path that will eventually change everything about his life, even his name.

While I demanded interpretation from Bregman, Jacob does not interpret his dream. Instead the dream interprets him.

That is, the dream asserts through powerful images a reality more real than the ground on which Jacob rests. That reality challenges the ordinary sense of what is real by making vivid the existence of another realm of consciousness.

The dream is not only real; it alters Jacob's reality. That is why Jacob says, "How awesome is this place." Certainly, this stony ground where he lay his head did not appear awesome before the dream. What's changed is his gnosis: he now knows what he "didn't know" before; he has seen the realm of the invisible.

Jacob's initial response of awe feels right. It suggests Freud has everything backward when he writes, "Dreams are derived from the past in every sense."[1] The ladder dream doesn't come to tell Jacob something about his past. It comes from the future. Dreams are not the fruit of reality, but the stem.

Such dreams demand a response different from mere interpretation, if interpretation means recalling events or memories tied to the dream, as Freud suggests. Bregman would show me a different way to respond, but it did not come easily.

The promise of a dream is difficult to realize. The solid earth gives way reluctantly to the insubstantial etching of a dream. The idea that a dream comes from a divine realm—from a THEY, as Bregman put it—is too challenging, too strange and fantastic, too contradictory with respect to all we think of as real, to be easily accepted. We have to do a lot of work to accept the fact of the dream. Keeping faith, abiding with the dream, not interpreting it—this is the path Jacob eventually took, but not without a hard struggle.

He stumbles often. Jacob is very much flesh and blood, just as Ribera painted him—a man of doubts and conflicts. He is very human to us, with all his flaws and pain. He struggles greatly between his earthiness and his soulfulness. We can identify with him as he wakes in awe, and identify again as he falls away from the promise of the dream, in withdrawal and retreat. I could identify with him in my struggles with my own dreams, which I tried to interpret in practical terms, as if the ladder in Jacob's dream had been purchased the day before at the hardware store.

Jacob builds an altar at his dreaming spot. But then he makes a strange, halfhearted vow: if God will protect me, I will do this and that in return. Gnosis yields to calculation. He turns a brilliant promise into a mere bargain. As the rabbinic commentators note: "Jacob vowed and lost."[2] He made a vow he need not have made.

Because he doubts his dream, Jacob will strive with those of a similarly pragmatic cast of mind, like his father-in-law, Laban. He must wrestle with himself and his doubts, and it's not until he wrestles the angel that Jacob acquires the name Israel, signaling his real transformation. *Jacob* means "the heel"; he grabbed his brother Esau's heel in the womb. Jacob remains a heel to his father and brother, and this is his main predicament in life. But *Israel* takes all his struggling to a spiritual level, for it means "one who contends with the divine," and that is the true situation of his soul.

Part Jacob and part Israel, we live halfway between the predicaments of waking life and the promise of our dreams, and we have difficulty moving from one to the other.

It's naive to think one dream can instantly change the mental habits of a lifetime, the carefully constructed mask of the outer personality. Nor can the images of the dream, however sovereign, withstand the barrage of doubts that follow inevitably when we wake. We return from the clarity of the dream to the confusion of life, from the clarity of image to the welter of words. To reorient oneself completely to a revelation dream would require major changes in personal psychology, if the narrative that follows Jacob's dream is any indication. Jacob knows that the place he dreamed is awesome, yet he can't seem to stay in this place of awe. His wavering is something mystical teachers have always understood. As Rabbi Kalonymus Shapira wrote in *Conscious Community,* "When we are truly moved and awake, we understand, without any conscious effort, that God's presence extends from the unreachable heights right down to us.

"In our own way, in this elevated emotional state, we understand how exquisite is the moment."

But, "it is difficult to stay on this level and hold on to this state of awareness."[3]

Shapira, the last great Hasidic master of Poland, died tragically in a concentration camp. He was a devoted educator who lived near Warsaw and wanted to raise the spiritual level of people who had to balance practical life with a life of the soul.

In *Conscious Community* he writes of the dilemma of ordinary people who might attain very high levels of consciousness in their meditations, but who also must then return to the business of daily life. We let go of the moment of revelation, the rebbe writes, for two reasons:

First stress and sadness crop up and this causes emotional contraction.
Second, the habitual mind returns, looking for descriptions and
explanations. This mental level cannot contain the higher dimensions
of thought. It is pointless to try to decipher this experience in your
normal state of mind.[4]

To illustrate the idea, the rebbe tells a parable of a dream:

A pauper, God help him, goes door to door, begging. He dreams one
night he has become the king, but in the morning he is upset and he cries:
"Just to keep my family alive, I have to beg door to door. Now that I am
promoted to king, the whole royal entourage is dependent on me. How
will I ever have the strength to beg all over the world?"
   He views his kingship through the prism of his poverty. He supposes
that he will have to support the army by begging, just as he supports his
family now. He cannot transcend his poverty long enough to realize that as
king, his whole means of sustenance will be qualitatively different.[5]

The rebbe uses the parable of the pauper's dream to explain how we lose
grasp of the moment of enlightenment. The difficulty of holding on to an inner vision in the face of the pressing demands of mundane daily life applies
not just to individuals, but to communities and whole traditions. Not only
have we lost the memory of last night's dream; our culture has lost the promise of the ladder. We need a way to work with dreams that come by night, so
as to keep their promise in our days.

   That is why whenever I asked him to interpret, Bregman answered that he
was "facilitating" the dream instead. He asked me to do "homework," which
means: to visualize key images in the dream, to keep them alive hourly in
consciousness. This homework recalled the imaginal exercises of Colette,
though with additional power, because the images, after all, came out of my
own dreams. Through homework my dreams became meditations exactly
tailored to my spiritual condition.

   Sometimes these homework images were very difficult and challenging: they touched on profound feelings and stirred up the depths. In other
cases the dream was really a warning, only I couldn't feel it because I was too
numb.

   In fact, K de G proved to be a warning dream—not as dire as Abimelech's,
but a warning all the same. If I had the strength to accept it.

Jacob's story also shows him struggling along the path of living with and from his dreams.

But this is not the main path of the biblical tradition. There is an inner and outer history of dreams: the history of our dreams, and the history of how they are received. That outer history begins with Joseph, the paragon of all dream interpreters.

Chapter 12

JOSEPH THE DREAMER AND
JOSEPH THE INTERPRETER

The problem of interpretation defined my struggle with Bregman at the outset. I kept waiting for him to interpret my dream; he kept wanting to "facilitate" the dream, which for a long time I didn't understand. I wanted to know, and he wanted me to feel.

Week by week I insisted he interpret. *Give me the answer, Geshtin-anna. Tell me what it means.* Week by week Bregman returned me to my dreams, to face the images and feelings there.

I did not want to do my homework. I did not want to abide with the fear or the sadness or the rage the images presented me. My reflex response to a dream is to read it. Read it like a book.

This reflex is so widespread, it feels entirely natural. Yet there is no inherent reason a dream should be interpreted into words; it's just what we do. I've been a reader since I was five. I've been reading and reading and haven't stopped believing that I can find the answers to any question in books. So why wouldn't I read dreams the same way?

As a child, when I first read the Joseph story I identified with him in many ways: as a loner in his large family, as a revealer of secret messages, as a reader of dreams.

But in rereading Genesis, I was surprised to discover two Josephs. I'd remembered only Joseph the interpreter. But before Joseph the interpreter comes Joseph the dreamer.

He's a son in a troubled family rife with competition and rivalry fostered by his father, Jacob, who "loved Joseph more than all his children, because he was the son of his old age." His brothers "hated him" for that.

Now Joseph dreamed a dream, and he told it to his brothers; and they hated him even more. He said to them, Hear, I beg you, this dream which I have dreamed; For, behold, we were binding sheaves in the field, and, lo, my sheaf arose, and also stood upright; and, behold, your sheaves stood around, and made obeisance to my sheaf (Gen. 37:5–7).

This is a remarkable dream. The image is remarkably potent. "My sheaf arose, and . . . stood upright." The erect sheaf is phallic, a sign of power.

The brothers are outraged: they "hated him even more for his dreams"—and "for his words."

It is bad enough to dream, worse to declare your dream openly to the world. His brothers' response launches Joseph into a life of peril. He is dumped in a pit, sold into slavery, accused by Potiphar's wife, imprisoned. By the end of this series of misfortunes, he is no longer a boy. He has learned firsthand about the seductions and duplicity of the world. False accusation, false imprisonment have been his fate. If he has more dreams, he keeps them to himself.

One lesson seems clear: a dreamer does not come to power merely by announcing his dream. But no matter. Joseph's dream of the sheaf is always true. Even in prison, the warden notices his special quality, and he is put in command of the other prisoners. Wherever he goes, Joseph stands upright like the sheaf. The dream has given him a great gift, an essential image of his life.

The dream of Abimelech is a warning; the dream of Jacob reveals a whole world. Joseph's dream of the sheaf shows another gift of the revelation dream: to reveal you to yourself. Not as you are now, but as you are in essence. These are the three gifts of the revelation dream in Genesis: Abimelech's, Jacob's, and Joseph's. Somehow we have misplaced them all.

The essential image is a great gift of the dream. Joseph sees the situation of his soul; he sees how he is seen by God. The image may have nothing to do with how others see you now. It may contradict what you know of yourself or what others know of you, the figure you cut in the world.

The erect sheaf exemplifies an archetypal dream in Bregman's work, which often includes magical or miraculous events. In this case the miracle is a sheaf that stands upright on its own. This can happen only if it's being supported invisibly. That points to the inner meaning of the dream.

Such dreams are not often well received by others. Joseph's dream infuriated his family. He was "a lad of seventeen," powerless. How could it be that his older brothers are bowing down to his sheaf? In a second dream, Joseph sees eleven stars bow down to him, along with the sun and moon. The stars represent his brothers; the sun and moon, his parents.

His father, Jacob, reacts angrily and asks Joseph how he dares imagine that his father and mother will bow down to him. But then Jacob retreats and reflects. He has second thoughts. The brothers "envied" Joseph, but Jacob "kept the matter in mind" (Gen. 37:10–11).[1]

Keeping the matter in mind is an important concept. It is the opposite of interpretation. It means remaining with the wonder, the awe, and even what's irrational and inexplicable in the dream—as opposed to fitting the dream into a rational context, a simple comment on some past activity or present relationship. Let the dream and its images play in consciousness, and especially learn how the images change how you feel. To reduce the dream to a tidy interpretation is to cheat it of its deeper power.

Joseph, like his father, kept the matter in mind, for though he will be the great interpreter, he never interprets his own dream. He lives into the dream as the strange image of the erect sheaf becomes more and more the story of his life. The world eventually comes to see him as God sees him in the dream.

Because we think of Joseph as the personification of a dream interpreter, it's surprising that the first interpreters in Genesis are actually his envious brothers. According to the Zohar, their malevolent interpretation seals his fate—and theirs.[2]

The brothers' "interpretation" is a snap judgment, self-involved and tainted with envy; but maybe all interpretations are tainted with self-regard, especially those we do for ourselves. The brothers hate Joseph's dream. In their fearful reaction, we see the first gush of that huge tide of anxiety Joel Covitz describes in his research, the massive phobia about the dream.

Dreams engender anxiety. This theme runs through the rest of the story as Joseph is carried into Egypt. Imprisoned, thanks to Potiphar's wife, Joseph sees the baker and butler of Pharaoh "distraught" and "downcast." Why? "Because there is no one to interpret our dreams."

Joseph interprets their dreams. The baker will be executed, the butler freed. But Joseph exacts a promise that the butler will remember him to Pharaoh. Years pass. Now Pharaoh comes onstage, likewise agitated by his dreams. He complains, too: "There is none who can interpret [my dream]."

Now the butler remembers Joseph. He tells Pharaoh, "As he interpreted to us, so it was"—a phrase the rabbis quote with approval.[3] Joseph is summoned from prison.

Pharaoh said to Joseph, "I have dreamed a dream, and there is none who can interpret it; and I have heard say of you, that you can understand a dream to interpret it."

Joseph answered Pharaoh, saying, "It is not in me; God shall give Pharaoh a favorable answer."

"It is not in me"—an important point. The brothers interpret out of their own blind spots, the jealousy and rage that arise from the competition and envy in the family.

But Joseph indicates that the source of his interpretation is not personal. His interpretation comes from the same place as his dream of the sheaf: his connection to God.

Pharaoh recounts a pair of dreams: seven thin cattle devour seven fat ones; seven withered ears of wheat devour seven fat ones. Joseph quickly solves the dream equations that have stumped everyone else: seven good years will be followed by seven years of famine. "Now therefore let Pharaoh select a man discreet and wise, and set him over the land of Egypt."

The "discreet and wise" man is Joseph, who in a stroke catapults himself from prisoner to dream interpreter to high official, second in command to the ruler.

He stands in this powerful position when his brothers arrive years later fleeing famine in Canaan. They don't recognize Joseph, but as they bow down to him, Joseph recalls the dream of the sheaf. The rabbis calculate that twenty-two years have passed. All this time Joseph kept faith with his dream. Now it has come to pass.

The mystical commentators of the Zohar tell us:

A dream that is not remembered might as well not have been dreamt, and therefore a dream forgotten and gone from mind is never fulfilled. Joseph therefore kept his dream fresh in his memory, never forgetting it, so that it should come true, and he was constantly waiting for its fulfillment.[4]

Joseph did his homework.

Joseph the interpreter did not interpret his own dream, but kept the matter in mind. Abiding with dreams returns the dreamer to the seriousness of an inner life; interpreting leads to practicalities. Interpretation makes something useful of dreams.

Interpretation delivers Joseph to the height of power. Dream interpretation is always about power in one way or another: power over the dream, power over the dreamer, power over some part of ourselves. This is what we most remember from the story, whereas the gift of the sheaf that kept Joseph going is less prominent.

The Joseph story has glued together dream and interpreter so firmly that we still can't unstick them. We don't think of one without the other.

The transition from Joseph the dreamer to Joseph the interpreter marks an important moment in the struggle between the image and the word. The dream is the center of Jacob's story. Now the interpreter replaces the dream.

In the earlier stories—Abimelech, Jacob—dreams come from God; with Joseph's story, interpretations come from God. In the early stories there is no interpretation; after Joseph there is only interpretation. "As he spoke, so it was," says Pharaoh's butler about Joseph. It's a God-like power, one that Freud and other dream interpreters appropriate for themselves, thinking that they have reasoned their way to the secrets of dreams.

We forget that Joseph is more modest than Freud. He tells Pharaoh about the source of his interpretation: "It's not in me."

Joseph has become for us the hero of interpretation. But in the mystical tradition, Joseph is remembered differently, as the dreamer who keeps faith with his dream. In kabbalah he is identified with the *sefirah* of *yesod,* the phallus, which recalls the upright sheaf. (We would say: Joseph is a stand-up guy.)

Joseph's abiding with his dream gets overlooked, and so does the "essential image" of his dream, which reveals to him the situation of his soul as it stands in relation to God. I call this "the second gift of the dream." In the work with Bregman, this powerful gift means recovering your own "essential image"—that is, seeing how your soul stands in the archetypal world. But I could not receive this gift until I turned away from all the old paragons of interpretation, from Joseph to Freud, and turned back to face the dream.

After the story shifts from Canaan to Egypt, Joseph interprets four dreams. The narrative firmly establishes his technique as a model of interpretation. In each case, he replaces the images in dreams with words, restoring the established order of waking life, in which words dominate images.

Yes, "images are sovereign in the mind," the unconscious mind. They thrive in the unconscious, unruly and undefined. Interpretation replaces images with words, which are crisper, more orderly and definite, but more abstract. Images are private; words are social and political. The move toward dream interpretation in the Joseph story parallels a huge cultural shift that is also reflected in the history of writing: the shift from images to letters, from pictograms to cuneiform, from hieroglyphs to alphabet.

The setting for the Joseph story reminds us that ancient Egypt (along with Sumer) is the great homeland of writing. Writing is always subject to interpretation. "You are a dead man," spoken right to your face, is not.

Jacob is the last dreamer in Genesis who hears a voice. All the dreams in the Joseph story are silent, the way the written word is silent. They are literary dreams, meant to be read.

In the four dreams Joseph interprets (baker, butler, two of Pharaoh), the images are very weak. They have been reduced to signs, as in algebra, where letters stand for variables in an equation. In the baker's dream, 3 baskets = 3 days. In Pharaoh's dream, 7 cattle = 7 years.

The baskets or cattle or wheat have been stripped of all mystery or resonance. No one would reflect on these images for twenty-two minutes, let alone twenty-two years. When the equation is solved, they lose all potency.

Certainly I could find very little of potency in the images of K de G. I dream of myself reading a book, at best a joke about my aloneness, my addiction to reading. Other men dream of hunting lions or flying through the sky; I am a bookworm whose big dream is reading a book.

And how to read a dream of reading? That would be a mirror reflecting a mirror.

Chapter 13

The Untimely Disappearance of the Dream

Numbers and Deuteronomy

To the mystics, the Torah is a dream and every character in it is you. At some point in your life, you have been Abraham inspired by an inner calling. You have been Sarah laughing when an angel tells you good news. You've been Joseph the dreamer declaring the essence of your soul, or, sadly, you have despised your brother's dream.

In the dream of Torah, Joseph and his brothers personify the struggle between the image and the word. Joseph triumphs when his dream comes true and his brothers bow down to him. But who wins the struggle in the long run? The internal and external history of the dream take different tracks, and Joseph stands at the switch point.

It's a paradox: to fulfill the promise of his dream of the sheaf, Joseph becomes a dream interpreter.

At first in Genesis, God is behind the dream; now God is behind the interpreter. And after Joseph? Surprisingly, his story marks the end of dreams in the Torah altogether. The revelation dream begins with Jacob; the first interpreters are his sons. The rise of Joseph the interpreter marks the downfall of the revelation dream.

There are several ways to interpret how much dreaming goes on in Genesis, but the text specifically mentions eleven dreams.[1] The word *dream* does not appear in Exodus or Leviticus. In Numbers there are no dreams—but there's a pivotal story about them.

Again, no dreams in Deuteronomy. Just this: "That prophet, that dreamer of dreams shall be put to death" (Deut. 13:1–5).

The word *dreamer* also appears in the mouths of Joseph's brothers: "When they saw him from far away, even before he came near to them, they conspired against him to slay him. And they said one to another, Behold, this dreamer comes" (Gen. 37:19).

Both contexts promise death to dreamers. The Torah, then, speaks in two voices about dreams, but which voice is stronger? Genesis, or Deuteronomy? Joseph, or his brothers?

We have inherited this ancient ambivalence. For us, too, a dream is both a promise and a vain delusion. We don't kill dreamers, we just ignore them; we don't kill dreams, we just forget them.

Deuteronomy's animosity to the prophet-dreamer is first announced in Numbers 12. This dramatic story establishes a hierarchy of revelation.

Miriam and Aaron have spoken out against Moses because he married an African wife. They assert their own prophetic authority: "Has the Lord indeed spoken only by Moses? Has he not spoken also by us?" (Num. 12:2). The Lord overhears them and weighs in on the dispute.

He said, Hear now my words; If there is a prophet among you, I the Lord will make myself known to him in a vision, and will speak to him in a dream. (Num. 12:6)

The implication is that the Lord has at some previous point spoken to Miriam and Aaron in a dream. But the dream will no longer be the preferred method of prophecy, for the Lord adds:

Not so with my servant Moses, for he is the trusted one in all my house. With him I speak mouth to mouth, manifestly, and not in dark speech; and he beheld the form of the Lord. (Num. 12:7–8)

Note that Moses not only sees God but hears God. This is another of those contradictory seams in the text. It seems to assert that Moses has seen God, and indeed in that special intimacy he is also able to hear God's word directly.

Why then were you not afraid to speak against my servant Moses? The anger of the Lord was kindled against them; and he departed. (Num. 12:8–9)

It's clear that the revelation dream is now considered second-rate. Just to underline the point, as the Lord departs in wrath he touches Miriam with leprosy (Num. 12:10).

The female prophet and the dream are demoted in one stroke.

After Moses, the prophetic mode is about receiving the "word" of God. The prophetic formula is generally: "The word of the Lord came to ..." Whether it's Amos or Hosea or Jeremiah, prophets hear the word of God and have it speak through them. Hebrew prophets are prophets of the word of the Lord. The only prophet who dreams is Samuel, and he dreams of hearing a voice.[2]

There are two exceptions: Isaiah and Ezekiel.

In a vision that encompasses a few verses, Isaiah sees the heavenly throne and angels surrounding it.[3] Isaiah's images inspire liturgy known as Sanctus in the Church and the "*Kedushah*" in the synagogue service. Jewish worshippers act out Isaiah's vision by standing on tiptoes and praising God as the seraphim do: "Holy holy holy is the Lord of hosts; the whole earth is full of God's glory" (Isa. 6:3).

Ezekiel's vision of heaven is far more elaborate. In a time of loss and exile, he sees a huge waking dream of angels in the form of living creatures, descending together as a throne.

This throne later came to be known as the "chariot," or merkabah.

The rabbis found this vision uniquely powerful, and carefully restricted the study of Ezekiel to the learned old and wise. They tell a cautionary tale of a boy who broke their rules. When he came to the mysterious word *chashmal*, a fire leapt out of the text and burned him to a crisp.*

Ezekiel's prophecy carries such fire because of the "sovereign" power of the image in the mind. As a unique waking dream prophecy, Ezekiel's vision was a great magnet for mystical speculation and inspired "the work of the chariot," which is one half of Jewish mysticism.

The visions of Isaiah and Ezekiel endure in the imagination perennially. We stand on our toes, we see angels, and some dream of reaching God's throne and even seeing God's face.

The imagination is irrepressible and images arise anew, unruly and untamed. An image can't be canceled by a word. Nor can the memory of the

---

Chashmal is what scholars call a hapax legomenon, a word used once and therefore difficult to define. *Chashmal* is often translated as "electrum" or "amber." It is full of mystical secrets.

revelation dream. The case of the disappearing dream is not a murder mystery but a kidnapping: the revelation dream is hidden away, but it can still be recovered.

However, just as the rabbis restricted the study of Ezekiel, they also restricted carefully the revelation dream. They remembered Jacob, but they followed the path of Joseph and took the path of interpretation, a path our culture is still on today.

Chapter 14

THE RABBIS AMELIORATE
THE DREAM

To the vast majority of people in the world, including many Jews, the Talmud is a rather obscure subject. Many know little of the ancient rabbis or sages, those first-, second-, and third-century teachers of Israel and Babylon who are the elite group discoursing in those sacred books. But I believe that the legacy of the sages goes beyond Jewish thought. The rabbis were the first to respond seriously to the mixed heritage of Genesis about the dream. The choices they made have had a hidden impact on Western thought.

Their views of the dream run in parallel to the views of their counterparts in the early Christian Church, known as the Church Fathers. Also, Freud adopted many features of the rabbinic approach to dream interpretation. So it's a useful perspective to look at how the rabbis reconciled the contradictions between Jacob and Joseph, revelation and interpretation.

How could those living in the era of the "hiding of God's face," the time of exile and loss after the destruction of the Second Temple, ignore the great promises in Jacob's dream? "Behold, I am with you and will keep you in all places you go."[1] And especially the promise to Jacob's descendants: "To you I will give [the land of Israel], and to your seed" (Gen. 28:15, 13).

The sages cherished this dream promise but were uneasy about the revelation dream itself. They didn't want anyone in their own time claiming to have had a dream like Jacob's. That would give too much authority to a dreamer. The written Torah—the revelation given to Moses at Sinai—was the ultimate and final authority, and they brooked no rivals to it.

They were brilliant psychologists, very shrewdly aware of the power of interpretation, the power of the word, the power of their logic and discourse.

They had great skill as interpreters, so the key was to make the dream a kind of text.

They followed the lead of Joseph, whose interpretations already move in the direction of turning dreams into writing. The Babylonian sage Rabbi Hisda (217–309) makes the comparison explicit: "A dream uninterpreted is like a letter unopened."[2]

The dream is a text, a letter. Another sage, Hisda's contemporary Rabbi Huna (216–296), insists: it must be interpreted.

Only interpretation opens the letter of the dream. But the rabbis take Joseph a step further: interpretation determines the outcome of the dream. With approval, Rabbi Eleazar repeats the butler's praise of Joseph: "As he interpreted, so it was." Interpretation completely determines the outcome of the dream.

The rabbis had plenty of competition. Dream interpretation was a thriving business throughout the Roman world, part of the common culture of Greeks, Romans, and Jews. The best-known dream interpreter of the classical world, Artemidorus, was a second-century contemporary of the sages, as was Tertullian (160–230), the first great Latin writer of Christianity, and the first Latin author to compose a sustained study of dreams.

It's reported in the Talmud that Rabbi Bana'ah said, "There were twenty-four interpreters of dreams in Jerusalem." This seems like a large number for a relatively small town. "Once I dreamt a dream and I went round to all of them and they all gave different interpretations, and all were fulfilled, thus confirming that which is said: All dreams follow the mouth."[3]

Meaning, a dream will follow its interpretation.

The rabbis recognized that a shamanic power falls to anyone who interprets dreams, and they didn't want that power going to charlatans and scoundrels. The rabbis wanted to claim that power for themselves and their Torah.

But the sages had a broader agenda than beating the competition. They wanted to establish firmly their ultimate authority as interpreters of the written Torah and subordinate other sources of revelation.

In three folio pages of the Babylonian Talmud "Blessings" (Berachot 55a–57b), the rabbis contend over the prophetic significance of dreams.* Some offered symbolic interpretations; some scoffed at dreams completely—as

---

*Some scholars believe this was once a separate book, known as the rabbinic dream book.

straw and chaff, or as references to everyday events. Others upheld the revelation dream. Some sought to split the difference:

> *When the third-century Babylonian scholar Samuel had a bad dream, he used to say, "The dreams speak falsely." When he had a good dream, he used to say, "Do the dreams speak falsely, seeing that it is written, I [God] do speak with him in a dream?"*[4]

Samuel's equivocation feels very contemporary, for often we also prefer to remember the good dreams and forget the bad. In the competing voices of the rabbis, we can hear echoes of Sir Francis Crick's total dismissal of the dream. We hear some Jung and a good deal of Freud.[5]

But the main argument that emerges in the rabbinic dream book is that every dream must be interpreted, and every dream will follow its interpretation.

The rabbis tell a story that illustrates their power over the dream. A woman came to the sage Rabbi Eleazar and said, "I dreamt that the beam of my house was split." Eleazar told her, "You will bear a son." She did. A second time she came to him and said, "I dreamt the beam of my house was split." Eleazar told her, "You will bear a son." She did.

The third time she returned, Eleazar wasn't around. She came to his students and told them, "I dreamt the beam of my house was split." The students said, "You will bury your husband."

She passed Rabbi Eleazar as she left. He asked his students, "Why is this woman weeping?" They told him their interpretation.

Rabbi Eleazar said, "You have murdered a man."

"Dreams go according to the mouth," he tells them. "As Joseph interpreted it to us, so it was."[6]

But Rabbi Eleazar out-Josephs Joseph. If a dream means whatever an interpreter says, then what inherent meaning does the dream have? Yet this becomes the mainstream rabbinic position. No matter what the dream says, it will go as the rabbis interpret. This marks a major defeat for the image and triumph for the word: interpretation overwhelms the dream.

The rabbis mostly used this power benignly. A student dreamed his nose fell off. His teacher gave it a positive spin: "This dream is good: 'anger' will drop away from you." (In Hebrew, *af* means both "nose" and "anger.")

They taught that you can turn your own dreams to the good by reciting the right biblical verse immediately on waking. After seeing a river in your dreams, one rabbi advised, rise early and say: "Behold I will extend peace to her like a river, before another verse pops into your head, 'Distress will come like a river.'"[7]

If all else fails, the bad portent of the dream might require a dream fast (*taanit chalom*). And since even a poorly remembered dream contains an omen, if you can't remember the dream very well, you are advised to recite a prayer during the priestly blessing. These practices have all but died out in our time, but one rabbinic practice has proven durable. It's called "amelioration of the dream"—literally, making the dream good, *hatavat chalom*.

If one has a dream which makes him sad—says Rabbi Huna b. Ammi—he should go and have it interpreted in the presence of three. He should have it interpreted! . . . he should have a good turn given to it in the presence of three.

Let him bring three and say to them: I have seen a good dream; and they should say to him, Good it is and good may it be. May the All-Merciful turn it to good; seven times may it be decreed from heaven that it should be good and may it be good.[8]

The Talmudic text specifies certain therapeutic verses to ameliorate the anxiety-provoking dream. More liberal denominations of Judaism know little of this practice these days, but Rav Yitzhok Adlerstein, a teacher in the Lithuanian yeshiva world who lives in Los Angeles, affirmed that in his community, "when people are disturbed by dreams, they will do *hatavat chalom*."

Amelioration can be seen as a brilliant social invention of the sages. It takes a disturbing private experience and reconnects the anxious dreamer to the community and to the Torah.

Any Dumuzi can understand why the rabbis might have created ceremonies of amelioration, and even why they work. Most people would be more content to relieve the anxiety of a dream than to go deeper into it. Because when dreams take us to certain difficult feelings, we do all we can to run the other way. Dumuzi calls out to his sister for relief. Pharaoh begs Joseph for an answer. The Hebrews of their time called out to the rabbis. *Give it a good turn. Make it good.* The problem is that a "bad" dream has the power to warn us so we can change: amelioration takes the sting out of the dream.[9]

I've done a private version of *hatavat chalom* all my life, sweetening dreams for myself. I find three convenient "witnesses" in my own mind: habit, logic, and practicality. All swear that the dream is good, or if not, they whisper under their breath that the dream is meaningless.

If a dream means whatever you say it means, then what happens to the power of the revelation dream? If it can mean anything, or nothing, how can a dream change you? The rabbis left us this problem. Although they cherished the promise of Jacob's ladder, ultimately the emphasis on amelioration led to a neglect of the revelation dream.

The Talmud may be full of debates, but a consensus emerges. According to Rav Adlerstein, the consensus in the yeshiva world today emphasizes the most skeptical statements in the rabbinic dream book. Yes, dreams may contain a grain of prophecy, but the vast majority of dreams are more straw than wheat.[10]

Just as Joseph marks the end of dream stories in the Torah, so the rabbinic dream book concludes the mainstream discussion of dreams in Jewish religious literature. While other parts of the Talmud receive extensive commentary, little is devoted to dreams in the following centuries. Dreams became a closed book. The revelation dream became a story remembered, not a lived reality. That didn't mean the revelation dream died out altogether. But it would never be an important focus for religious experience for most Jews.

The rabbinic sages had good reasons for carefully sequestering the dream. In the first centuries, their spiritual authority was being challenged by all sorts of dreamers, including those waking dreamers who descended to the chariot, some of whom became Jewish Gnostics and others Jewish Christians.

Amid this opposition and contention, in the despair and difficulty following the destruction of the Temple in 70 c.e., they systematically closed the doors of scripture, prophecy, and dream.

They closed the sacred canon in the year 90; thenceforth no more sacred texts would be produced. (They argued over the Song of Songs; they argued over Ecclesiastes.) They closed the door on oracles—which once functioned for the High Priest. They closed the door on prophecy—dating its end to the time of Ezra. Henceforth, they said, prophecy belongs to children and fools.

Following the lead of the books of Numbers and Deuteronomy, they closed the door on the dream.

Dreams are made to be interpreted, primarily to relieve the anxiety of the dreamer. Revelation lost its power to interpretation, and interpretation collapsed into amelioration. I believe that this ameliorating habit is widespread and deeply ingrained. It became clear in my working with Bregman that when it came to my own dreams, I was much more interested in amelioration than I was in the truth.

. . .

The rabbis did not close the door to revelation completely. At least one sage left the door open to the revelation dream. He is Raba (280–352),[11] the most important rabbinic authority of his time in Babylonia, then under the rule of the neo-Persian empire and the main center for Jewish life and learning.[12]

Raba was a practical man, who acquired wealth and political influence in the court of King Shapur II (310–379), assets that he used to protect his community. But he was also a mystic, initiated into esoteric matters by his teacher Rabbi Joseph. He was a merkabah meditator. And he was a champion of the mystical dream.

Raba went so far as to assert that in a time of need, God would reverse his decree in Numbers 12 and bring back the revelation dream.

Commenting on the curse in Deuteronomy "And I will hide My face in that day," Raba said, in the voice of the Lord, "Although I hide My face from them, I shall speak to them in a dream."[13] Raba, in effect, reinstates the dream as a vehicle of prophecy.

Raba's precedent was followed in later ages. Over time, influenced by the inner journeys of the merkabah mystics, a mystical theory of the dream emerged in the medieval era. For the kabbalists, the dream became a nightly journey of the soul to a heavenly realm: in dreams one can see revealed the hidden life of the soul.

But for the average person, the main concern about dreams remained the anxiety they provoke. For them the consensus of the rabbinic dream book prevailed: the proper remedy is amelioration.

Another group of religious thinkers worked on the biblical heritage of the dream. The Church Fathers—the earliest Christian theologians of the first through fifth centuries—wrestled with the power of the imaginal and the troublesome authority of the revelation dream.

When their work was done, these Christian thinkers had parsed and compartmentalized revelation dreams, restricting them to certain saints only. Yet even so, like Jacob, groups of mystical Jews and Christians kept the matter of revelation in mind.

Chapter 15

PETER SEES A DREAM, AND JEWS AND CHRISTIANS PART WAYS

I t does take courage to assert, as Bregman did to me, that dreams have revelatory power. The idea of public prophecy of any sort has become repellent in our highly rationalized technocratic society. In our conventional wisdom, dream prophets fare little better than Joseph did with his brothers. They are lumped in with fanatics of all stripes, end-time babblers, crazed street preachers.

This general skepticism is very old and often sensible, as in the wry Hasidic story Reb Zalman told me about the young man who dreams he is destined to be a great spiritual leader, a rebbe. He takes his dream to an old established rebbe, who tells him, "When a hundred people dream you are rebbe, then you will be a rebbe."

The old master believes that not every dream means what the dreamer would like it to mean. But the punch line acknowledges how powerful it can be when a group of people dream the same dream.

Hasidism itself arose among the impoverished Jews of eighteenth-century eastern Europe in a feverish wave of dreams, tall tales, legends, visions and miracles, signs and wonders. The Baal Shem Tov, the first of the rebbes, engendered a swirl of legendary material. He journeyed in dreams to heaven many times on behalf of his followers, his Hasidim. Valuing closeness to God over the study of books, the new movement triumphed despite the more learned authorities who opposed it.

Hasidism was the last flowering of mass mysticism in Jewish history, but not the first. The early sages lived through the rise of Christianity, which emerged as a Jewish sect fueled in part by visions and dreams. In studying this history it becomes very clear how dreams and visions can disrupt old lineages, and create new ones.

In any established tradition with a sacred text, spiritual authority passes in a continuous chain from teacher to student. The lines of transmission are carefully preserved and often memorized. For instance, I once heard a Buddhist teacher recite a fifteen-minute lineage statement before presenting a teaching. He explained that he learned it from his teacher, who learned it from a previous teacher, and so on; he named names going all the way back to the Buddha. Only then would he present the teaching itself.

There are similar Jewish lineage statements. For a time, I thought "K de G" referred to a book in my library that also had a blue cover.

The Sayings of the Fathers According to Rabbi Nathan is a commentary on the Pirke Avot ("The Sayings of the Fathers"), a classic rabbinic lineage statement found in the Mishnah.

The Mishnah in turn is the codification of oral law, the authoritative extrapolation of law from the written Torah.* Thus from Rabbi Nathan to Pirke Avot to Mishnah to Torah we have a chain of books commenting on books, each dependent on the next. Likewise "The Sayings of the Fathers" delineates a chain of authority from Moses to Joshua, from Joshua to the elders, to the prophets, to the men of the great assembly and to the rabbinic sages—each of whom received a special sacred oral teaching. This is the essential Jewish lineage statement of the rabbis.

But what is the lineage of the first Christians? How do the apostles receive their authority? Whereas the rabbis assert a direct oral transmission from teacher to student known as the Oral Torah, Christianity takes a different approach. Some authorities, like Peter, knew Jesus as a teacher during his lifetime. But merely being a student of Jesus is not the basis for apostolic authority; rather, authority came to those who had certain visions and dreams.

In that sense, every time a group of people dreams the same dream, a new religion gets born. Shared dreams and visions establish a new order, disrupting the careful lineage of teachers, their sacred books, and their authoritative

---

*The name *mishnah*, means, in effect, "repetition" or "recapitulation."

interpretations and statements. Dreams upset the applecart and sometimes the dining table: that's exactly what happened in early Christianity when the laws of Leviticus about food were overturned by a dream.

Early Christianity was an entirely Jewish movement. Obviously, Jesus himself was never a Christian. The original apostles were all Jews. As described in the book of Acts and elsewhere, both Peter and Paul were Jews who first preached in synagogues.

Even though their message was often better received among Gentiles than Jews, the earliest apostles strained to keep the movement within the bounds of Jewish law. But even in the land of Israel, where Peter lived, it became difficult to maintain the purely Jewish character of the sect.

One important boundary line with Gentiles is Jewish dietary law. Based on proscriptions in the written Torah about forbidden and permitted food, the laws of kosher food (kashruth) as elaborated by the rabbis made it nearly impossible for Jews and Gentiles to share a common meal. How do you organize a community when people can't eat together?

Some Jewish Christians upheld the laws of circumcision and kashruth; others sought flexibility while somehow remaining Jews. A dream decided the issue for Peter, the most important of the Jewish Christian leaders.*

Peter was staying at Joppa, near modern Tel Aviv, and went up on a roof to pray. He became hungry and wanted something to eat. While the meal was being prepared, he fell into a doze or trance. In a dream—a waking dream or a vision—the heavens opened and a large piece of cloth was let down to earth by its four corners. The cloth held four-footed animals, kosher and nonkosher, as well as decidedly nonkosher reptiles. A voice told him, "Get up, Peter. Kill and eat."

"Surely not, Lord!" Peter replied. "I have never eaten anything impure or unclean."

The voice spoke a second time: "Do not call anything impure that God has made clean."

This happened three times, and immediately the cloth was taken back to heaven" (Acts 10:9–17).

As an observant Jew, Peter finds it impossible to eat forbidden food, even though a voice seemingly from God commands him three times. He is still wrestling with the implications of the dream when he receives a strange

---

*Scholars argue over the terminology and say Peter had a waking vision and not a dream. To me, for reasons that should be clear at this point, the difference is not highly significant.

confirmation: a messenger arrives and tells him that the Roman centurion Cornelius has been dreaming about him.

Up to this point, Peter has not preached to Gentiles. But the news of Cornelius's dream confirms his own waking dream. He goes to Cornelius and tells him, "You know how that it is against our law for a Jew to associate with a Gentile or visit him. But God has shown me that I should not call any man impure or unclean"(Acts 10:29).

Peter preaches the story of Jesus to Cornelius and his household, and they become followers without first converting to Judaism. This arouses opposition when he returns to the Jewish Christians of Jerusalem.

"The apostles and the brothers throughout Judea heard that the Gentiles also had received the word of God. So when Peter went up to Jerusalem, the circumcised believers criticized him and said, 'You went into the house of uncircumcised men and ate with them' " (Acts 11:1–3).

But when Peter repeats the story of his dream, they have no further objection. From now on the mission is not exclusively to Jews, but also to Gentiles.

One could say that Judaism and Christianity part company over Peter's dream. Until then, it was still possible to be Jewish and Christian, to follow the rules of the Torah while believing in Jesus as Messiah. Peter represented such Christian Jews.

But his waking vision raises the stakes. To say that God would send such a dream to a believing Jew runs against the forbidding words in Deuteronomy cited earlier,[1] which condemn any prophet or "dreamer of dreams" who wishes to "add to" or "diminish" the commandments.

To the rabbis, a dream like Peter's cannot be from God. Indeed, they go further and say that even if Peter was hearing a voice from heaven, he must disobey it. The Torah was already given at Sinai. The door to new revelation is closed.

This is clear from a rabbinic legendary tale in which a dispute arises between Rabbi Eliezer and other sages. Rabbi Eliezer calls on miracles to show that God is on his side of the dispute.

"If the law is as I say it," Eliezer says, "let the carob tree bend." And the tree bends. "Let the river flow backward," and the river flows backward. "Let a voice come from heaven," and a voice from heaven declares that Rabbi Eliezer is right.

"Then Rabbi Yehoshua stood up and said: 'The Law is not in heaven' (Deut. 30:12).'What does this mean?' asked Rabbi Yermiyahu. 'It means that since the Torah was given to us on Mount Sinai, we no longer require a heavenly voice to reach a decision, since it is written in the Torah: Follow after the majority' (Exod. 23:2)."

Later Rabbi Nathan encountered Elijah and asked him how the ruling was accepted on high. And Elijah said: "At this the Holy One, blessed be He, smiled and said, 'My children have overruled me!' "[2]

The meaning of the anecdote is clear: interpretation of the written Torah has passed firmly into the hands of the rabbis, who, through the lineage of the Oral Torah, are authoritative in this domain. Even the voice of God, let alone a dream or vision, cannot shake this strongly held tradition, established by a long lineage of teachers and students discussed in the Pirke Avot.

How did the rabbis view contemporary developments in early Christianity? It's possible they did not "view" them at all, because, as one author remarks, in those early years this particular sect led by Peter would have been no more noticeable than a new storefront church in a big city today.

Surely, though, had the sages been aware of Peter's dream in Joppa, the events that followed would have confirmed to them what Deuteronomy 13 had already told them: that a dreaming prophet who contravenes the Torah is anathema.

Peter becomes the chief apostle to the Jews and "the rock" on which the Christian church is founded. His counterpart is Paul, the Jewish apostle to the Gentiles who is transformed by visions. The second half of the book of Acts recounts his story.

As Saul, a student of the rabbis, he never knew Jesus in his lifetime, and vigorously persecuted the early apostles until his dramatic conversion. "As he neared Damascus on his journey suddenly a light from heaven flashed around him. He fell to the ground and heard a voice say to him, 'Saul, Saul, why do you persecute me?' 'Who are you, Lord?' Saul asked. 'I am Jesus whom you are persecuting,' " he replied (Acts 9:4–5).

What actually happened to change Saul to Paul? The whole question of imaginal realities is raised by this story. Paul touches on the matter in a passage that many scholars believe alludes to a merkabah experience.

Paul writes: I knew a man in Christ who fourteen years ago was caught up to the third heaven. Whether it was in the body or out of the body I do not know—God knows. And I know that this man—whether in the body or apart from the body I do not know, but God knows—was caught up to Paradise. He heard inexpressible things, things that man is not permitted to tell (2 Cor. 12:3ff).

Scholars have supposed that the "man in Christ" is Paul himself.[3]

"In the body or out of the body"; "in the body or apart from the body." Paul professes indifference on the subject but raises the question nonetheless. Was it a waking dream, vision, hallucination, or actuality? The same question arises in our own dreams: is it live or is it Memorex? Is it real real, awake real, or just dream real? And if it's "dream real," does that make it any less real?

That becomes the question in the struggle between the Church and Christian Gnostics. As for the Jewish Gnostics, who are better known as kabbalists, the dream became for them a nightly journey of the soul.

Chapter 16

THE GNOSTIC HERESY AND THE MYSTICAL DREAM JOURNEY

During the first four centuries of the common era, the early Church struggled against Gnostic Christians and others it deemed heretics, many of whom claimed authority from dreams and visions. In this struggle, the status of imaginal experience became a crucial issue.

A major discussion centers around the resurrection, and those who claimed to see Jesus in the flesh after his death. Elaine Pagels, in the opening chapter of *The Gnostic Gospels,* argues that the early Church was very sensitive on this point. Papal authority derives from a lineage going back to the apostle Peter. Peter's authority rested on the claim of his being the first witness of the resurrection.

This was the original test for apostolic leadership. It was not enough to have heard Jesus, or even to have been an eyewitness of the crucifixion. Only those who actually saw the resurrected Jesus in the flesh were included. Pointedly, Mary Magdalene was excluded.[1]

Pagels writes, "New Testament evidence indicates that Jesus appeared to many others besides Peter.... But from the second century, orthodox churches developed the view that only *certain* resurrection appearances actually conferred authority on those who received them. These were Jesus' appearances to Peter" and to the disciples. According to the account in Luke, Pagels explains, after a forty-day period, "the resurrected Lord abruptly withdrew his bodily presence.... Henceforth, for the duration of the world, no one would ever experience Christ's actual presence as the twelve disciples had during his lifetime—and for forty days after his death."[2]

The Gnostic Christians took a less restrictive view, Pagels explains. They looked on all appearances of Jesus as, in effect, imaginal. That did not make such visions any less authoritative to them.

Writes Pagels, "The author of the Gospel of Mary [Magdalene], one of the few Gnostic texts discovered before Nag Hammadi, interprets the resurrection appearances as visions received in dreams or in ecstatic trance."[3]

Some Gnostic Christians did not limit such revelations to the past. They put forward the possibility that later dreamers and visionaries could receive teachings even more profound and authoritative than those the apostles themselves received.

Obviously, this doctrine would endanger the lineages that establish the Church hierarchy. The more restrictive view carried over into the discussion of dreams. The Church Fathers who defended Christian doctrine against opponents and heretics were in a bind similar to that of the rabbis when it came to the question of dreams. They had to respect the authority of past revelation dreams and visions—but didn't want new dreamers to compete with the old.

Tertullian (c.160–230), the first Latin and Christian dream authority, acknowledges that dreams are essential to spiritual life. He affirms in his "On the Soul" that "just about the majority of people get their knowledge of God from dreams."[4]

However, Tertullian speculates that some dreams come from God but others from the devil so that it's hard to know which is which. Augustine (354–430) concurs, believing that even a true dream might be used by the devil in a confidence game:

"Our designing foe, in proportion as he is utterly unable to get the better of them when awake, makes the deadlier assault upon them asleep." The evil spirit "transforms himself, according to Scripture, as if into an angel of light, in order that, once having gained his victim's confidence in matters that are manifestly good, he may then lure his victim into his snares."[5]

Later Christian authorities go so far as to say that because of such concerns, Jesus would forgive a person who ignored a prophetic dream.

Traditional Jews make similar arguments. Joel Covitz writes, "A Chasidic rabbi once explained to me why he gives no value to dreams. Since the Talmud says that a dream can come from either an angel or a demon, this

rabbi rationalized that he was better off ignoring all dreams, as he was un-
sure of his ability to identify the source of a dream."[6]

I would argue that the rise of interpretation exacerbated this divide. If
we interpret dreams in a self-interested way, saying that this dream is good
or that dream is bad, it soon follows that a dream may come from either an
angel or a demon. It's notable that the dreams of Genesis all come from God.
Nonetheless, by the medieval era, ambivalence about the dream has gone so
far as to bifurcate the dream at its source. Instead of seeing all dreams as essentially good or whole, the rabbis and the Church Fathers create a strong
uncertainty about the very nature of dreams. Some dreams come from God,
some from the devil, and it's hard to know which is which. This same bi-
furcation reappears in modern psychology as the distinction between manifest and latent dreams and is at the center of the dispute between Jung and
Freud. Jung views the manifest dream as a "natural phenomenon," whereas
Freud sees the dream as devious and tricky, requiring a great deal of discernment to ascertain its real meaning.

The Church Fathers likewise assert that certain individuals have a "gift
of the spirit," which they call "*discernio*," or discernment. This is the ability
to distinguish demonic and divine dreams. But in keeping with the Church
Fathers' overall program of restricting access to the revelation dream, only
saints have this gift. Gregory the Great (540–604) writes:

"The saints . . . can distinguish true revelations from the voices and images
of illusions through an inner sensitivity. They can always recognize when
they receive communications from the good Spirit and when they are face to
face with illusions."[7]

Once the Church gained full power and authority, beginning in the era of
Constantine, Christian Gnostics who believed that their dreams and visions
could still be authoritative were persecuted as heretics. In 326 Catholicism
became the state religion of the Roman Empire. Gnostics were forbidden to
assemble. In 350 the Church banned Gnostic writings.

The dream and the vision were now severely constrained. Just as the
rabbis believed that not even a voice from heaven could overturn the Torah,
so, writes Elaine Pagels, "Christians who stand in orthodox tradition, Catholics and Protestants, expect that the revelations they receive will confirm (in
principle, at least) apostolic tradition: this, they agree, sets the boundaries of
Christian faith. The apostles' original teaching remains the criterion; whatever deviates is heresy."[8]

Henceforth, in both traditions, the revelation dream in the West can have no authority independent of the already established religious teachings. No new dream had the authority to directly challenge established doctrine.

Yet people did not stop having such dreams or stop believing in their prophetic power. On one occasion, the monk Wetti of Reichenau had visions of Charlemagne (742–814), which the Church used as leverage to criticize the emperor's sexual behavior. In Carolingian times (the eighth and ninth centuries), the dreams of the emperor and other dignitaries were consulted as important omens for political decisions.

Because of doubts about the source of dreams—God or the devil—the distinction between a waking vision and a night dream became increasingly important to Christians in the Middle Ages. In autobiographical works of saints or of converts, a waking dream was considered more likely to be divinely inspired than a vision of the night.

Hildegard of Bingen (1098–1179), a nun living in the Rhineland, is celebrated today as a mystic, composer, artist, and creative spirit. She reports numerous visions in her three autobiographical works, but, writes Jean-Claude Schmitt, "she is careful to describe [her visions] as neither dreams . . . nor the result of madness . . . or sensory experience, but rather wakeful visions of the soul." To Schmitt, "This speaks of the enduring suspicion of dreams—gateway of the devil—and of the mistrust of the body and the senses. For this pioneer of 'female mysticism,' the wakeful *visio* is the highest form of revelation."[9]

The religious dream remains important in the lives of individuals in the medieval period. Numerous dreams show up in stories of religious conversions. But the dream had no power to make changes in religious doctrine. There would be no more dreams or visions like Peter's on the roof in Joppa. The word, the official interpretation, had the upper hand; the revelation dream in the broad sense was carefully controlled and circumscribed.

Pagels tells how Irenaeus, the bishop of Lyon and an early Church Father, successfully combated Gnostic Christianity and defended the apostolic lineage. Yet from time to time in medieval Europe, dissident Christian groups arose to challenge the Church, and they have been identified with Gnostic ideas. Among them were the Bogomils in tenth-century Bulgaria and the Cathars in eleventh-century southern France.

Some scholars speculate that Gnostic influences on kabbalah came through exchanges with Cathars. Although Gershom Scholem (1897–1982), who established the modern scholarly study of Jewish mysticism, did not believe this proven, he notes that "in Narbonne and Toulouse, important Jewish centers at that time, there were stormy disputes and incessant clashes between the hostile camps" of Catholics and Cathars. "It was precisely in these regions that the Kabbalah made its first appearance."[10]

In Judaism, Gnostic ideas had a fate very different from the Christian story. Amazingly, they entered into the heart of the Orthodox tradition as kabbalah. They brought with them the vivid imagery of dreams and visions.

The roots of kabbalah are the visionary ascents of the merkabah mystics. Gershom Scholem describes the merkabah as "one of the Jewish branches of Gnosticism."[11]

Scholem finds strong Gnostic influence in the masterpiece of kabbalah, the Zohar, which emerged in Spain in the year 1300.

Some Gnostic systems are frankly dualistic. They describe an utterly transcendent remote hidden God and a lower creator god, the Demiurge, who is associated with evil. In kabbalah, too, there is a remote hidden God, the *Ein Sof,* and there are ten emanations of this God known as the *sefirot.** However, the kabbalists insists it is all one—a monotheistic Gnosticism. There is one God, and yet in a certain way God is ten. God has ten powers, attributes, lights, crowns, numbers—all represented by the ten *sefirot.* The sefirotic system underlies the Zohar and is basic to Spanish kabbalah. In essence, the *sefirot* are images or faces of an invisible God.

The personal revelation dream must have strongly influenced the medieval kabbalists' speculations about the nature of God and the universe, or how we see the faces of God.

If Scholem is right that the Spanish kabbalah has roots in the merkabah experience, then it's also plausible that once the secrets of the merkabah were lost, mystics would continue to seek direct experiences and make heavenly journeys. Then the dream became the chariot for the spiritual journey, thereby fulfilling Raba's statement that someday once again God would show his face in dreams.

---

*The *sefirot* first appear in the Sefer Yetzirah, which is mentioned in the Talmud (Sanhedrin 65b), where we learn of two rabbis who studied the "book of formation" and learned how to make their own calf, which they ate for lunch. Attributed to Abraham and also Rabbi Akiba, it is the oldest Jewish mystical text.

The Zohar describes the dream journey succinctly:

"When a man retires to rest, he must first acknowledge the Kingdom of Heaven and then say a short prayer. For when a man goes to bed and sleeps, his soul leaves him and soars aloft. . . .

"Dreams originate on high when souls leave their bodies, each one taking its own route. There is a graduated series of intimations by which deeper knowledge is conveyed to men, dreams forming one level, vision another level, and prophecy a third level, in a rising series."[12]

During sleep the soul travels upward through a crowd of demons, all hoping to deceive it and prevent it from rising higher. How high the soul rises depends on how pure the soul is in life. This explains why some dreams mix together wisdom and nonsense. The demons interfere.

But if a soul is sufficiently pure to get past the demons, it rises to the realm of the angel Gabriel, who is the master of dreams and who works for the Shekhinah. There the soul receives dream prophecy, which, as the Talmud had said, is one-sixtieth pure prophecy. However, even this degree of insight is difficult to preserve, for the soul must now journey back down past the same demons it met on the way up, who will once more attempt to confuse the dreamer and mix in "straw with the wheat."

Some righteous souls ascend higher still to the lowest of the ten *sefirot*, the Shekhinah. A dreamer there receives vision. This is the level of the prophets, according to the kabbalists. It comes from a "dark mirror that shines."[13] The Shekhinah is called a dark mirror since it receives spiritual light from higher *sefirot*, but makes no light of its own.

Higher yet are the *sefirot* of "radiance" and "eternity" (*Hod* and *Netzakh*); this is the highest level of prophecy. It is what Moses received. Here is utter clarity; Moses himself is compared to a clear lens that does not distort the light.

The Zohar's mystical view of the dream as a journey of the soul became widely influential. Rather quickly after the first manuscript appeared around 1300, the Zohar became a canonical text in Judaism, and also came into Christian circles.[14] It was believed to be an authentic midrash or commentary on the five books of Moses from the first-century mystical sage Rabbi Shimeon bar Yohai, and that belief persists in some *haredi* circles today. Though Scholem proved that the book came from the fertile imagination and incredible industry of Moses de León (1250–1305), it nonetheless reflects a long development of Gnostic ideas and influences going back to the merkabah.

A further development is the kabbalah of Isaac Luria of Safed (1534–1572) in the land of Israel. He was known as a dreamer who journeyed nightly to the heavenly academies. He came even closer to the idea of seeing the face of God, because he reconfigured the ten *sefirot* into five visages, known as *partzufim*. In effect Luria saw the *Ein Sof* manifesting in five "faces" of God, though these were certainly not something that could be seen in any sense by human eyes.

What we can read through all of these developments in kabbalah is the yearning through millennia of exile to make some contact in some way with the withdrawn or hidden face of God. Whether meditating on the *sefirot* or the *partzufim*, the mystic believed he, too, was making the heavenly ascent.

Kabbalah originally meant any special teaching passed by word of mouth, from teacher to student. This trend in Jewish mystical thought originates with the merkabah of the first centuries, gets transmitted to Europe through early medieval Germany and France, and emerges more fully in medieval Spain.

As the texts were written down and published, the teachings gained a wide influence and, as with any tradition based on the image, eventually proved disruptive to the established order based on interpretation of the word. Kabbalah fueled speculation that drove the career of the false messiah Shabbatai Zvi (1626–1676), who for a time captured the popular imagination.

A more lasting religious influence of kabbalah came with the rise of the Baal Shem Tov (1698–1760) and the teachings of Hasidism. Kabbalah, which had been an esoteric account of the cosmos, of God and creation, was recast by this masterful teacher in vividly personal and psychological terms. The psychological dimension of the ideas in the Zohar and the Lurianic kabbalah were taught by charismatic teachers in eastern Europe known as rebbes, and the movement spread in an imaginal feast of legend, miracles, dreams, visions, heavenly ascents.

Nachman of Bratzlav (1772–1810), the great-grandson of the Baal Shem Tov, is the greatest Jewish mystical dreamer, so great his dreams shaped his unique tales, for which he is known today. His vivid, colorful tales are shot through with Gnostic ideas and beliefs that touch on the experience of dreams and the role of the unconscious in spiritual life. Nachman affirmed that the imagination is necessary to faith, that faith without imagination is impossible.

Freud's contemporary Martin Buber (1878–1965) translated Nachman's tales into German in 1906 and the legends of the Baal Shem Tov in 1908, bringing Buber's romantic recasting of Hasidism to the attention of German-speaking Jewish intellectuals who were searching for an alternative religiosity just a few years after Freud published *The Interpretation of Dreams*.

Some authors have speculated on the direct or indirect influence of Jewish mysticism on the psychoanalysis of Sigmund Freud.[15] However, Freud was a "firm atheist" and not interested, as Buber was, in bringing to the fore the hidden wisdom of Jewish mysticism. Instead, he approached dreams from what he believed was a strictly scientific viewpoint.

The revelation dream and the waking dream vision had been marginalized, shunted aside, and hidden away by mainstream religion, but the imaginal life of the soul survived with great force among Jewish and Christian mystics. When a new Joseph arose in Vienna to restore the dream to the forefront of modern thought, he added a new chapter to the history of interpretation, though he did not bring back the lost ladder of his father, Jacob.

Chapter 17

SIGMUND AND IRMA

The Secret of Dreams Revealed

Genesis is the first great dream book of the West. *The Interpretation of Dreams,* by Sigmund Freud, is the second. But like Genesis, Freud's book proves ambivalent about dreams.

Freud is the father of the modern dream, and like any pioneer, he made mistakes. But it should never be forgotten that he opened the territory and put the unconscious on the map.

He was so confident about the significance of his dream book that he had the publisher deliberately alter the date of publication on the title page from 1899 to 1900 so as to dramatically mark a new era. In a letter to his best friend Wilhelm Fliess, he shared a fantasy of a marble tablet at Bellevue, the house where one night he had a most significant "specimen dream," the dream of Irma.[1] The tablet read:

> **In This House, on July 24ᵗʰ, 1895**
> **the Secret of Dreams was Revealed**
> **to Dr. Sigm. Freud**

Freud's pride and audacity are extraordinary. To discover "the Secret of Dreams," and to compose a book around it! He called it simply *Die Traumdeutung* ("The interpretation of dreams"). He was consciously setting himself up in competition with all the hundreds of dream books of the exact same title through the millennia, in Greek and Latin, Arabic and Hebrew. The *Oneirocriticon* of Artemidorus is one—and Rabbi Almoli's *Pitron Chalomot* another.

Freud cites Artemidorus and knew of Almoli's sixteenth-century kabbalistic work, but he was certain his book would sweep its predecessors aside by establishing dream interpretation once and for all on a scientific basis.

Fittingly for such an important project, he composed the book very carefully. The opening chapter, he wrote to Fliess, is like a walk in a dense woods.[2] The woods are thick with theories of the dream, fighting for the light. He points out each idea, literary or scientific; discusses its merits and its failings; guides us past them all, leaving us almost in despair that the truth will ever come out of such a dark tangle of contradictory opinions and evidence.

But when we turn the page to a new chapter, we come to "[a] cavernous defile through which I lead my readers—my specimen dream with its peculiarities, its details, its indiscretions and its bad jokes."[3]

This is the "specimen dream" of Irma. With it, we have left the woods. "We find ourselves in the full daylight of a sudden discovery."[4]

Freud carefully fills in the immediate background. He had been treating Irma for "hysterical anxiety." But they broke the treatment off because she refused Freud's proposed solution.[5]

The morning before the dream, his friend and fellow physician Otto pays a visit. Otto has just recently seen Irma's family. "I asked him how he had found her and he answered: 'She's better, but not quite well.' I was conscious that my friend Otto's words, or the tone in which he spoke them, annoyed me."

To make matters worse, Freud's wife is planning a party, and she has invited Irma. With these thoughts in mind, that night Freud dreams:

Dream of July 23–24, 1895

A large hall—numerous guests, whom we were receiving. —Among them was Irma. I at once took her on one side as though to answer her letter and to reproach her for not having accepted my "solution" yet. I said to her: "If you still get pains, it's really only your fault." She replied: If you only knew what pains I've got now in my throat and stomach and abdomen—it's choking me. I was alarmed and looked at her. She looked pale and puffy. I thought to myself that after all I must be missing some organic trouble. I took her to the window and looked down her throat and she showed signs of recalcitrance like women with artificial dentures. I thought to myself that there was really no need for her to do that. . . . She then opened her mouth properly and on the right I found a big white patch; at another place I saw extensive whitish grey scabs.[6]

Now he calls in several colleagues to examine Irma in turn: a senior colleague identified as "Dr. M.," also his "friend Otto" and his "friend Leopold" (both physicians and former associates of his). Dr. M.'s diagnosis confirms Freud's; however, he makes very strange comments. Then we learn that Otto has given her an injection of a concoction of chemicals, "a preparation of propyl, propyls . . . propionic acid . . . trimethylamin."

In his presentation, Freud emphasizes the strangeness of the manifest or surface content of the dream.[7] "No one who had only read the preamble and the content of the dream itself could have the slightest notion of what the dream meant. I myself had no notion. I was astonished at the symptoms of which Irma complained to me." The second part of the dream seems to him even more inscrutable: "Toward its end the dream seemed to me to be more obscure and compressed than it was at the beginning."[8]

Overall, Freud sees the dream as a difficult puzzle to be solved, like Pharaoh's dreams. His first step is to double up the dream into manifest and latent.

The manifest dream is simply the dream as reported by the dreamer, with all its images and incidents. But hidden below the surface, Freud believed, is the latent dream, which expresses an unconscious wish. Only the latent dream will reveal "the Secret."

Is this doubling into manifest and latent a real feature of dreams, or an artifact of the act of interpretation? In her signal essay "Against Interpretation," Susan Sontag notes that interpretation "presupposes a discrepancy between the clear meaning of the text and the demands of (later) readers. It seeks to resolve that discrepancy. The situation is that for some reason a text has become unacceptable; yet it cannot be discarded."[9]

This critique applies to Freud. His dream of Irma seems unacceptable at face value because, he claims, it makes no sense to him. Therefore, interpretation must uncover the latent dream.

To Freud, "The dream which the dreamer recalls, the 'manifest dream,' does not picture the real wish, but masks it. The essential cause of the dream, the trigger which sets the process in motion, is the hidden, unacceptable wish."[10]

Freud spoke of the dream work as the unconscious process of confecting the manifest dream out of the latent. Interpretation undoes the dream work to uncover the latent dream and its wishes.

The dream work models for him the workings of the unconscious. Neurotic symptoms, he argues, are like dreams: both make no sense at the manifest level but can be explained as the distorted expression of a hidden wish. The secrets of the dream are the secrets of the unconscious.

Freud looked forward to our own time, when it would be possible to investigate the dream in the laboratory the way Dr. Hobson and Dr. Kahn do, directly measuring changes in brain activity during dreams. Lacking EEGs and PET scans, he saw the dream as nonetheless providing indirect evidence of brain processes that ultimately would be understood better, but for now could be described as psychic processes—namely, the ego censoring unacceptable wishes and urges. In the meantime, he also endeavored to ground dreams on as scientific a basis as he could by studiously tying the dream back to verifiable events in the past.

In keeping with this plan, Freud insists that "a dream begins with the event of the previous day that set it in motion."[11] "This view is confirmed by every dream I look into whether my own or anyone else's."[12] (This view has not, in fact, been confirmed.)

Freud also uncovers more distant memories in dreams. The important point for him is to relate every event in the dream to a memory, near or far. For Freud, a dream event has no immediate reality of its own, but only insofar as it recalls a memory or registers the pressures and distortions of one of his theorized psychic forces, such as repression.

Freud, in a loose way, is often compared with Joseph, a comparison he slyly encourages in his landmark book. (Joseph the interpreter, of course; not Joseph the dreamer.) Yet Freud, as a "firm atheist," has no interest in Joseph's statement that interpretation comes from God and is "not in me." Instead, Freud asserts that the ultimate authority is science.

For Joseph, dreams are always messages about the future, but not so for Freud. "And the value of dreams for giving us knowledge of the future?" he writes at the end of *The Interpretation of Dreams*. "There is of course no question of that. It would be truer to say instead that they give us knowledge of the past. For dreams are derived from the past in every sense."[13]

Freud is closer to the spirit of his rabbinic predecessors than he is to that pillar of faith Joseph. Scholar Ken Frieden argues that Freud's dream theory owes a lot to the rabbis.[14]

He clearly subscribes to Rabbi Hisda's idea that "a dream uninterpreted is a letter unread," that a dream is essentially a text. His focus on words rather than image is very striking in many of his dream analyses.

Also, his style of dream analysis closely follows the style of rabbinic midrash. The rabbis took considerable freedom with a biblical verse. Instead of commenting on it as a whole, as we might do, they often took the verse out of context and broke it into small phrases and responded piece by piece, or *ad locum*.

This is exactly parallel to Freud's procedure with the images in dreams. "I put the dream before [the patient] cut up into pieces." The dream is considered *en detail* (in detail), he says, not "en masse." He then asked his patients to free-associate to the pieces, further removing the interpretation from the original context of the dream. The patient gives a series of associations to each piece, which Freud believed corresponded to the "background thoughts" of that particular part of the dream.[15]

Freud did not associate his *ad locum* method with midrash, which it so closely resembles. To give his interpretive approach a scientific air, he deliberately uses terminology from chemistry, such as "the day residue" for memories that lie at the bottom of the dream like substrate in a test tube. He sees himself performing analytical chemistry on the strange and bizarre material of the dream, sorting out the elemental substances out of which it was composed. This shows his general tendency of viewing the dream as inscrutable and bizarre, a baffling mixture that required clever operations to be sorted out.

I once tried the same Freudian chemistry with those mysterious letters "K de G" to determine where they came from, what portion of my daylight hours they emerged from.

One day it clicked. I belong to a marching society in New Orleans, a Mardi Gras krewe—the Krewe de Jieux (the crew of Jews). Every year we parade on foot through the streets of the French Quarter in absurd costumes with exaggerated rubber body parts. We give out bagels we have decorated by hand. We bake the bagels hard, paint them gold or silver, then sprinkle glue and glitter. "Krewe de Jieux" is too long to fit on a bagel, though.

I always paint on mine "K de J."

So if Freud's approach is right, the great rabbi of my dream was once blue glitter on a bagel.

Freud's method of free association is very fertile and in itself can actually enhance the power of the dream, but only if it does not distract from the main point.

Through free association, every dream accumulates a huge raft of memories. If you can bring your whole life into the dream, the dream can move your whole life. Bregman follows Freud in seeking associations, but for a different purpose.

The goal of Freud's free association is to find a path out of the manifest dream to the latent dream. Critics today, including William Domhoff, ask why a free association conducted after the dream should necessarily lead to the thoughts that produced the dream.

In *The Interpretation of Dreams,* however, Freud does not always use free association, because in many cases—forty-seven in all—he interprets his own dreams. In these cases, he searches his memory for the background thoughts so as to theorize about the hidden wish that he thinks lies at the bottom of every dream.

reud assumes that the dreamer creates the dream down to the smallest detail and does so to serve his own egotistical interests. Discussing Irma's pains in her throat and abdomen, for instance, Freud asks, "I wondered why I decided upon this choice of symptoms in the dream."[16]

Freud answers that these odd physical symptoms express his wish to be exonerated. If she is physically ill, it's not his fault if Irma is "not quite well," as Otto had said that morning, because Freud is not treating her for an organic illness, only for hysteria. His dream, he concludes, expresses a hidden wish that gets Freud off the hook.

He admits: "I had a sense of awkwardness at having invented such a severe illness for Irma simply in order to clear myself. It looked so cruel." He invents the illness; his ego is the sole proprietor of his dream. The logic of Freud's charming rhetoric is that the more dastardly and egotistical his confession, the more valid his theory of repression seems. After all, why repress a wish unless it is nasty or embarrassing?

Freud now analyzes the second part of the dream: "I at once called in Dr. M. and he repeated the examination and confirmed it." Otto and a third doctor also examine Irma. All the doctors agree: she has an organic illness.

The dream gets "more obscure and compressed," says Freud; the doctors say and do absurd things. Dr. M. says not to worry, dysentery will cure Irma's white patches. Otto confesses he gave Irma that weird concoction of chemicals. Propyls ... propionic acid ... trimethylamin. Freud's wish to be safe from criticism has already been fulfilled, so why, Freud asks, does the dream continue?

Freud must necessarily uncover a second wish.

It is revenge on Dr. M. and on his "friend Otto" for annoying him. Again the dream is solely Freud's product: he has both doctors spout nonsense to humiliate themselves.

Freud writes with satisfaction, "When the work of interpretation has been completed, we perceive that the dream is the fulfillment of a wish."[17] Exoneration in part one, revenge in part two. With that, we have "the Secret of Dreams . . . Revealed." The puzzle is solved.

Or is it? Suppose the dream is not so bizarre. Suppose Freud was wrong, right from the start, about his "specimen dream."

Chapter 18

THE TWO BELLY BUTTONS

To approach Freud's dream as Marc Bregman would, you would not be ranging far and wide for obscure memories or digging for hidden wishes. You would not suppose there is a latent dream. Instead, the meaning of the dream—the white spots on Irma's throat, the doctors spouting nonsense—appears right on the surface.

Nor would you break the dream into fragments, *ad locum*, or free-associate from them. Those interpretive procedures, however wonderful for creating imaginative elaboration, would tend to destroy the wholeness—the gestalt—of the dream and take you further and further from its intention.

Instead, the manifest dream is clarified to deliver its message. The noise is reduced so the signal can come through. The dream is not the distorted product of a dream censor's struggle to conceal hidden wishes of the dreamer. Therefore, it doesn't necessarily require extensive free association just to uncover its secret. The meaning is often right on the surface even if the dreamer is the last one to see it.

The direct power of Bregman's work derives in part from his simply taking the dream seriously at the manifest level.

The dream is not a creation of the dreamer. It's a blunt message, like Abimelech's dream, that wants to be heard, though the dreamer doesn't always want to hear it. Facilitating the dream means breaking through the clutter of details, looking for wholes (gestalts), not parts (*ad locum*).

The question becomes, Who is Irma, and what is she trying to tell Freud-in-the-dream?

Freud assumes, without question, that Irma in his specimen dream refers to Irma in real life.

It's a subtle error. Freud sees Irma, so he thinks the dream is about Irma the patient.

It's not necessarily true that Irma in the dream is the same as Irma the patient, though Freud especially insists on it because he claims that most dreams come from the events of the preceding day.

Who is Irma-in-the-dream, or "Irma" for short? Who is " Freud" for that matter?

Within the precincts of his dream, the character "Freud" is not necessarily bound to behave as the very accomplished physician and psychoanalyst Freud knows himself to be in waking life. Dream-Freud has more freedom of choice than that.

"Irma" tells "Freud" that he ignores her pain. "Freud's" response seems logical to Freud, but to Marc Bregman it is a highly significant error, and the "belly button" of the dream.

Freud, interestingly, uses the same term. In *The Interpretation of Dreams* he writes, "There is at least one spot in every dream at which it is umplumbable—a navel, as it were, that is its point of contact with the unknown."[1]

He elaborates on "navel" on another page of *The Interpretation of Dreams*. "There is often a passage in even the most thoroughly interpreted dream which has to be left obscure. This is because we become aware during the work of interpretation that at that point there is a tangle of dream-thoughts which cannot be unraveled and which moreover adds nothing to our knowledge of the content of the dream. This is the dream's navel, the spot where it reaches down into the unknown."[2]

Freud's navel and Bregman's belly button are not the same. Freud's navel is the dead end of the elaboration of free associations, whereas for Bregman it is the main point of the dream.

By "the unknown" Freud means that the net of possible associations to any given point in the dream—the "tangle of dream-thoughts"—is so complicated that the recondite meanings can no longer usefully be tracked down. Freud locates the navel of the Irma dream in a very different spot than Bregman. The navel is Irma's "recalcitrance" when her throat is examined, which leads Freud to recall a second patient who also suffered from symptoms of hysterical choking. This speculation in turn, Freud writes, leads too far afield for him to continue to trace it out. Therefore, he's arrived at the end point or navel.

For Freud, the navel of the dream is where you give up interpreting. But for Bregman, the belly button is the most important part of the dream because it leads to a choice that requires feeling.

When dream-Irma says to him, "I am choking," dream-Freud has the choice of responding with feeling. But he does not allow himself to feel. There's an emotional blank spot.

This numbness can be found in many of Freud's dreams.

"Irma" is saying, You ignore my pain—you are choking me—you are cutting me off.

What part of "I am choking" does "Freud" not understand? Yet he doesn't take "Irma's" complaint to heart. He can't respond in the dream as a human being.

"Freud's" response is to look down her throat. If you think of this as two human beings trying to talk about their feelings, then "Freud's" response borders on the insane. But he sees it all backward:

"I took her to the window and looked down her throat and she showed signs of recalcitrance like women with artificial dentures. I thought to myself that there was really no need for her to do that."

"Freud" is puzzled that she resists. He doesn't get the irony. She won't open her throat. But he won't open his eyes. The meaning is manifest, not latent. The dream does not fulfill a wish; it holds up a mirror to his own behavior.

"Irma" comes to him with her pain. But to Freud, "Irma seemed to me foolish because she had not accepted my solution." In a footnote to this he adds, "I was forced to admit to myself that I was not treating either Irma or my wife very kindly in this dream; but it should be observed by way of excuse that I was measuring them both by the standard of the good and amenable patient."[3]

"Good and amenable." But "amenable" means taking the doctor's advice. (Even if, as he admits in the footnote, it is sometimes at the cost of his patient's life.) Good—to Freud—is amenable.

Good is what is good to Dr. Sigmund Freud, a male physician of the Viennese high bourgeoisie with a superior attitude toward his wife, wives, women, patients, especially women patients.

But my point is not only feminist; Freud has received his drubbing on this point at better hands than mine. The point is that most dreamers make the same mistake, at least in the early stage of doing the dream work. It's what I kept doing with my dream of K de G. For Bregman this defines a first stage of dream work: what's good in the dream is bad, and what's bad is good.[4] Freud is clearly such a stage-one dreamer, though that's not surprising. Most of us naturally are.

"Irma" represents a voice Freud needs to hear and know. She feels deeply, and she carries deep feeling. But he misses the opportunity. Instead "Irma" is suppressed, ignored, and condescended to.

"I at once took her on one side ... to reproach her for not having accepted my 'solution' yet. I said to her: 'If you still get pains, it's really only
your fault.'" Freud admits, with some hesitation, that he may well have said
these words to Irma in waking life.[5]

The dream tries to warn him against the extreme arrogance of such statements and offers him an opportunity to respond in a different way to "Irma"
than he responded to Irma the patient. Instead of examining her throat, he is
being asked to examine his life. This is a warning dream, like the first dream
in Genesis, Abimelech's.

All of this is manifest content. It is right on the surface. Hidden in the
obvious. All you need to do to see it is to strip away the preconception that
"Irma" deserves the behavior she's receiving in the dream and that Freud-in-
the-dream is required to respond purely as a physician.

That is, you have to strip away the professional arrogance of Dr. Freud.
Then it's plain as day. Freud can't see it because he has a blind spot. He can't
see "Irma" as a person because he can see himself in his dreams only as a
doctor, an authority of some kind. This need to be always authoritative mo-
tivated Freud throughout his life, a clear pattern in many of Freud's dreams
recounted in *The Interpretation of Dreams*.

The so-called recalcitrance of "Irma" is his projection. It's "Freud" who
resists her. Freud-in-the-dream misses an opportunity to be warned, and to
change. When "Freud" fails "Irma's" challenge, the dream mocks his pretentiousness by sending in the clowns, those doctors with their silly diagnoses.

This is Bregman's explanation for the second part of the dream. Once
"Freud" fails the moment with "Irma," the story goes haywire.

Marc Bregman told me, "You can trace a dream back to the point where
you make a mistake: at that point everything goes to shit. Basically you can
completely change your dreams just by being a good student. If you do the
right thing, no matter how hard it is, if you do exactly what they tell you, you
will grow."

The clownish doctors mirror Freud's own pomposity, making fun of him
the way the cop in my dream made fun of my bicycle. But Freud doesn't get
it any more than I did. You usually need someone else to show you your own
blind spot.

Yet "Irma" continues to haunt Freud. Her voice resonates throughout *The
Interpretation of Dreams*; the whole book is structured around his interpretation of this "specimen dream." It receives more attention than any other,

referred to in twenty separate passages apart from the chapter devoted to it. Remove "Irma," and the book loses its hidden muse.

Dream-Irma's voice secretly works on him while he artfully dances away from her with his dazzling arguments, charming apologies, and brilliant excuses. His interpretation allows him to ignore the real demand for change that she presents. In this sense Freud is also carrying out an amelioration of the dream. The real accusation of the dream is never faced or even heard.

True, in the course of his explanations he confesses to many dastardly egotistical motivations, but only in the wry manner of a sophisticated man of affairs.[6] He winks and nods to the reader, saying, in effect, "You, too, my good fellow, would do the same in my position." Irony, condescension, humor, charm—these are literary tools, but they are also how the ego blocks the door of the dream. The written word of interpretation triumphs over the "living word" of Irma. Instead of a secret being "revealed," a dream is ameliorated. Freud does not feel any call to change. He will not change: he is going to be, always, Dr. Freud, the revealer of secrets. In and out of the dream.

Who "Irma" is and what she might further teach Freud become more apparent if you apply Bregman's approach to look at other dreams, as we will see. But Freud himself never gets there. Instead, "Irma" will always be just a "female patient," and Freud feels entirely justified in shutting her up, lecturing her, peering down her throat.

Then, to make things worse, he hauls her into his book, where she gets to be a specimen. Dr. Freud the interpreter adds a self-justifying interpretation that doesn't deal with the surface of the dream at all, but instead imagines hidden wishes shaping the dream. A third layer is packed around that: the entire superstructure of his dream theory, with its initial division of latent and manifest, that takes us to increasingly abstract considerations of psychic forces. Freud is very good at describing the id, the ego, the dream censor, the dream work, repression, distortion—so much so that we still use such terms, though their scientific shelf date has expired. But all these ideas take him further and further from hearing the "living word" of Irma. A word intended for his ears.

Freud believed that all dreams are egoistic, or, as he put it nicely, that they have an "egoistic lining."

I have spoken . . . of the egoism of children's minds, and I may now add, with a hint at a possible connection between the two facts, that dreams have

the same characteristic. All of them are completely egoistic: the beloved ego
appears in all of them, even though it may be disguised. The wishes that
are fulfilled in them are invariably the ego's wishes, and if a dream seems to
have been provoked by an altruistic interest, we are only being deceived by
appearances.[7]

Though Freud backs off this point in later footnotes and additions, he was certain that the wishes fulfilled in the dream are the wishes of the "beloved ego."

Freud would certainly reject the model of Abimelech's dream. Dreams are not judgments or warnings, he believes; they are riddles. Only in the closing pages of *The Interpretation of Dreams* does Freud briefly address the question of their possible "ethical significance."

"I do not feel justified in answering these questions, I have not considered this side of the problem of dreams further . . . would it not be right to bear in mind Plato's dictum that a virtuous man is content to dream what a wicked man really does? I think it is best, therefore to acquit dreams. Whether we are to attribute reality to unconscious wishes, I cannot say.

"I think . . . that the Roman emperor was in the wrong when he had one of his subjects executed because he had dreamt of murdering the emperor." To Freud, only "actions deserve to be considered . . . not the impulses expressed in dreams."[8]

Freud knocks down a straw man. The issue is not legal, but how dreams can change you from within. I would learn from Marc Bregman that for a dream to change your behavior, you must treat it as if your actions in the dream are real, most especially those actions that are "ethically objectionable."

For these embarrassments are shown to you for a reason. They dramatize powerfully the holes in your story, the blind spots.

To respond to the dream's inherent moral accusation—Jung calls it "judgment" in his last great theoretical work[9]—you must take the feelings in it as seriously as if you had them when awake. You must act as Abimelech did, who immediately obeyed the voice in his dream. Only if you can do that can the dream change your life.

For the dream comes, as the archaic torso of Apollo came in Rilke's sonnet, to say, "You must change your life."

If you don't feel remorse when you see yourself in the dream acting arrogantly or unkind, the dream can never touch you with its charge. Freud's technique of association is useful in binding the dream to waking life. But the dream is not subordinate to waking life; rather, the dream displays a template of waking behavior. Note the reversal of direction: instead of the meaning of the dream being tied exclusively to a memory, memory adds to the power of the dream. The belly button of K de G would prove to have nothing to do with bagels.

Working with a feeling of distaste for your dream behavior, you change from the inside out.

That is the gist of the work Marc Bregman showed me in stage one, though that simple summary tells you nothing about how difficult this work really is. I struggled against it mightily, using all my powers, including my own powers of interpretation, my education, my reading, my books. My ego was just as beloved to me as Freud's was to him.

In a certain way, Freud believed that the dream was designed to ameliorate itself, for he wrote that the whole point of the dream distortion is to prevent "the generation of anxiety or other unpleasant affect," which might disturb sleep.[10] In his psychodynamics, the dreamer's id or superego expresses uncomfortable wishes, but the dream censor distorts and disguises them. So for Freud, the dream doubles up into manifest and latent. The latent-dream theory gives Freud an escape hatch to avoid what "Irma" and the doctors are trying to show him. Freud never sees the real belly button of the dream, which is not the end point of interpretation, but the genesis of feeling.

Carl Jung, Freud's main antagonist, took a very different approach to the dream. He writes in his autobiography,

I was never able to agree with Freud that the dream is a "façade" behind which its meaning lies hidden—a meaning already known but maliciously so to speak withheld from consciousness. To me dreams are a part of nature, which harbors no intention to deceive but expresses something as best it can, just as a plant grows or an animal seeks its food as best it can. These forms of life, too, have no wish to deceive our eyes, but we may deceive ourselves because our eyes are shortsighted. Or we hear amiss because our ears are rather deaf—but it's not our ears that wish to deceive us. Long before I met Freud I regarded the unconscious, and dreams, which are its direct exponents, as natural processes to which no arbitrariness can be attributed, and above all no legerdemain. I knew no reasons for the assumption that the tricks of consciousness can be extended to the natural processes of the unconscious. On the contrary, daily experience taught me what intense resistance the unconscious opposes to the tendencies of the conscious mind.[11]

Rosemarie Sand, a contemporary psychoanalyst who trained in the Freudian tradition, cites research that confirms the importance of the manifest content of a dream, meaning the dream as recalled and reported by the dreamer.

"[The researchers] ... after summarizing results of a number of dream studies ... noted that 'the manifest dream content carries a great deal of meaning. ...' [T]he weight of the evidence argues against viewing the manifest content as a largely meaningless conglomeration of camouflage devices, such as Freud spelled out."[12]

Sand concludes that the ancient theory of the dream is closer to the mark. The manifest content displays the message of the dream. It's a picture, a pictorial representation—that is, an image.

This is also true of the prophetic dream stories in Genesis: Joseph's dream of the sheaf, and Jacob's dream of the ladder. These dreams represent the real gifts of the dream in Genesis, and with them we can find the true "Secret of Dreams" revealed.

With Freud I can bring to a close the case of the disappearing dream. The trail begins when Joseph's brothers introduce interpretation into the story in their reaction to the dream of the sheaf. That is the turning point. All the dreams in Genesis before that did not require interpreters. All the dreams thereafter do.

Joseph as interpreter returns images to the realm of words; the rabbis follow in this path for the most part and add the idea of amelioration; the Church Fathers also indicate that dreams are so tricky that only saints can really discern whether a dream is from God or the devil.

The overall result is that interpretation of one kind or another has become the dominant response to dreams. Interpretations may well come, as Joseph's did, from God; but for most of us, the interpretation is just as likely to come from "Joseph's brothers"—that is, from our blind spots.

With Freud, this same struggle between image and word, dream and interpretation, reappears, not only in his personal conflict with Jung, but also in his division of the dream into manifest and latent.

Freud adopts many strategies of his rabbinic predecessors, frequently focusing on words and language in dreams more than images, and reading the dreams "*ad locum,*" as the rabbinic midrash reads the Torah. He consciously assumes the mantle of Joseph the interpreter. "It will be noticed that the name Josef plays a great part in my dreams (cf. the dream about my uncle). My own ego finds it very easy to hide itself behind people of that name, since Joseph was the name of a man famous in the Bible as an interpreter of dreams." Freud mentions Joseph three times in *The Interpretation of Dreams*.[13] He does not mention Jacob or the ladder once.* For Freud, only interpretation matters, because only interpretation can establish the science of the dream.

So who should be accused in the case of the disappearing dream? Freud or the rabbis or the Church Fathers? Or Deuteronomy or Joseph's brothers? All are plausible suspects. Another answer is: the butler did it.

That is, Pharaoh's butler, who in distress begs Joseph to interpret his dreams. The butler personifies our fear of the dream's accusation, a fear that leads to one form of amelioration or another.

The butler did it. The whole history of dream interpretation is shadowed by fear and anxiety.

But fear is not the whole story of the dream in Genesis. There are also great promises and three great gifts.

First, there's the pointed warning of Abimelech's dream; then, there's the dream of the sheaf, which reveals an essential situation of his soul to Joseph; finally, there's the dream of the ladder, which indicates an entire new realm of consciousness. Those who respond by keeping "the matter in mind," who abide with the dream in life and dwell on its images, learn to heed the dream's warnings and change. They come to see their essential spiritual condition, and can explore the dream life of the soul.

Dream Revelation in Genesis

DREAMER	DREAM	REVELATION
Abimelech	"You are a dead man."	Warning
Joseph	Dream of the sheaf	Essential image
Jacob	Dream of the ladder	Realm of consciousness

The merkabah mystics followed the text of Ezekiel to find a way into the same consciousness that Jacob experienced in his dream. When the secrets of the merkabah were lost, Jewish mystical dreamers continued to explore the

---

*Interestingly, Jakob is the name of Freud's father.

world of the chariot by using the chariot of the dream. These explorations underlie the theosophy of the kabbalah, and the teachings of the original Hasidim.

What surprised me in working with Bregman was to learn that these ancient gifts of the dream could be rediscovered in our own time. They are hidden in the obvious, right on the surface of the dream, though often they can't be seen by the dreamer.

Chapter 19

BLIND SPOTS REMOVED
WHILE YOU WAIT,
AND THE BOOK OF
K de G SPEAKS

To Freud, dream content seems distorted and "nonsensical," and requires interpretation to unearth the dream's secrets.

Not in Bregman's approach. For him, the manifest dream may offer an obvious message, but not one the dreamer is willing to see. Because he wrote about his own dreams, it was harder for Freud to account for his own blind spots.

Admittedly the dream can feel confusing. Especially because, as Freud shows so clearly, any moment in a dream can lead to an immense tangle of memories and associations. Once you apply the intellect to all this tangle, you can produce a very elaborate interpretation, but you may have missed the main point.

Suppose, however, that in dreams you take the road less taken, that other path Joseph took with his dream of the sheaf, the path of abiding with the images in the dream. You stay with the manifest content instead of looking for a hidden explanation. You give yourself time to see the images in the dream. It's not something you can do easily for yourself. But a good guide can point out exactly what you're not seeing because of your blind spots. Then the manifest dream begins to acquire power and consistency. Then it seems that, contrary to Freud, the real "Secret of Dreams" was never hidden in the first place, but simply overlooked.

. . .

Dreams may ultimately lead to a spiritual journey, but the path begins where you are. And where you are will remain the issue of your dreams until you allow the dreams to teach you certain facts about yourself that may, at first, be unpleasant to acknowledge.

After several years' apprenticeship with Bregman, I became a student teacher and began to work on dreams with clients. One was William T., a fifty-year-old professor who came to me initially because he wanted to return to his early love of painting, which he had abandoned in his twenties.* He'd been a talented painter who won prizes, but he thought there was just too much competition in that field. As a practical matter, he put up his brushes and went to graduate school in art history. He is a very successful academic who teaches at a prestigious college on the East Coast, with a large number of books to his credit.

But he's not happy in his academic work. He'd like to start painting again but can never find the time. His success has gotten in his way. He's got too many lectures and commitments.

In his dream William is on the beach—always a happy place for him. He loves the beach; swimming is his greatest pleasure. He sees a little girl about eight years old, who walks up to him, holding a crayon drawing. When I asked him, he told me he liked her very much and loved her drawing.

A man in a business suit comes walking along the beach. He asks William to come with him, to look at a new museum on a college campus. Without hesitation, William abandons the little girl who'd won his heart and trudges off with the man across the sand.

—Why did you decide to go off with him? I asked when we had our session on this dream.

Because when I go traveling to give lectures, if my host wanted to show me a new building on campus, naturally I'd feel obliged.

—So your obligation to him was more important than the little girl with the drawing?

Yes.

---

*I have changed certain details to disguise his identity.

He didn't see anything wrong with that. But Bregman stresses that the choices you make in dreams are important. In this case, my client William thinks he has good reasons for choosing the man.

And it's a big mistake.

At first William's response seems logical enough. He's making a choice in the dream exactly as he would make it if he were awake. He operates from his waking reality and from his practical considerations. He goes off with the man in the suit without even thinking about making a choice. He leaves the little girl behind.

I've left out a little part of this dream, and it's somewhat significant. It's what Bregman calls the "hole in the story." When we were discussing the little girl, William T. told me that after looking at her drawing he became anxious because he couldn't find the girl's parents.

I asked why.

Again he applied waking logic: If you saw a little girl all alone on the beach, wouldn't you be concerned?

Fine. But then here comes the hole. As soon as the man in the suit shows up, William T. dumps all that "concern" and leaves the little girl behind. Which seems to indicate that concern wasn't very important.

William T. doesn't see that hole because he's so convinced that going off with the man in the suit is the practical thing to do. What about his feeling for the little girl with the drawing—that initial delight and joy he felt just seeing her? Feeling is our guide in the dream, and William feels something for her, he acknowledges. It's just not strong enough—in this dream—to overcome the pull of the practical. She is his heart's delight. If he can't choose her over Mr. Practical in his dream, when can he choose her?

I want to say such dreams are true in the sense that they expose us as we truly are. Certainly you could use the dream as a sort of diagnosis: William T. is too obsessive about his work. Or you could start trying to figure out why he did this, what incident in childhood led him to be so practical and so shut down to his feelings.

But the dream doesn't work that way. The dream presents the drama in a three-character play. William T. has probably been in this sort of dilemma every day of his life. The dream portrays vividly how William chooses what's important to do—whether to make a painting or give a lecture, go with his feelings or obey his obligations. Dreams show us beautifully the flavor of a person's situation in life.

That is how manifest dreams begin to be revelations: they manifest the truth about us. This is a very remarkable thing, and not at all expected. That dreams tell the truth about us is a powerful argument for contemplating their images and dramas instead of throwing them away.

However, dreams are tricky—not because some of them come from demons, but because the dreamer is often the last one to get the point. Based on his long experience, Bregman distinguishes dreamers by stages. He says the beginning or stage-one dreamer is characterized by a persistently backward response. For stage-one dreamers, what looks bad is good and what looks good is bad.

I t's best not to make a hard and fast category, because confusing what's good and bad can happen to any dreamer—but the stage-one dreamer does it fairly consistently.

As a result of this confusion, the stage-one dreamer will often overlook or dismiss the very character who is most important, as "Freud" did with "Irma."

A second dream illustrates how this dismissal can seem perfectly justified to the stage-one dreamer even when it is strikingly inappropriate.

Olivia, a piano teacher from a small town in Missouri, was beaten and kicked by her father as a little girl. She also received very little support from her mother as a child. She is wracked with a constant feeling of worthlessness, even though she is an accomplished teacher with many successful students.

Olivia dreams she is sitting in a café with her daughter. She's feeling panic because she doesn't have enough money to pay the bill. She looks out the window and sees two women wheeling a bloody man tied up on a dolly. They've practically killed him. "He's looking at me. I see his bloody eye. I feel he's done something horrible to them and deserves whatever he gets."

The bound man pleads to her with his eyes, but she reacts negatively. To justify her reaction, she says that she "knows" he's committed crimes. This is a good example of how projection hides within a blind spot. Projection fills the holes in the story with a fantasy—in this case, a dramatic story that justifies her reaction.

When asked by Bregman gently, "How do you know?" Olivia answers with exquisite illogic that once she was assaulted by a man in a coin laundry. Therefore, she assumes that these women wouldn't harm him if he hadn't hurt them first.

Sometimes in life we do just know, but in a dream such knowing more often indicates projection from a blind spot. To get someone to reconsider this prejudice, Bregman often uses the technique of treating the dream existentially; he applies real-life tests to the situation. He asks Olivia, If you saw a bloody man wheeled down the street on a dolly, what would you actually feel?

Clearly, it would be a disturbing sight. Yet even though the man appeals to her with his eyes, the communication does not lead anywhere further. She does not allow herself to feel anything for him, at all. The bloody man is in her blind spot.

Olivia feels that her assessment of the man on the dolly is the only correct assumption, and this carries over into everyday life. She mistrusts men in general in exactly this way. The underlying emotion driving her is shame, a sense of worthlessness. That comes out in the first part of the dream when Bregman gently probes. "Is it true," he asks, "that you are so broke you can't afford a cup of coffee?" Olivia laughed, but Bregman had made the point.

Her emotion at not having enough money stems from her lack of self-worth. So does her reaction to the "bloody man," for reasons that would become clear in later dreams.

The bloody man is her "Irma." She won't let herself feel his pain. Later she'll learn how her shame keeps her from responding to him. For now, the manifest content of the dream simply shows where she's stuck. Unless she can work through her shame, the dream will be the script she follows again and again.

Emotions run Olivia and William T. in dreams and in life, reactions and projections. Feelings are missing or muted in these dreams. Finding the feelings and feeling them more strongly is the thread that leads out of the dream labyrinth of stage one.

The first day we met, Bregman had told me that emotions and feelings are the signposts of the dream. I laughed to myself; I had so much condescension toward him. I thought, The words are synonyms. What kind of signposts can they be? I went into a whole huff about this dyslexic postman and his misuse of language. I didn't understand yet, because I hadn't experienced the difference clearly in my own dreams.

Yes, in ordinary talk we use those words interchangeably, something Bregman knew full well. But from the point of view of the dream, feeling and emotion are completely different experiences.

Emotions drive; feelings lead. Emotions are reactions, usually set routines and stereotyped behavior. Feelings lead us away from such stereotyped reactions. So they are liberating. A stronger feeling for the little girl in William's dream might have allowed him to explore more deeply who she was and what the creative joy she represented was, instead of trudging off in the sand to meet yet another obligation.

I don't want to underestimate the difficulty of making the right choice in a dream. The pragmatic or practical or ego-adjusted sensibility doesn't disappear just because my head is on the pillow. It persists within my dreams.

It's easy to talk about someone else's struggle, but I knew from experience that the distinction between feeling and emotion is subtle and has to be worked out dream by dream. We are not used to thinking this way, and our everyday language is inadequate. Each person brings a different life to the dream, and Bregman's work is subtle and particular. He lets the dreams guide him.

To Bregman, "Everything in a dream is a reflection of a feeling or an emotion. Every dream is full of clues as to which is which."

Following the clues is key, because Bregman's work is empirical and interactive. The dreams of Freud, Olivia, and William T. show us dreamers driven mostly by emotional reactions, who never get to genuine feelings. In each case there's a blind spot. In each case they can't see or hear or respond to other persons in the dream who do carry feeling. "Irma" *feels* in Freud's dream much more than he does. The bloody man is full of pathos and suffering in Olivia's dream. The little girl in William's dream expresses pure child-like creative joy.

But because of blind spots, these figures full of feeling are ignored, overlooked, rejected by the dream-ego, the I-in-the-dream.

A blind spot justifies itself as an instant reaction, the "of course" reaction. "Of course" "Freud" treats "Irma" as recalcitrant; she's just a patient. "Of course" William T. goes off with the man in the suit. "Of course" Olivia's bloody man deserves what he gets.

"Of course" in my dream of K de G, I get lost in a book and forget all about who sent it to me. . . .

One way Bregman gets you past your blind spots is to use a technique from Frederick Perls's gestalt therapy. Perls was a psychotherapist who attracted a wide following in the 1960s and 1970s after his workshops and seminars at the Esalen Institute made him well known.

Gestalt is the German word for "wholeness," and the aim is to see the dream whole, not cut up into pieces. Though Perls started out as a Freudian, he became dissatisfied with the Freudian approach of fragmenting dreams to interpret them. For Perls, "all the different parts of the dream are fragments of our personalities. Since our aim is to make every one of us a wholesome person . . . we have to . . . put the different fragments of the dream together. We have to re-own these projected fragmented parts of our personality, and re-own the hidden potential that appears in dreams.

"Instead of analyzing and further cutting up the dream, we want to bring it back to life. And the way to bring it back to life is to re-live the dream as if it were happening now."[1]

In my work with William T., I asked him to talk to the little girl and ask her who she was and what she was doing in his dream. If Bregman were working with Freud, then Freud would sit across from Irma and hear at last what she had to say. This process is called, informally, "doing a gestalt," or "gestalting" the dream.

When Bregman worked Olivia's dream of the "bloody man," he got her to question her assumptions about him through a gestalt. She sat in a chair and saw the bloody man in the empty chair across from her. She had assumed he was tied up because he'd done a crime. Now she could ask him.

"Bloody man," she asked, "why are you tied up like that?" Then she switched chairs and, speaking in his voice, answered herself: "Because they are trying to keep me from you." Through that answer she came to realize her projection onto him and the fact that the women who were binding him were not the "good guys" in her dream, nor was he a "bad guy."

Sometimes such gestalts are very hard to do; at other times, the empty chair talks.

When I brought in K de G and we'd discussed it for a time, Bregman asked me to do a gestalt. In itself, my dream of K de G was technically harder to gestalt than Olivia's. There were missing persons in my dreams and also missing feelings. I'm a fairly solitary intellectual guy who spends hours every day musing over words and reading books. At least William T. had three characters on his beach; I had no one from my dream to talk to.

However, Perls had the idea that not only the people in dreams but the objects could be made to talk. A man dreams of a blue car at the bottom of a lake and sees a rusty license plate. Perls had that man speak to the license plate.

So Bregman asked me to talk to a book. I sat across from an empty chair. I spoke and then switched seats, and spoke back as the book of K de G.

Yes, I was sitting in his office having an interview with a talking book from my dream. . .

Here's how the dialogue went. Bregman supplied my lines, and the book answered back.

Me: Book, why are you being shown to me?

Book of K de G: *Because I fascinate you.*

Me: What are you trying to show me that fascinates me?

K de G: *You love what's doubled up. You love the commentary on the original.*

Me: What's wrong with that?

K de G: *There's nothing wrong with it if you're not scared, but it's keeping you from your destiny.*

Me: How?

K de G: *Because you get lost in it. Instead of starting from the beginning, telling your own story, you comment on somebody else's.*

Me: What do you mean, my story?

K de G: *It's your genesis. It's your origin.*

When I heard those words spoken by the book of K de G, I was surprised. Gestalts don't always work for me, because I get too self-conscious. But in this case I really felt that the voice of the book was saying something I didn't know. I could feel that in getting the book of K de G to speak out loud to me, I was being lured deeper into accepting the viewpoint of the dream. It was strange and magical. I felt that the dream was coming out into the world and speaking to me in its own voice. I could no longer stand outside my dream and interpret it, by searching for memories, or according to any fixed equation of symbols. Instead, the dream was now interpreting me.

Worse, according to the dream, I was falling short because I was looking in a book for the answer instead of looking within.

I had thought the point of the dream was that K de G stood for "Kamenetz on Genesis." That is how I did my own amelioration.

I thought the book of K de G was a friendly image of the book I would be writing.

The gestalt ruined these happy thoughts. Considering how much energy I'd spent tracing the history of dreams in Genesis, what the talking book said was anguishing but also funny.

Who was in charge here? Was I writing about dreams, or was this talking book from my dreams going to tell me what to write?

Who would win the battle, me or THEY?

The book of K de G asked me to choose.

Between Genesis and my genesis. Between my deep love of books and reading and—what? Or who? What was meant by "your genesis" and "your origin"?

For the moment I didn't know. The lesson I drew from Freud's dream of Irma applies to my dream of K de G. The I in the dream is not the I who interprets on waking. THEY—whoever THEY were—were showing me a path of transformation, a path to becoming a different I, someone I knew not of.

I had missed my own blind spot. The dream comes to us disguised in everyday concerns. My waking concerns were the book I was writing, *this book*.

I'd read the dream backward.

Looking into Genesis had been fine. But the dream hadn't come to reassure me. It's just THEY knew that writing the book was more important to me than doing my "work" in Bregman's sense, the work of spiritual growth in dreams. THEY got my attention the only way THEY could—through the image of a book.

The whole point was not Genesis but "your genesis" and "your origin."

For a dream to transform you, you must enter fully into its imaginal reality. You must endure the grip of the actual angel on your thigh—the pain in the dream must be your pain—and that sort of participation can come only with a long entrainment, an extended friendship with your dreams and a willingness to abandon your old words and ideas, and take seriously the images that come to speak to you.

Obviously I had a huge blind spot. My blind spot happened to be a big blue book. It blocked the view of my father, who'd sent it to me. The dream was showing me that my fascination with books is not entirely healthy because it was keeping me from knowing my father. That hurt to know. It hurt exactly like that gut punch from the first day.

Chapter 20

HOW DREAMS ABOLISH TIME, AND THE SECRET OF K de G AT LAST

Physicians speak of "guarding a wound." It's how the body adapts to an injury—with an involuntary tightening of muscles. In each of us is a wounded place, an eternal moment that reverberates in every other moment, seemingly permanent, unchangeable, unchanging.

It is our point of shattering. The dream teacher Tarab Tulku referred to it more dryly, in that Tibetan way, as "vulnerable self-reference."

The wound seems fixed and forever, and though its traumas could surely be traced to a particular date or time, the pain lives on perennially—unless it is possible to go back to that past and change it.

And it is possible, because dreams abolish time.

So the dead mingle with the living in our dreams. The more mystical rabbis believed this. In one Talmudic tale, Raba asks his beloved teacher Rabbi Nachman, on his deathbed, to visit him in a dream after his death.

He does just that, and Raba asks Nachman, "Did you suffer pain?" "No," Nachman answers gently, "as little as removing a hair from the milk."[1]

To the mystical rabbis, dreams had no boundary of time or of space. They associated dreams with both ends of life. They likened the dream to the womb, where they believed you could see from one end of the universe to another.

Time and space, life and death, past and future—all meet in the dream.

Therefore, making a new choice in the dream changes the past. This is the incredible experience in the dream work. It is not a question of magic or mystical belief. Simply, a dream brings an old moment vividly to life so it can be reexperienced as real. Then the old wound can be healed, the damage reversed.

Colette spoke of "reversing." For people with traumas, she gave an exercise. You were to vividly visualize the painful incident and then slowly wipe the whole scene clean with a sponge—"always to the left," she insisted, for she believed that was the direction from the present to the past.

That sort of imaginal exercise has difficulties. It is not so easy to recall a traumatic scene at will. The wound has been guarded too long, or it has been covered over with amnesia. There is a second-degree hiding of pain, too. Not only is the deepest pain hidden from memory, but it is hidden from us that it is hidden.

But our dreams take us back to the past and heal it. This is the astonishing power of "the work" in stage one. It's something I saw happening to many people who worked with Bregman, and it happened to me.

In the dream you relive vividly what was once a frozen memory. By making a new choice in the existential moment of the dream, a profound anamnesis or unremembering takes place. The wound no longer needs to be guarded. You unlearn an old hurt; you remake an old relationship. From that place one can heal. Through "the work," I learned to feel a love for my father that I thought had been lost.

My distance from my father was measured in miles and years. All that first year with Bregman, I'd dreamed of my wife and children many times, my sisters and brothers, my deceased mother, but never once of him. He never appeared in my dreams. The first hint of him was the dream of K de G, and that was only an e-mail. I would have to do a lot of work before my father appeared and spoke in person in my dreams.

The important persons in your dreams approach gradually. Sometimes they are mentioned before they are seen. They might appear in a photograph, or a film. Sometimes they call on the phone, but the distance is measured by the faintness of the voice, or static on the line. It may be a long time before they truly stand before you, and even longer before you can see them as they truly are.

The dreamer gets distracted and misses the opportunity. I didn't see that by focusing so much on reading the book of K de G, I was forgetting that it was a gift from my father.

Dreams probe the tender spots of your relationships; with father and mother, with brothers and sisters, with your wife or lovers, with your children.

In stage one, dreams are showing you what's wrong, what's missing. What's clear already in the dream of K de G is simply: my father is missing, and instead there is a book. What got clearer is how in dreams and in my life I'd grown up with books as a substitute for a father.

Before I could see him in a dream, I had to get past the book, because whenever it appeared in a dream my fascination with the book became pathological. K de G was not the only book in my dream library; the entire collection could be filed under the Dewey decimal code for "anxiety."

I mention to Famous Poet that his poem is in the book I'm holding. Famous Poet asks to see it. I thumb through the book, but now I can't find it.

_____

The teacher has written a passage on the blackboard: God can save us from depression: we don't have to do anything. *I don't even dwell on the meaning. Instead, I believe I am a fellow teacher, though no one says I am.*

Since I'm not prepared to contribute, I figure I'll fake it by finding the statement quoted in a book. For some reason, I believe it comes from II Chronicles in the Bible.

Now I'm holding a book I think is a Bible. As I thumb through it, looking for II Chronicles, I see economics charts, and narratives of World War II. I'm tearing through the pages searching. There's not even a table of contents I've forgotten the teacher and the teaching completely.

My dream books get out of hand; they multiply; they mutate as I search them. It's an acutely anxious moment when I turn to a book for support and it starts to turn on me.

I'm in a private house where my literary hero, the Argentine master Jorge Luis Borges, is speaking.

I open his Ficciones, *and the first page describes a boat trip I just completed. The coincidence astounds me. I want to tell Borges all about it.*

I raise my hand, and the master walks toward me. I thumb through his book to show him the passage I just read. But now I can't find it. Acutely embarrassed, I say, "It just fell open to the page before." As he stands over me, I am searching the book; ridiculous little slips of paper fall out. I lose all sense of his presence. . .

Each dream boils down to the same absurd triangle: me, an authority—
and a book. In each dream I make a choice: I choose the book.

Then my father appeared:

My father and I were sitting at a long table with another father and son,
who were studying a book together. (It was a text about two kinds of fish.) I
thought to myself: two kinds of fish, how silly. But then on second thought,
I felt that the love shared between the father and his son was more impor-
tant than the text they studied together.

As for me, I looked down and saw a word I didn't understand: feffer. I
looked up and saw my father across the table and felt he understood it, but
I didn't say a word to him.

"Why didn't you ask him?" Bregman said.

For homework, I was to see my father's face and ask him what he knew.

I practiced seeing his face and asking. It was painful. My pride didn't like
it. I had built my whole life as a man around not asking him for help—my
father, or any father, mentor, or male rival. I found my own authority in
books.

The homework was a meditation like Colette's but arising from my dream
and pointing directly at my life. This is where contemporary spiritual practice so often failed people—in not engaging them at a specific enough level
where a spiritual problem has it roots in a psychological issue.

How could I seek the face of God if I couldn't even see my own father's
face? How can I relate to God as a father if I can't relate to my father? We need
images of our relationship to God that touch the heart, but we are blocked
from them because of the pain and trauma in our lives. Our spiritual questions are psychological, and our psychological questions are spiritual.

I called up the image of him sitting before me and felt my own stubbornness and pride. I did not know how to ask him for help. As far back as I could
remember, I had always been too proud.

I did the homework and felt something melting. The answer could not be
found by looking at the book, or staring at that silly word *feffer*. The answer
could be found only by asking my father for help in the dream.

It was a breakthrough, and after this homework, my father became a regular in my dreams. Now I had a wonderful opportunity, which I thought I'd
never have again in my life. The opportunity to repair and recover what had
long been lost.

It still wasn't easy. There were still difficult feelings to work through, but now my father was in my dreams at last. No more e-mails. No more books in the way. Just him and me.

Sometimes I reacted to him in the dream just as I often had in life—with aloofness, distance, criticism. Once it came to rage; that was like a thunder burst. I woke shocked and chastened by my own stupidity.

That gave the dreams a new opening, and with that shift I could overcome the ancient distance between us that Bregman had touched on in our first meeting through the cop-and-bicycle dream.

In new dreams, I came to core feelings of hurt and sorrow—and I came in the end to love. It's strange to say, but over those months I renewed my relationship with my father, strictly through dreams.

With Bregman's help, I reached the point where I-in-my-dream was no longer the I that I had been. From the dream-side out, I'd changed the "ID" that those cops had been asking for in my first dreams. My dream-ego was no longer so defensive or angry; "I" grew younger, more a boy, a son who could admit he needed his father and call for his help.

I dreamed the walls of my house were collapsing all around me. I called out like a little boy, "Dad, it's a disaster!" I called out from my heart for his help, and he appeared like magic and saved the day.

It's remarkable that changing how you behave in dreams can change your waking life.

The inner work precedes the outer. The dreams sweetened my feelings for my father in the last years of his life.

It was an everyday miracle to Bregman; so many clients had recovered lost relationships with parents or with children, revived marriages or ended them, changed occupations, and renewed their lives. Bregman took no personal credit for this; he simply called it "the work." But the forces he was guiding had remarkable powers of healing and recovery, and he deserves more credit than he took.

Over years, my feelings about Marc Bregman also sweetened. In the beginning, he was another male rival to overcome, but over time I came to understand how to learn from him. The great teaching of so many of my dreams is how to be a student.

'd come a long way from the guy who thought Bregman would make an amusing chapter in this book, from the scared guy on the bicycle who did not get the cop's joke, from the aloof son with his nose in a book.

I'd learned how to take the warning of the dream to heart, as Abimelech did. By changing my behavior in my dreams, I changed in my life. This was a huge gift already. But there was more to learn and further to go.

The personal work is wonderful, but there is a story beyond the personal, which Bregman spoke of as second-stage work.

The book of K de G spoke of it, too. The mysterious phrase "genesis and origin" refers to a deeper level of life than personal autobiography. It expresses the mystery I'd been wrestling with since I met Bregman: the mystery of THEY and their part in the dream life of the soul.

3

DREAMS

So God created man in his own image,
in the image of God created he him;
male and female created he them.

—GENESIS 1:27

God created man WITH his image....

—RASHI ON GENESIS 1:27

Chapter 21

THE THREE GIFTS
OF THE DREAM

The interpretation of dreams is a stubborn reflex, with a long history, not easily undone.

As soon as I wake, I say, "That was a good dream," or I say, "That was a bad one." "That was an interesting dream." "That was boring." Those first thoughts are already interpretations, based on what some part of me thinks is good, bad, interesting, boring.

Which is not necessarily what the dream thinks.

Dream interpretation in the usual, popular sense represents an enduring victory for the word in its struggle with the image. How we react reflexively to dreams is consistent with how we think in general. The word strives to keep its place on top in the conscious mind, and awareness of the image remains partly or wholly submerged. The dream has its place and time at night and in private, but interpretation rules by day. The reflex is so strong that a powerful force must drive it. But is that force on our side? Dreams come to bring depth. But we resist. It is as if another person inside us wants to fend off the dream. A voice that says: Don't go there. Don't open that door. Don't look.

For now, let's call that force within "the opposition."

The opposition wants to keep the dream safely lodged in the darkness where it belongs, not out in the light of day. The opposition uses numbness to keep us unaware of feeling; it infiltrates interpretation with amelioration. We go along with the opposition because we don't want the images in dreams to stay active in daylight, gnawing at us, worrying us. Because these images can be disruptive. They can pull us deeper when we prefer to stay "on top of things."

But to take dreams as a path to soul we have to learn a very different move. Take the images seriously, take them in, abide with them, suffer them, go deeper with them.

This is the move I made when I turned away from the books in my dreams to face the dream image of my father. It was very humble and simple—about feelings, finally, and not complicated or "doubled up."

I simply learned to love my father better in my dreams.

I think that was a lot. I learned that dreams can lead us to feel much more deeply.

But first the reflex of interpretation had to be broken.

In that sense, my history of interpretation is best understood as an exorcism.

I've cleared the busts of the dream doctors off the shelf—all those brilliant rabbis and Church Fathers who taught us how to interpret and ameliorate the dream, and most of all Dr. Freud, who remains, though slightly chipped, our little plaster god of dreams.

Once I swept them from the shelf, the descent into dreams began in earnest.

When I first met Marc Bregman, my intellectual concerns were with religion and spirituality—but my dreams showed me wandering lost in strange cities. What did such dreams have to do with God or soul or enlightenment?

On the face of it, nothing. But I was wrong, because dreams open a cellar door to depth. They show you how to shift from being driven by external events and internal emotions to being centered on your soul or psyche, which is rich, powerful, and generative.

In an age when so many are disillusioned with organized religion, this is the great promise of the descent into dreams: to go deep within yourself, to learn the tools to go deep, relying on what happens at night and finding a way to learn and grow. To find out where you are blocked from growth, to rediscover a nature that was part of you at one point and has slowly been lost. To be able to get back down to the source of your being and recover a grounding and honesty with yourself that's been gone for so long.

But the descent begins where you are. For most people, that's at the ground-floor level of everyday conscious thoughts and emotions, worries and troubles. From that perspective, even the first dreams can seem puzzling.

A woman doing the dream work has various crises. Her husband is a gambler, and she just found out he's been stealing money from her bank account. Her son was caught driving while drunk and totaled the car. She's being sued for fraud, and she's having trouble sleeping. She's upset and anxious, but as she tells it, she's coping.

One night, she dreamed she was chained in the basement.

From her waking perspective, her dream seems bizarre and nonsensical. But as you feel into the reality of the dream, it opens into a larger drama. Why is she chained? Who chained her there? A man standing next to her chats casually. He's Bob Barker, the game-show host. Why a game-show host? What's Bob Barker doing in her dream? Is he friend or foe?

Then her teenage son comes downstairs to see her before going off to school. She says, Have a nice day.

Why doesn't she ask her son to unlock her chains? It turns out that she feels nothing at all about being chained. Not a thing. It just feels normal to her.

This numbness is the issue. It's even more bizarre than the chains. It's a failure to feel deeply or with imagination. A failure to feel her own pain. For many people, numbness is the barrier to depth.

A man dreams of a long needle inserted into his knee. He says, I didn't feel a thing.

The next night he dreams he's sealed in a space capsule, all alone. It's the same dream, really. He's hermetically sealed, isolated, headed for outer space.

The dream wants to show us inner space. It shows us our predicament, how we really live. But you have to be willing to feel something about your predicament, because there's no other way in.

The dream isn't speaking in a language that makes literal sense. The man is not an astronaut. The woman is not chained in her basement. These dreams do not speak in the language of the dreamer's daily concerns or preoccupations.

The dream speaks its own special language.

The special language of dreams is forceful, poetic, metaphorical—and for most people, very unfamiliar. It appeals to imagination and creates an imaginal space where eventually you can move around and explore. This is the move I'm talking about, and it's very, very different from interpretation as it has historically been done, and as we usually know it. So different that I could call it "uninterpretation." But it's the only way to receive the gifts of the dream.

I nterpretation cannot lead you to these gifts. Amelioration will only help you avoid them. Turning away from the manifest dream to the latent, as Freud did, only helps the opposition. In the chapters ahead I will sometimes return to Freud's own dreams to show opportunities he missed. But mainly I will use my own dreams to illustrate how I opened the three gifts of the dream.

The first gift: dreams reveal through powerful images and dramatic situations your predicament in life—where you are blocked, stuck, lost without even knowing it. You have to learn what causes your predicament and overcome it.

Then, deeper down, comes the second gift. You have a pivotal dream where you glimpse the situation of the soul. I call mine "the orphanage dream," but it would take a different form for each person.

As for the third gift, a whole sleeping world awakens for you that you carry with you always. It is the world of the soul and its encounters with the divine.

These three gifts correspond to three dreams in Genesis: the dream of Abimelech, Joseph's sheaf, and Jacob's ladder. In that sense they fulfill the promise of the dream made so long ago.

But before I can tell the story of how I received these three gifts, I have to rewind back to the start of my work with Bregman, long before the dream of K de G. That's when I had my own predicament dreams. The images I saw were not so dramatic as being chained in the basement. They were simply dreams of being lost.

I start with them not because I think these dreams so special or rare, but exactly because I think they are all too typical. They struck me as boring.

Yet that was already a mistaken interpretation that played right into the hands of the opposition—because it kept me from fully appreciating the predicament the images were trying to show me.

Chapter 22

LOST AND
WANDERING
DREAMS

The Predicament

A t first, it did seem better to forget my dreams. At least the ones I was having when I met Bregman.

It was not easy to begin. Because many dreams, when we wake, just feel boring. I dream of driving a car, looking for the address of a shop to buy a book. I find the right number, but it's the wrong street. Then I find the right street, but the wrong number. Now the streets aren't named or numbered at all. I get angry. I tell my wife, *They* should have better signage. It's all the fault of the city fathers, or the store owners. It's not my fault I get lost.

The dream, at this stage, is a contemporary labyrinth—roads that lead you in circles. That's a very common and mild form of the nightmare. You are driving your car, which is to say, you are in charge of your life. Whichever way you turn is wrong. Whatever you try to do to help yourself makes things worse. In classical literature, a labyrinth is a maze with a monster in the middle, but for a long time I do not see the monster.

I hadn't gone two steps deep. I was still centered in my waking consciousness and everyday life.

I had a variation of the lost dream, set in railroad stations. I'm supposed to catch a train, but I never catch the train. Something always goes wrong.

I'm not sure when the train is leaving or exactly where I am going, so I ask directions. A group of clerks in railroad uniforms—black coats with shiny buttons—sit at tall desks above me. They have nearly identical features, like wooden dolls.

I wait a long time at the counter, looking up and trying to get their attention, but they sit placidly at their desks, staring into space, and no one acknowledges me. Finally I shout up to the clerks, "Can one of you come to help me?" And I add in frustration, "You don't look like you are doing anything to me."

Nasty. But they are mild mannered. They don't pay me much mind. One clerk says, "You can talk to me." But how will I get to him? I look up, and the distance between us enlarges and expands. I climb up complicated narrow winding stairs, all the time wondering if I am missing the train. I am moving between the offices where these officials work. The offices are empty or the men in them ignore me. I go down corridors lined with blank walls. Finally at the end of a long corridor I find an official sitting alone in his office. I say, "Well, it must be you, you're the last one left." He shakes his head no.

I descend some stairs, and at the bottom I see another clerk sitting in an identical office.

Now that I've found him, I realize I don't know what to ask. Because in all my worry about missing the train, and all my anger about not getting answers, that's a hole in my story. Until I arrived at this last desk, I didn't realize it, but I don't know my destination.

I cover up because I'm embarrassed. I tell the clerk, vaguely, that I know the train I want is going north. (How do I know this? I don't know it. I'm making it up—lying, really.) "Maybe Vermont?" I add. (I'm just improvising.) I feel silly and humiliated and angry and put upon.

The clerk doesn't respond. So I say, "Well, can you just tell me the next few trains going north? I'm sure it's one of them." I feel better saying that, even though I have no idea if it's true. I'm trying to solve the predicament as best I can. I've come all this way through all these corridors to find this clerk, so now I want an answer. Maybe knowing when the train is leaving will help. The clerk takes a slip of paper and writes down "8," with "03" in smaller numbers beside it double underlined, and then he writes "13," with an "02" double underlined. He slides the paper across the desk. I think: well, they wouldn't want me to wait until 13:02. That would be one o'clock in the afternoon. Come to think of it, is it 8:03 in the morning or 8:03 in the evening? I really don't know. As I'm thinking, I look down below to the main floor of the station. Is that my wife? Maybe she can help. But then as her face comes into focus I see it's a stranger, an old woman with distorted features. How can I have mistaken her for my wife?

Now other people crowd into the room to ask the clerk directions. I grab the slip of paper and say, "Well, it must be the 8:02," and the clerk says as I leave, "You must be in luck because that's right now."

I can't help feeling he is being sarcastic. Because I hear the whistle blowing as he speaks. I look at my watch. It's exactly 8:02. Panicked, I dash down the stairs, only as I run, the stairs multiply at my feet. The faster I hurry, the more turns and twists there are. Now the stairs fill with piles of folding chairs, which I have to leap over. At every landing I have to twist around bureaus and desks. Minutes go by, and when I arrive at the platform, I see in the distance the last car of the train leaving the station.

Not exactly a screaming nightmare, but certainly unpleasant, uncomfortable, frustrating . . . Yet when I deal with the officials, I am so sure I am in the right. I become immediately indignant when the clerks don't answer my questions. I'm certain they are holding something back from me, deliberately mocking me.

All that anger and frustration made me overlook a very important hole in my story.

I don't know where I am going.

I had these kinds of dreams often when I first met Bregman: the car dream where I get lost, the train dream where I miss the train, dreams of wandering on foot, lost in city streets. Silly stuff, dull nightmares, and easily dismissed. I say, They are only dreams.

But suppose these lost dreams are not really about the trivial events of daily life, like getting lost or missing a train. Suppose instead they hold a clue, not only to who I am, but why I am supposed to be here. Suppose it is possible for me to change so that I can get on the train I keep missing and that it will take me somewhere new where I need to go. Suppose being lost in the city is meant to lead me somewhere new, if only I'd let it happen.

Then again, why should I care? These dream labyrinths I'm wandering in at night—on foot, in the car, in the train station—don't mean what they seem to mean, do they? They can't mean that my life is that trivial, that frustrated, that stupid.

At times I became sick of it. I didn't want to record any more dreams. Bregman or no Bregman. I just wished these boring dreams would end. I didn't think these dreams were leading me anywhere. But I was wrong. They were leading me to an orphanage.

. . .

began with the predicament of being lost. Lost is where many begin the descent into dreams. There are variations: a lost car in a parking lot, a lost wallet, or a lost purse.

You dream of losing something, or being lost. It's a similar feeling either way. You've lost something—or you've lost someone, or you've lost yourself. Who is lost? What has really been lost?

I was having dreams of being lost when I first began work with Bregman. I had the train-station dream in many variations, but I never got on the train. Or I had the driving dream, where I looked for a store and couldn't find it. Or I had the dream of walking the city streets.

I wandered on foot in a strange city on vaguely familiar streets. The city was unfamiliar and then familiar, because it started out as one city and changed to another. I tried to stay on top of it, find my way, but I couldn't. The emotion in these dreams seemed to be increasing frustration, anxiety, sometimes boiling over into anger.

Ordinarily, I think, you dream such dreams and shrug them off. Just dreams, you say. You don't want to look closer, don't want to know: these dreams are a snapshot of the predicament of your life.

If the dreams are boring, perhaps it is because you have wasted the spiritual potential of your life. You are lost—but you don't know it. In your pride, you think you can eventually find your lost car, your lost wallet or purse, that you can find the road out of the baffling duplicitous city. But you don't see what's really going on.

The emotions in these dreams—dissatisfaction, anger, and frustration—are a very real undercurrent in everyday life. Thoreau wrote: The mass of men lead lives of quiet desperation. The lost dreams show that desperation inescapably, vividly, in living color. Not as some event in the past but as an inner predicament suffered and endured.

I kept having these "lost dreams" over a period of weeks. They represented my predicament in life. Many people have such dreams all their nights. They are bad news. That's why we try to forget them, or if we can't, we ameliorate. Probably in time, were it not for Bregman, I would have stopped thinking about them, dismissed them. "My dreams are boring," I would say if asked. They are about everyday events, trivial conundrums; there's nothing really important there.

But something else happened because of the patient way Bregman had me slow down and work the images. These dreams of predicament led somewhere eventually, to dramas where I had to make real choices. They challenged me to find a deeper way of seeing my feelings, of knowing myself. They opened doors. They led to spiritual encounters I couldn't get to as long as I tried to figure everything out for myself, and as long as I relied on "reading the signs" and interpreting them in my old way. As long as I tried to stay the same me in the dreams that I was when awake, full of pride and blame. As long as the opposition had the upper hand.

The lost dream morphed. This is part of how the descent into dreams works. You have a dream and then it repeats and varies, until the opposition weakens and you change your response in the dream, and then the dreams can change, too. And you take a step deeper down. It's a slow process: there's backing and filling; it's not smooth, it's not linear; you get stopped. But if you persist, eventually you do work yourself out of your predicament and go deeper.

In one of those changes, finally I saw a dream that meant a great deal. I went back to it again and again in my mind. I named it "the orphanage dream." The lost dreams had finally arrived at a destination.

I want to show how the orphanage dream felt and the gift that it led me to, the second of the three gifts of the dream, the situation of the soul. Through the orphanage dream I came in time to encounters with important persons, very important persons.

But before I can show how the orphanage dream felt, or introduce the VIPs I met, I need to clear some ground. I need to open up more completely a topic I've skirted.

It has to do with our internal resistance to our dreams, which so far I've called "the opposition," though it has other, more difficult names.

Because until you can see the opposition for what it is, the dream descent stays stuck near the surface. You remain in your predicament.

At first this opposition hides within the dream-ego and can't be seen. Then it appears dramatically in the open, as a separate character. When that happens, your life, and your dreams, change dramatically. Because then you can receive the first gift of the dream. You can unlock the chains, leave the space capsule, find your way home from being lost.

Chapter 23

THE OPPOSITION:
GRAVEL GRANDMA

This is the hard part. Almost everyone who does this work with dreams comes up against a predicament, something unpleasant that has to be faced. You might see yourself chained in the basement or flying numb and oblivious into outer space. You might see your inability to feel or see yourself putting up with being violated. Or, as in my case, you might see yourself acting like an aggressive and presumptuous jerk. These are predicaments our dreams show us in.

The anger and blaming I saw in the railroad dream were an all-too-familiar reaction. The dreams simply threw me into a situation where this behavior was triggered, and made me starkly aware of it as a pattern.

Until you get through this part of the work, the dreams are unrelenting; they come at you with tremendous persistency and force, one after the other. And they work different angles of each issue, and once they've worked one issue they go to another. It's like a whole curriculum of basic faults. Here's a series on your imposture. Oh, here's a new series on your intellectual pretentiousness. Here's a series on your lies. . . .

It doesn't happen for everyone, but if you have a strong ego to begin with—and lots of pride—then the dreams slice away and show you these pictures of your behavior.

I don't want to exaggerate my faults. For some dreamers this part of the work is much more difficult and shattering than what I've described because what's seen in the dreams is darker and uglier than they can bear.

But that's not the whole story. Because if a person is crushed and broken already, the dreams behave very gently and this stage of the descent is very different from mine: the dreams can patiently build the person up for a long time before revealing the negative. The dreams seem to know exactly how much you can take.

I didn't need the building up, so I got the breaking down.

I got cops who kept asking me for a driver's license; they wanted to know "Who do you think you are?"

I got black folks. I first saw them in another train-station dream. I panicked at night in a dark parking lot just outside the station. I was in urban New Jersey, convinced some young black guys were going to kill me. When I talked about the dream, I was ashamed to admit it because it sounds so racist. I didn't like the idea that such stereotypes were running around in my unconscious. That is a good and interesting point, but it wasn't the point of the dream. Bregman told me: face your fear of these young black guys. And I did. In my homework, I saw myself in the parking lot of the train station again. I saw the young black guys standing next to a cab, and I looked into their faces. Something softened: I realized I had no reason to be afraid.

The homework took effect quickly. In the next dream, a black family—father, mother, two teenage kids—moved into the basement of my house. In the next dream, we were all living together, for I sat at the kitchen table with a mother and her son. These black folks in my dreams told me things I needed to hear. They weren't lessons about race: they were about me. I started listening. And as I grew closer to them, I started changing. I looked in the mirror and saw myself turning black. I had dreadlocks in one dream, and I got the pun: the locks on my dread had been broken; I had no reason to fear. Again the dreams were telling me: *Who do you think you are?* But this time they were also saying: *You are beginning to change.* I was being shown a new layer: below the arrogance in the other dreams was fear.

"Who do you think you are?" was the general theme. I've been teaching at the university for many years. So I think of myself as a teacher. I had a whole series of classroom dreams that led to a surprise.

I walked into a classroom. The students were sitting around a seminar table. I sat down and thought, I haven't really prepared a lesson. I decide I'll just start teaching and maybe figure out what the course is about. I say something I consider to be smart—but the students don't listen. They are still talking among themselves. I call on one, but he just looks away. I'm frustrated, but I figure I'll do my job, so I plunge ahead—just like I might in waking life in that situation—even though I don't have clue one what the class is about or what I'm supposed to be teaching.

As I'm talking, some of the students get up and walk around the room, look out the window. I get angry at these unruly, disrespectful students. "Wait a minute here, I'm trying to teach," I say. They ignore that, too. Several more drift toward the door and walk out. I am frustrated, confused, and angry. What's wrong with these students?

I had this dream in many variations. The opposition fought these dreams every inch of the way. I interpreted the dream as a reference to my everyday life. I said to Bregman after each dream, "Well, I'm a teacher. So naturally I think I am the teacher in the dream. That's what I do every day. I walk into classrooms and I'm the teacher."

He patiently went back to the dreams. He pointed out that the students didn't seem to be listening. He asked: "How come you don't know what the class is about?" He asked: "How do you know you're the teacher? Does anyone in the dream say so?" He didn't see the dream as a reference to my waking life. He saw it as being about my inner life.

The dreams kept coming. In one dream, as I spoke, the classroom slowly enlarged and expanded. Now it was a lecture hall. Once again I didn't know the subject matter, but I was casting about for something clever to hold the students' attention. I gamely blabbed on. The students ignored me. A bell rang. Students abruptly walked out. Other doors opened. Students trooped across the room on their way to other classes. My classroom had become a sort of corridor; the room was now enormous, an auditorium.

I felt insignificant and hurt. This was actually a significant change within me. Instead of reacting—turning out my discomfort and blaming the students—I turned inward and felt the pain of being abandoned and rejected. As homework, I replayed that bewildering moment as the students walked out.

Then the time came where I actually got it—in the dream. This was much later, but it finally happened.

I walked into the classroom and sat down at the table. I looked around at the faces of the students, *my fellow students*. I waited for the teacher as they had been waiting in my dreams all along. I was "just" another student. I didn't need a lesson plan because I wasn't supposed to be teaching a lesson. That was a great relief. I was there to learn.

The classroom dreams, I came to understand, were not really about my teaching career at all, though I kept trying to interpret them that way. The classroom was an interior space: the dreams dramatized an inner attitude I brought to nearly every encounter in my life, where I played a know-it-all. In any given encounter, I'm the teacher, so you're the student. The dreams brilliantly exposed this flaw. You could give it a name like "arrogance" or "pride." But the images were more useful than a label because I could work with the feelings they offered. The image of the students walking off was something I could replay in my mind and feel into more deeply. This is how dreams give you leverage to change.

I could ask, What is behind that? Why do I always have to be the teacher? Why do I have to offload blame? Why, if I didn't know where I was going, did I get angry at the clerks? The dreams indicated the nature of an opposition I couldn't yet see. The opposition that drove my interpretations also drove much of my behavior. It had to do with pride, intellect, superiority. I was helpless when it got triggered. In a tight spot, I blamed someone else. Or if I was lost, I tried to figure things out for myself; I didn't ask for help. I didn't allow myself to get vulnerable or to feel my hurt. There was the key to my predicament: I was seeing me and my father, me and Bregman, me and most anybody.

It wasn't enough to be aware of these patterns and try to correct them from the top down, which is the usual procedure when we run up against our flaws in a moral context: the "you should"s—you should do this, you shouldn't do that. Because that doesn't usually work; exhortation just doesn't do the trick. Shame and guilt make things worse.

Freud proposed a different approach, a clinical model. There is an illness—neurosis—and there is a cure: if you know the etiology of your symptoms—if you can find the smoking gun—you can eliminate them.

That approach may also work in some cases. But to reflexively reference every dream to actual events in the past, as Freud does, is to miss much of the profound work dreams do.

Bregman's approach is not limited to the personal domain, though he certainly includes it. But if you bring everything back exclusively to your autobiography, then you are stuck inside your story as your ego knows it. If you're a teacher in life, then you are a teacher in your dream; if you are a doctor in life, then you are Dr. Freud in your dream.

You are also stuck with your personal history. You can't change what happened in your childhood. Where does that lead you?

Personal history takes you back to a past you can't change. The diagnosis feels like a permanent stain on you that can't be erased. And that's not the whole truth of it. I had to go deeper.

What's really at stake is how these forces work within you now, and how they lead to your predicament: wandering lost or numb in outer space or chained in the basement.

The first step is to let the dream display the behavior so you can see it. What was in shadow steps into the light of the dream, and then you see it. In my case, I had to admit that the guy playing me in the dreams was a jerk.

It didn't come easy. You struggle to accept this first difficult gift of the dream. Because there's really no way to go deeper if you are dragging the opposition along with you.

Bregman helped facilitate the process by slowing the dream down, by asking me to fix on the image and asking me to tell what I felt in that moment: when the clerk didn't answer, when the students left the room.

The feelings deepen, and so does your conscious sense of aversion to the opposition. It may happen quickly, or it may take months of working patiently with the dreams before you step down through this dark fog.

What's whirling in it varies from person to person: every particle of the struggle, every step through the dreams, is different depending on your predicament. The amazing thing to me was how brilliant and knowing the dreams were about my faults.

It's a strange miracle: dreams tell you the truth about your basic predicament. To me this is most amazing. After all, dreams could be just random bits of misinformation, neuronal garbage, totally jumbled irrelevant nonsense. But somehow they aren't: somehow, if you learn how to feel them, they are very clear dramas of your life's struggle.

For some people the fog you step down through is really, really dark and thick. For some it's light gray. There are some people, Bregman says, who are "good to go" when they begin the dream descent. Maybe they are born with this clarity, or maybe they've already done work on themselves. There are those who move quickly on to all the good stuff. It depends on how you were conditioned and formed, abused or traumatized, or whether you have worked through this material in other ways. The dreams always begin the lesson where you are. Not where you think you are, but where you are.

They display your behavior straight up, like the Irma dream or my train-station dream. They make you wonder, Why do I always act like Mr. Know-It-All or Ms. Doormat or Ms. Indifferent? Why am I a numb astronaut flying into space? Why am I letting myself be chained in the basement? What's inside me that makes me do it? Because surely I don't want to be the person I'm seeing in my dreams.

At first this opposition may be completely cloaked within the I of the dream, the dream-ego, the dream-I. You can't see it in the dream, in the exact same way that you can't see it in your life. Something happens and you react;

that's all. (Or something happens and you fail to react.) But why you reacted, or why you remained numb—that you don't know. Or maybe you do know, but you don't like to think about it. Maybe it crops up in your intimate relationships, or you get a glimpse after you've been pushed or stressed.

Then you say: "I'm sorry, something came over me." "I didn't mean it." "I didn't know what I was doing."

What something?

Who meant it if I didn't?

Who was doing it if it wasn't I?

Now, if this opposition could step out of the shadow, if it could acquire a body and a voice and a personality, then you could know the hidden force that you are reacting to. And that is exactly what certain dreams do for you.

They personify the opposition.

Instead of being hidden inside you, you see a man on the beach in a business suit. Or Bob Barker is standing beside you while you happen to be chained in the basement. You may not get it even when the opposition is personified. You may actually go off with the man in the suit, or be content to chat with Bob Barker while you are bound in chains.

But eventually, if the opposition keeps showing up, some dreams come where you get a stronger feeling of aversion for this opposition and the evil things it does to you:

I am sitting on a screened-in porch with my daughter, who is a young girl in the dream. I hear footsteps in the dark clumping across the gravel. My daughter is speaking intently to me in a way I love, but now abruptly I interrupt her—"Shh, she can hear you." An old lady appears on the porch. "Be nice to your grandma," I say. This is very strange, because this old woman is not anyone whose face I know.

Here the opposition comes out in the open and acquires a body. She clumps across the gravel. "Shh, she can hear you." Why do I react to her instantly and interrupt my daughter?

Then it gets worse: "Be nice to your grandma"—sounds like good advice, but is really just a way of telling my daughter to knuckle under to her the way I am knuckling under. That's a gesture destructive of our relationship. Whoever this figure is, she isn't anyone's grandma, and being nice to her is not a good idea.

The dream dramatizes inner workings that in other dreams are hidden from conscious awareness. We have these inexplicable automatic reactions that seem natural: in the train-station dream or the classroom dream, I blame others when things go wrong. It's an instant reflex. I didn't realize the reflex had a motivation; I couldn't stand to look bad in front of gravel grandma.

When I'm not consciously aware of her, I'm still reacting to her. When she makes me feel guilty, I try to shift the blame onto someone else. More dreams fill in the picture, but the basic point is that the dream gives me a picture: I see the opposition clearly as a separate character.

What does gravel grandma want from me? How does she manipulate or control me? What emotions does she evoke when she appears? Guilt? Shame? Anger? Panic?

The dreams show me all this over time. But instead of a pejorative label like "pride" or "superiority complex" or a reconstruction of childhood history going back to one parent or another, I had something much more valuable: an antagonist in an inner drama, staged nightly.

To see what so often drives you personified as a distinct and vivid character is to more fully receive the first great gift of the dream. I liken it to the difficult gift Abimelech receives when he is bluntly warned in that first dream in Genesis. He is going to lose his life if he doesn't change.

In the same way, the dreams show you how a force within you is snatching you away from your true life. The fear of gravel grandma's disapproval led me to always seek to be blameless, and if necessary to cast blame on others. I figured it out eventually: I was trying to be perfect for her.

This made me seek out situations where I was sure that I was on top, the teacher to any student. It also made me highly competitive with male figures, like the cop in the bicycle dream.

The dreams gave me a perspective on my predicament by showing the hidden role of the opposition. Imagine, the one pushing my buttons all those years was really no more than an old lady clumping across the gravel. This is a liberating revelation. The opposition comes out in the open where it can be seen and dealt with. Then your predicament can change.

In my case the opposition acquired the body of an older woman, but for others it can be a seductive man, a cruel father figure, or a pliant woman. Each of these general types appears in different guises in various dreams, yet over time the consistency becomes clear.

Bregman calls the opposition a deliberately ugly name: pathology. Sooner or later these sorts of dreams show up and allow you to see who pushes your buttons in those moments when you feel, "This isn't really me."

This recalls a climactic scene in *The Wizard of Oz*. Dorothy and her three allies—Scarecrow, Tin Man, and Cowardly Lion—have completed their mission for the Wizard and returned with the broomstick of the Wicked Witch of the West.

Now they ask him to keep his promises to them, but he puts them off with a fearsome display: the giant head of the wizard floats over his throne, with smoke and thunder. His mighty voice roars, so that Dorothy and her friends are knocked off their feet. But then the little dog Toto runs to one side and pulls at a curtain. You see revealed an older man furiously working the controls of his machinery, which spews all that smoke and roar. When he sees that the curtain is open, and that he is exposed, he says into the microphone, "Ignore the man behind the curtain. I am the great and powerful Oz."

But it's too late. Dorothy and the others have seen him for the humbug he is. The pathology doesn't like to be exposed like that. Because when it is, it loses a certain power over you. And you gain freedom, the freedom to say no or refuse to listen. You don't have to be intimidated by the Wizard of Oz or the Wicked Witch of the West. A pull of the curtain, and he's exposed; a splash of water, and she melts.

When the opposition shows up personified, whether it's a grandma or a seductive movie star or a cruel, demanding man or a glib game-show host, there's a chance to win your freedom right there in the moment of the dream.

You may miss that opportunity, too. That's more or less what happens in one of Freud's dreams where the opposition appears as an older woman. Not gravel grandma, but a staircase maid. Understanding what she does to Freud makes clear how the opposition blocks further growth, and what you gain by separating from it.

Chapter 24

The Opposition:
Freud's Staircase
Dream

In *The Interpretation of Dreams,* Freud interprets forty-seven of his own dreams. Among them is "the staircase dream":

> *I am very incompletely dressed, and I go from a flat on the ground-floor up a flight of stairs to an upper story. In doing this I jump up three stairs at a time, and I am glad to find that I can mount the stairs so quickly. Suddenly I notice that a servant-maid is coming down the stairs—that is, toward me. I am ashamed, and try to hurry away, and now comes this feeling of being inhibited; I am glued to the stairs, and cannot move from the spot.*[1]

Freud explains the setting: his apartment is upstairs from his office. When the workday is over, he's accustomed to pulling off his collar and tie on his way up to his apartment.

Freud emphasizes that in the dream he's in an even "more advanced" state of undress. This unbuttoned quality—really nakedness—signals that he's not the serious Dr. Freud of the Irma dream. He's not just running up the stairs; he's jumping three steps at a time. The workday is over; it's time to let loose. There's a boylike joy. Just then, a mysterious female figure steps out of the shadow on the landing—and immobilizes him.

Who is she? Why does she have the power to paralyze him? Why does he feel so ashamed? How much does fear of her drive him in his life?

None of these questions come up in Freud's interpretation. As is his typical procedure, he relates the dream to events of the previous day, when he unbuttoned his collar on the way up to his apartment. But that doesn't explain his shame or his paralysis. Instead, Freud searches his memory for other maids, other incidents on staircases.

All of this association could be very valuable preparation for going deeper with the dream; it's something Bregman uses all the time. But by itself, this widening of the interpretive circle from maid to many maids, from staircase to many staircases, distracts Freud from the core truth about the opposition. It's as if she doesn't want him to know who she is.

Because the maid is clearly very powerful, and if she can remain hidden inside him as the opposition, she remains capable of paralyzing him anytime she pleases should he decide to act a little too unbuttoned or boyish.

How does she have such power, considering she's supposedly just a maid, and according to Freud "elderly" and "curmudgeonly," "surly, and by no means attractive"? If the I in the dream is the same as the I on waking, how is it that Dr. Freud who faces down a thousand intellectual opponents in the world could be "inhibited" by a maid on the staircase?

It's clear she, whoever or whatever she is, is in opposition to the half-naked, carefree fellow vigorously skipping up the steps. She won't let him act the boy.

Freud's interpretation leads him very far from any of these considerations. He ends up discussing his smoking habit and how it might be causing a heart condition. He talks about this maid resembling a maid in the house of a woman he's treating. He talks about spitting on the staircase and pharyngitis and everything but the main point.

What he doesn't talk about is his pain. His interpretation doesn't touch on it, and it's clear he doesn't feel his own pain. This is another important way the opposition can assert control: it numbs us.

The image is vivid: he is "glued to the stairs." He doesn't seem to feel enough about this extraordinary paralyzing power of the maid. His interpretation even takes her side and gives reasons why he ought to be ashamed.

But suppose the "old maid" in the dream isn't someone to side with. Suppose she's there to stop him from going any further in this running-up-the-staircase, half-naked, "unprofessional," happy way of being. She doesn't like that sort of thing in him at all.

The staircase dream gives us a peek inside Freud's "dream-ego." It shows the hidden mechanism that drives his arrogant behavior in the Irma dream.

You can imagine that the staircase maid doesn't want him to listen to "Irma" or care about her pain. She wants him always to be fully suited up as the supreme authority, the über-doctor who is always right. If "Irma" refuses to open her throat, why then, she's being recalcitrant. He can't acknowledge "Irma's" pain. The staircase maid doesn't allow him to acknowledge his own.

Freud is seeing in his staircase dream the opposition within him to feeling more deeply, which Bregman calls pathology. In the Irma dream the pathology hides within his dream-ego and he's not aware of it. But it's out in the open in the staircase dream—because the pathology has acquired a body. As she comes out of the shadows, the effect on him is clear enough: she inhibits him. This is an image of what happens within Freud's dream-ego in the Irma dream.

D oes everyone have an opposition, a pathology?

Most of us do, though the opposition takes many different forms or shapes and degrees of darkness, individual to each dreamer. In Freud's case it's personified in a female form; for others it's male. In some cases it's highly sexualized; in other cases it's about ego and pride. Sometimes it's a controlling older woman, as in my dreams or Freud's; sometimes it's a seductive philandering male or a harsh father figure or a compliant mousy woman. Yet over time, in looking at a person's dreams, certain characteristic figures appear with an impressive consistency, though in many disguises and variations.

Is the opposition an actual person in your past, from your childhood, a mother or father, or mother figure or father figure that has somehow been internalized? In some cases the origin of the opposition is very very clear in the dreamer's childhood history and becomes the subject of dreams. In other case, it is murkier. It's inevitable and tantalizing to locate the origin of the pathology in family dynamics. It's not wrong; it is important, and it needs to be understood. It's how we obsess about it, often how we feel it. "My mother didn't love me." "My father overlooked me." In some cases it's just inescapable: I was abused, I was exploited sexually, I was abandoned. But finally, the past is not the focus of Bregman's dream work.

The dream isn't coming only to show you history, but also presence. You see how the opposition operates in you now, regardless of how and when it was installed. That's dramatic and powerful—when you see it step out as a character and you have to confront what it's doing to you, how it keeps you apart from those you love. How it keeps you from your heart.

Occasionally, in a voodoo mood, Bregman calls it the "demon." And the dream work can feel like an exorcism—driving the demon out. Bregman is a skillful teacher and varies the terminology depending on the person.

How does he know that a given figure in a dream is pathology? You have to look at how it behaves in the dream, how it relates to other characters. A character in a dream who lies is most likely to be pathology. Stock characters commonly associated with dishonesty—a used-car salesman, or the glib game-show host in the basement dream—are likely to be pathology. A character who paralyzes you, numbs you, makes you feel guilty or ashamed—who one way or another freezes you in your tracks emotionally—is likely pathology. A sarcastic guy who scoffs at feelings and talks in intellectual abstractions is likely pathology. If you have a friend with these qualities, the pathology may appear in the guise of that friend. A character who seduces you, or who separates you from those you love—likely pathology. Any character who separates you from a child—very likely pathology.

There's no hard or fast rule, though. Every person is different, so recognizing pathology in a dream requires skill and experience. The dreamer is often the one most easily fooled.

Pathology is a term Jung borrowed from clinical medicine. To a physician, pathology is simply a disease process. However, for most laymen the connotation feels very negative.

In *Re-Visioning Psychology*, James Hillman offers another take when he examines the etymology of the word *psychopathology*. He points out that *psyche* at root means "soul," *pathos* means "suffering," and *logos* means "meaning." Therefore *psychopathology* is the meaning of the suffering of the soul, or how the soul suffers meaning.[2]

The soul suffers; it suffers in this world, and as it suffers it throws off symptoms in waking life, and images in dreams.

When the pathology appears in a dream, it steps out of the shadow where it's been hiding. We have a chance to see it in three dimensions and as a living character. We see that it's unpleasant and that the name "pathology" fits. It feels like some disease process, a foreign growth we wish we could remove. The word *pathology*, as Bregman uses it, is almost deliberately painful. It can put people off, be disturbing, but that's just the heat that's needed to cook up change.

The good news is, the dreams give an opportunity to weaken the influence of pathology in the psyche. This is to receive the first gift of the dream: knowing the cause of one's predicament in life. I call it the gift of Abimelech because the dreamer not only hears the warning in his dream but, like the king, heeds it.

Bregman is very skillful with pathology, which he views as a wily, tenacious opponent. First, he helps you see the pathology in your dream behavior. You may defend it initially, but over time you feel a deeper and deeper aversion. You feel ashamed, embarrassed, sick at heart, and worse. It depends on what the dreams are showing.

In the next phase, you see the pathology in action, as I did in the gravel grandma dream. I could see her effect. "She" made me feel instantly guilty and then pass guilt on to my daughter. As dreams like that accumulate, you become more and more averse to the opposition because of your awareness of how it separates you from your soul. At your peak of anguish over how horribly pathological you are, Bregman makes his jujitsu move.

He says very simply, "The pathology is not you."

It's not you. Even though for a long time, maybe all your life, your behavior has been pushed by it, the pathology is not you. It's foreign to you and your interests. Even if you've been friendly to it and have identified with it, the pathology is not you.

This becomes clear because the pathology is now appearing more and more in the dreams, personified, embodied. You can see her freezing Freud in his tracks; you can hear her clumping across the gravel. You see the cruel dark male or the mousy repressed prude. Seeing the dynamics of the process displayed instead of having it hidden within myself, obscured, I gain separation. It becomes a separate character. I see that indeed the pathology is not me.

Over time, as that awareness takes hold, the pathology is forced to change how it appears in the dreams. This is an amazing thing to see. It weakens. It may appear limping or diseased, or its voice on the phone may fade out to a hoarse whisper. It may appear with crutches or in a wheelchair as if to tell you, "I am losing force." In one dream I saw it falling apart, collapsing on the ground, unable to stand up. There are a hundred ways the dreams can show you the pathology losing its strength as the balance shifts. As you become freer in the dream, the pathology loses freedom.

It's forced into forms that are more and more obviously unpleasant, which the pathology does not like at all.

In some cases it may appear as an animal—for instance, an alligator. When you see those snapping teeth in the water, you get an idea of how dangerous this force actually is. In one dream I saw two rotting snakes wound round each other, their flesh falling off as they snapped at one another. Many people feel strongly attached to their pathology at first; after all, they've been living it with all their lives and have given it sweet names. They will defend it, but not when it appears in such a loathsome form.

That is its true ugliness, but you can't understand that fully until you discover the great richness the pathology has been keeping you from, which comes in further work.

The label "pathology" is painful and ought to be to an extent, to reinforce the aversion. It's a flinch word. We hear it as a sickness or a sin, a medical problem or a spiritual defect. Something to cure, or transcend. But in the dreams it is simply someone we see.

When you do see it, him, or her, as it resides within you, you gain freedom. More of its habitual lies and contradictions get exposed. You have the opportunity to make different choices. The old automatic power it has over you weakens the more it is forced to step out of the shadows.

In the drama of the dream, pathology is an evolving, shifting character. It hides in the blind spots. (Bregman says the pathology occludes the dreamer.)

When it hid in the shadows, you reacted to it reflexively: you were thrown into panic or spoke cruelly or skulked in shame or acted out of guilt and had no idea why.

I don't want to underestimate the trickiness or shiftiness of the pathology even as it begins to appear in the open. It has many wiles and tricks, and it knows you very well. Just when you get rid of it, it can come back in a different form. It's a shape-shifter. It knows how to fascinate you; it knows what you like. The work of separating from pathology can be subtle and painful, like uprooting a tumor that's thrown its tentacles around a vital organ. It feeds on the life of you. Its roots have to be skillfully snipped dream by dream, as a delicate surgery.

Sometimes—often—the person feels he or she is being attacked by the therapist, because, to the extent that I identify with my pathology, I feel its pain, or its fear. I may be fearful because it is fearful. This is a very deep process and not necessarily easy. This opposition or pathology can feel like a cherished part of you; in many ways it may be who you think you are. The pathology may wrap itself in good deeds, good acts, or great career moves.

That came out vividly in a discussion with William T., the beach dreamer. Through the dream process, he became more conscious of his pathology. He admitted what he saw in the dreams. But he wanted to compromise because he thought his pathology gave him benefits.

Although he knew he was neglecting his real feelings and that success came at the cost of his family relationships, William T. liked it that the pathology drove him to write book after book. It was the same pathology that appeared as Mr. Professional Obligation, a man in a suit who separated him from the little girl on the beach.

He understood how driven he was in that dream and could connect that to his everyday life. He admitted, "At any given moment I have a thirty-page to-do list."

But as we talked about it, I could almost hear the pathology defending itself.

"Isn't there a danger here," William said, "that I won't be creative anymore? If I would succeed in correcting this pathology . . . what's left? What else is there?"

—Your heart.

All right. It's possible that . . . In other words, I've lost touch with my heart and replaced it with a driven pathology.

—You haven't done it. It's done it to you. It wants to appear useful.

Isn't it possible that it is useful? Let me ask you this. I have thirty books. Would I have thirty books if I didn't have this pathology? What is William T. without those thirty books? Nothing. Do you understand?

He was getting pretty intense. And I said, "Yes—who is William T. without his thirty books? That's exactly the question we are trying to unravel—because the real you is who the dreams are trying to bring out. The pathology you made a deal with is not you."

He wasn't entirely convinced. Nor do I want to underestimate his struggle or mine. When the pathology is "marbled in," it's hard to separate. But in time, depending on how stubborn it is and how willing you are to follow your dreams, the separation happens.

The moment when the tables turn, when you no longer get sucked in, is a triumph. One time in a dream gravel grandma sat beside me on the plane. This time she took the form of a well-dressed middle-age woman, very articulate and sophisticated. She began to talk with me about a dictionary; she knows my fascination with books and language and words. Maybe in the past I would have been fascinated, but not this time. I knew what was up. I leaned forward and spoke to my wife, who was sitting in the row in front of us. At the end of the trip, the dictionary lady and I were standing outside the plane. She said, "Don't forget to call me about what we were talking about." I looked at her and said, "I'm sorry, I don't remember." I really didn't. She seemed to wilt, and she said in a weak voice, "Echoes in an empty room." That's all she had left of her voice, an echo. I walked away down the tarmac with my arm around my wife, and left her behind.

This moment came after months of work. It was just a moment, and there were more to come, but I was on my way. I had changed inside the dream, and this indicated changes in me—period. I'd received the first gift of the dream, Abimelech's gift. Now I knew not only my predicament, but the pathology behind it—and I was able to free myself.

The first effects I'd gained were a new way of relating to others without the pathology getting in the way. I was becoming more the student and less the teacher. I was less willing to follow the impulse to blame others. I was more patient with imperfection and perhaps even a little more kind. I was more open and vulnerable and receptive, in life and in dreams. That vulnerability was a very important gain. It allowed those I might have overlooked before—the student, the child—to become more distinct and prominent.

Pathology had driven me in circles, kept me lost and aloof, wandering in train stations and in city streets. That was about to change.

Now along with the dream-ego, and the pathology, there comes a new actor in the drama, and one with huge personal significance, for the child brings the second gift of the dream. I saw him clearly in the orphanage dream, though I did not recognize right away who he was to me. But with him, the lost dreams finally found their destination.

Chapter 25

THE ORPHANAGE DREAM

The Situation of the Soul

A t first, when I had dreams of getting lost on city streets, I responded as I would in life: by trying to figure things out for myself—a move Bregman calls "problem solving." It's applying your intellect where it has no traction.

I didn't notice any people on the street. But if there were, I ignored them. I didn't ask anyone for directions; I was too proud. Instead, I tried to find a familiar landmark. I would figure this out for myself. I looked closely at street signs. But as I gazed up at the letters, they wrinkled before my eyes; they seemed to be written in Arabic or Sanskrit.

I was reading street signs, reading in my dreams—and that reading was being defied and mocked in the same way K de G and the other dream books mocked me when they doubled and redoubled, or when I couldn't find a passage I was certain I'd just seen. But I didn't see the mockery of street signs that changed as I tried to read them, or of streets that began as familiar parts of Baltimore but turned into parts of other cities like San Francisco.

I kept having these "lost in the city" dreams over a period of weeks. Many people have such dreams all their lives. But in my doing the work with Bregman, eventually, slowly, something shook loose.

My dream-ego was changing, softening. I was feeling more. The work of outing the pathology had helped. I'd seen it first in my behavior in some dreams. Then I'd seen it step out of the shadows, and just seeing it personified began to change me, though the decisive struggles were still ahead.

I was a little more open, more willing to be vulnerable. More receptive.

I was trying to piece out where I was in San Francisco, because I was pretty sure I was in San Francisco, but I couldn't place the street. In other dreams,

I would have kept walking alone, trying to figure it all out. But this time, I noticed a black woman and her boyfriend across the street. This woman began to sing beautifully, spontaneously, and I was moved by the rich beauty of her voice. From across the street, I sang back to her in an impromptu duet—something I might not have done in "real life." It was just in my heart to do it. We finished together, "I Left My Heart in San Francisco"—belting out in harmony the old Tony Bennett finale.

When I come home to you, San Francisco,
Your golden sun will shine for me.

Singing with her gave me a feeling of exhilaration.

Then she stepped inside her house. Who she was, I didn't yet know. She was one of those mysterious important persons sometimes encountered in dreams, and I would learn more about her in other dreams. But for now she'd moved inside, and now I, too, found myself inside a huge institutional building many stories tall. I recall a rough-hewn stone structure like an old church or ancient hospital. The place was packed with boys. Boys everywhere. I climbed staircases looking for a door out, and on each floor I saw boys, playing ball, laughing, chasing one another. They were about eight or nine years old.

At first, I felt out of place. What was I, a grown man, doing among all these boys? But I was too proud to ask for help, and everyone working there seemed too busy to notice me.

Then it must have been getting into evening, because I saw attendants coming into the hallways and gathering the boys to their dormitories. I peeked in one room and saw them dressing in pajamas, brushing their teeth in the bathroom. For some reason, this sight ratcheted up my discomfort. I certainly didn't want to stay overnight with these boys. I have to get out of here, I thought, just have to.

I didn't think of asking anyone for help. I ran down hallways, up and down stairs looking for a door. I was convinced as always that I could figure a way out for myself. But in this massive stone building there seemed to be no exits. Now the discomfort built into inexplicable fear. I absolutely had to find a way out. It seemed a matter of life or death.

Just then a Hispanic kid appeared. He said, *You're going to need some help.*

He told me his name was Miguel. I had never seen this kid in waking life; he was completely a stranger, and yet oddly familiar. I liked him immediately.

Miguel showed me a vertical folding metal door, like one on a loading platform. Miguel pulled a chain and the door lifted. I looked down to a fifty-foot drop.

"I can't get out here."

Miguel answered, "*This is the way out.*" I looked again, and this time the drop was only a few feet. I stepped out. It was raining heavily. Funny, it had been bright and sunny before. The door slammed down behind me.

This was a pivotal dream, as it turned out, but also very puzzling, and I would go back to it frequently in my thoughts until eventually, through other dreams, I learned how to take it in. But I knew it was special at the time even though in certain ways I hadn't recognized in the dream where I was or what I was doing. I was no longer alone, or facing anonymous faceless clerks or students. A new character had emerged distinctly, and he had a name, Miguel.

When children appear, there's an invitation, Bregman says. Yes, but it's easy to miss the invitation. There was a lot I misunderstood. I didn't understand what it meant to see all those boys. I didn't know why bedtime at the orphanage panicked me, or who Miguel was or what Miguel meant by saying, *You're going to need some help.* Or what the help actually was. Most of all, I completely misunderstood the door. That is, I misunderstood which side of the door I was supposed to be on. I was still enough influenced by pathology to look at everything backward, including the door.

But later, when I had the chance to explore this space more carefully, I thought back on the scene with Miguel and knew that it was a very significant encounter. It came in the middle of a long series of dreams about boys, and marked a turning point.

You are essentially an orphan, the dream seemed to say. But I didn't recognize myself as an orphan. You belong in the orphanage, the dream seemed to say, with the other boys. Miguel is trying to help you. Not help you out that door, but help keep you in until you find the courage to stay. Because this is where you belong. You are one of us.

The fearsome drop was meant as one last obstacle to keep me with the boys. But the panic was too strong.

In time, I would understand. The orphanage was not a place to run from. It was where I belonged. I hadn't left my heart in San Francisco. I'd left it with the boys in an orphanage. My pride and adult way of thinking kept me apart from them. I just wasn't ready for that truth, that gift, at that time, in that dream. I just didn't know how to accept the invitation for change that Miguel offered.

Such missed opportunities are scattered all over my dreams, your dreams, anyone's. They are difficult to pick out unless you've been on the road, seen more of the landscape and inscape, the dreamscape . . . but in time, your eyes get accustomed to the light and you begin to pick out who is who. Not by any intellectual discernment or rule book; you navigate by heart.

I don't blame myself for blowing it; there's no need for blame. Eventually it got clearer and clearer who was who, who was my friend and who was my foe, and that inevitably led me to an understanding of what is meant by soul.

This dream had absolutely no reference to any experience in my life: never been to an orphanage, never sang on the streets of San Francisco. This was not a dream about my "predicament."

Everyone has what are called archetypal dreams. We see strangers with strange appeal like Miguel or the singing black woman, but we don't know who they are to us or what they mean. Weakening the hold of pathology helps us recognize them. As long as I was unable to admit I needed help, no one could help me. So it's significant that when Miguel says, *You're going to need some help,* I admit that I do.

Maybe in an earlier dream I would have dismissed this kid out of hand. I might have looked for some adult official or authority, the way I did with the clerks in the train station.

But at this point I'd been wrong enough times in dreams to admit that, yes, I need help. I knew my own panic and fear.

In my dreams and in life I'd become more permeable, more vulnerable. All those classroom dreams had made me more willing to be a student in life. And a whole series of dreams where I'd encountered children had led up to this as well. Now I was a little freer and looser, more open to hearing the song of the black woman, and that openness opened the door to the orphanage, too.

But as to what the orphanage really meant, why of all the places I might have dreamed as my soul's home I'd ended up in an orphanage, it would take time to be with that image and really live there before I would know. For the time being, I'd met Miguel, but by jumping out the sliding door I'd missed the opportunity to learn more.

Freud also had dreams where he saw children, and they were likewise invitations to go deeper. Freud had his own way of understanding and interpreting such encounters. As the genius who reopened for modernity the territory of dreams, he could never be blamed for overlooking features of the dreamscape, and yet certain of his dreams make you wonder what would have happened had he taken up one of his own missed opportunities.

One dream in particular haunts me—and I think it haunted Freud, too, based on what he writes about it in *The Interpretation of Dreams*, though I wonder if he finally knew why. He called it "the dream of the fleeing children":

On account of something or other that is happening in Rome, it is necessary for the children to flee, and this they do. The scene is then laid before a gate, a double gate in the ancient style. . . . I am sitting on the edge of a well, and I am greatly depressed; I am almost weeping. A woman—a nurse, a nun— brings out the two boys and hands them over to their father, who is not myself. The elder is distinctly my eldest son, but I do not see the face of the other boy. The woman asks the eldest boy for a parting kiss. She is remarkable for a red nose. The boy refuses her the kiss, but says to her, extending her his hand in parting, "Auf Geseres," and to both of us (or to one of us), "Auf Ungeseres." I have the idea that this indicates a preference.[1]

In his self-interpretation, Freud focuses on the parting words of his son, which are nonsense syllables in German. Attempting to solve the puzzle of "the absurd and unintelligible verbal form," he spins out brilliant and recondite associations, with "salted and unsalted caviar," and with Hebrew words. He discovers references to the play he saw the night before; he refers to the psalm "By the waters of Babylon we wept" and to the leavened and unleavened bread of Passover. His analysis is a literary exercise in intertextuality but can also be seen as rabbinic, not only because of the Hebrew references but because of his focus on the spoken words at the end of the dream. Of all the many details, these puzzle words in dreams most often command his attention. To someone familiar with the form, his analysis reads very much as a midrash on a sacred text.

Freud is a master of persuasion. But for Bregman, the dream is all about feelings. When we discussed Freud's dream, he zeroed in on the belly button. He noted that the whole atmosphere of the dream is terribly sad: the children are fleeing Rome. Freud is "almost weeping."

"If he can weep," Bregman said, "he's involved with his feelings. So if he were a client, we would work on the weeping."

In his self-analysis Freud mentions "by the waters of Babylon we wept" as an association, but Bregman said, "He doesn't take the step to connect it to himself: 'What about this weeping is my pain?' There's nothing. It's gone. He's totally in his head."

Freud reads away from the dream, not into the dream. He seems averse to learning why he's "almost" weeping. In particular, he doesn't think about the relationships between the characters in the dream.

One fleeing child is his own son. Yet strangely, Freud sits apart—on the edge of a well—and passively watches the nun hand him over to their father, who, Freud notes, is "not myself."

So there are two fathers in the dream. But why?

There are also two sons:

"The elder is distinctly my eldest son, but I do not see the face of the other boy."

So who is this other boy in the dream whose face he can't see?

Freud knows he is not the father. Is it possible that's because he is the son whose face he can't see?*

To Bregman, "That's the whole problem.

"Like in the Irma dream he is the doctor. When does he stop being the doctor and be the human being? When does he 'be' in his feelings? When does he acknowledge anything of his deeper sense? There's a traumatic door opening up to his pain, the children have to flee . . . What are those feelings? Well, he is feeling something, he is feeling along with these people who are leaving and trying to feel his own pain, his own loss.

"If you gestalted Freud, you'd gestalt the boys who are leaving. That's where you could find out about Freud's feelings. Because in the dream, Freud remains on the outside of his feelings, wondering what's going on. He's weeping—but just 'almost.' There is some great trauma or tragedy happening, and the way into this dream is through his feelings. Which he doesn't quite feel. "

Freud doesn't see that the feeling of "children fleeing the city" is about his own loss, his own separation from "the boy" whose face he can't see.

So also, I didn't see that my panic in the orphanage is about my feeling separation from the boys and Miguel. But I was more fortunate because I did see Miguel's face and even learned his name.

In general, the pathology or opposition separates the dream-ego from the child.

So gravel grandma came between me and my daughter on the porch. But the reverse is also true: separating from pathology can bring you much closer

---

*This recalls my friend David's dream, which I described earlier: there are two Davids. Is it possible there are two Freuds—one by the well, the other the "boy" whose face he can't see? It also recalls my own dream of two fathers and two sons.

to the feelings of the child. And this is a very good thing, because it brings you closer to the essence of who you are.

These two movements work together. The more you separate from the pathology, the closer you can come to the child.

At first, the approach of the child may be only partially successful or, in Freud's case, abortive, and that's realistic, because there's an internal struggle in the dream-ego against feeling what the child feels.

This is how you penetrate below the surface, how you break into the space capsule of your isolating numbness—by allowing yourself to feel what the child feels.

Whatever internal wall separates you from the child in your dreams is a barrier to renewing yourself. To live in your feelings instead of in your head requires becoming again a child. This is the experience I fled by jumping out the door of the orphanage.

It's the boy consciousness Freud is very separated from in his sad fleeing-children dream. The boys fully feel the sorrow the adult Dr. Freud can "almost" feel.

If we put this dream together with the staircase dream, the picture gets even more compelling. The force that separates him from the boys is the same force that freezes him when he's bounding up the steps. She—the "staircase maid"—doesn't want him to feel the vulnerability of a boy.

In some dreams, we see all three of these actors in the dream drama: the dream-ego, the pathology, and the child. I've mentioned the gravel grandma dream. Another example is William T.'s dream of the beach. He has to choose between the little girl with the drawing and the man in the suit. She is the child; the man is the pathology. The dynamic is clear: the pathology wants to separate the dream-ego from the child. In this particular dream, William feels much closer to the pathology than he feels to the child.

But as the dream descent goes on, such missed opportunities become real opportunities. Then the dreams take you deeper. It's not enough merely to see the child as I saw Miguel—or even to feel what the child feels.

Ultimately the dreams show you how to be the child. Only then could I really understand the answer to a question that truly puzzled me: Why, of all the types of children there are, was I being shown an orphan? What did that mean about the situation of my soul?

Chapter 26

BECOMING THE BOY

The Pins and the Desert

To return to the orphanage, I had to feel my way back to the child.

Early on in a long series of dreams, I got a glimpse of what becoming the boy is all about. It was one of those tricky dreams where you think you've just awakened.

I get out of bed, walk into the bathroom, and look in the mirror. I see pins in my face. Little white pins with black heads, like the pins used to attach a paper pattern to a piece of cloth. One pin is stuck in my right eyelid. I carefully remove it, hoping not to stab my eye. Another pin is stuck in my cheek, another in my upper lip. I remove them as well.

Where is my consciousness in this dream? What is the thinking of my dream-ego? I am actually thinking: *I can't go to work with these pins in my face.* I am centered in the waking workaday adult consciousness.

Only now that the pins are removed I notice something unusual in the mirror. My head has become smaller. Yes, it is decidedly smaller, and also I see that my hair is cut very short, just like when I was a boy and used to come back fresh from the barber's electric razor. I have that close-cropped look. My head is smaller; my hair is shorter; my head also seems to have a slightly different shape. It's a queasy feeling at first.

But then the queasiness gives way to wonder.

Do our dreams come to restore wonder, or is the wonder there all along, just waiting to be awakened?

Now the dream shifts. The setting changes, and the style. I am standing in the desert—somewhere in Arabia, a land not on any map. It is the end of the night. People move purposefully in the freshness before dawn. Tents and tables are being set up for a bazaar. An Arab merchant invites me to sit down at a small table. From a leather pouch, he spills out several polished stones: jade and picture jasper. He does not speak. He seems to tell me a story, pointing to the stones as symbols, but I don't understand. Some are just smooth pebbles; others are carved little white skulls the size of my thumb. An old woman steps out of the tent, and he gives her a stone. My eyes are wide open: I am new here.

That's it: I am new here. That's the overall feeling. I want to take in everything going on as when first arriving at a fascinating foreign land. The man gets up and borrows a metal teapot from a tea salesman. They bow to one another; I watch them closely. Then he returns and pours fresh clear water in my cup.

But now a boy standing a few feet away draws all my attention. He is about five, with blond hair and bright blue eyes. A man and woman—his parents?—stand behind him. He wears a simple white robe with fringes. He is laughing. There is a slight radiance to his face, a subtle rosy reflected light. Did I mention that he is extremely beautiful? My view of the landscape expands: a desert stretches away from my feet; at the horizon I glimpse a first glint of the rising sun. I have this thought before I wake—a vow: "I'll stay up until dawn, my first dawn since I changed."

Then I woke. I got out of bed. I walked into the bathroom. I looked in the mirror. No pins in my face. Nor did I look younger. But that dream of dawn presaged the change that would follow as the child came to light in my dreams and in me.

It's a recentering, a shifting away from adult attitudes to the boy.

The opposition lurks in the dream, hidden in the practicalities of the adult consciousness embarrassed by the pins and concerned about going to work. The opposition likes to cloak itself in such practical concerns.

But in the dream, the opposition is overpowered by a flood of wonder. That huge feeling transports me magically to a foreign landscape, foreign to my superficial way of living in the world, because it unfolds a hidden life within—a whole interior space full of strong, simple images: the vast desert and the rising sun. A space peopled with important strangers I feel deeply drawn to, like the Arab man with his stones—and the shining boy. I did not know yet who this boy was to me.

I had been descending through a dark fog, struggling to separate from the opposition, detaching from the ironic, verbal, sophisticated, bookish adult attitudes of the "dictionary lady" that make up the face I show the world.

With the pins removed, I could see the changes underneath: I had a new face.

As the darkness turns to dawn, a new depth in the descent comes in the engagement with the child. After the dark fog of pathology, a region of deep interior light opens. You see how the opposition has been keeping you from great wonder and delight.

The wonder of the descent into dreams is difficult to express. Another person's ecstasy is easy to distrust and discount. I need to risk expressing it because, having come to it after much struggle in the dark, this interior dawning feels more real than realism. It's emotionally powerful and convincing, a cup of clear water to draw on as the descent deepens. Underneath all the struggle with your predicament, this development has been going on—a development that leads to the soul.

Not that I got the significance of my new face or the shining boy at first, or easily. But with more dreams, the outline of this process of change grew firmer. First the opposition acquires a dream body where it gets exposed for what it is. Now in a countermovement, a deeply original part of you emerges into view, with the face of a boy or a girl.

It was the first glimpse of what the book of K de G must have meant in the gestalt by "your genesis and your origin."

I could watch the child born in a sequence of dreams, and feel it born in me.

First, dreams came where my wife is pregnant; then a dream where she nurses an infant. I dreamed my wife and I are adopting a baby boy. My father-in-law says, "There's no room in the house." But I answer, "We can make the house larger."

The "father-in-law" played the opposition with his pragmatic talk. But the optimism associated with the boy had the final word.

In these dreams there was still a subtle barrier between me and the child. That is, I saw the child as my child and saw myself as the child's parent. I was still interpreting from without to within, from the waking point of view. Though being a parent expressed my closeness to the child, it was still inaccurate. There was more to learn, and other dreams worked this issue from a different angle.

I see a woman and her rambunctious toddler. The child runs right into the wall, bounces off, and laughs. I laugh, too. "This kid is really amazing," I say to her. I feel joy and admiration for this child but have no sense of our true connection.

I am eating at a restaurant with a school principal and his son. It's a business meeting of some kind. In the middle of the meal I push my chair back and leave the principal. The boy and I walk outside and toss a football on the sidewalk. It's not clear to me why I do this. It feels right, though from a waking point of view it would be fairly strange.

Another dream in a restaurant. This time I'm with a Japanese businessman and his son. Again I abruptly leave the table to go off to play with the boy; we are laughing together on a green lawn. I tickle him under the chin. The boy asks me, "Would you like to come to my house?" I promise I will.

These encounters were positive, but in others I turned away from the child or let my adult attitudes dominate. I would condescend to him, or be patronizing. The dream work is hardly linear. There is zig and zag, approach and avoidance.

A woman is staying at a hotel with her mother and her son. She wanders through the halls and hears the sound of music. She opens a door and sees a three-year-old girl playing the piano. She sits down to listen, entranced because the child is playing so beautifully. It would be good to listen for a long time, but a pathological impulse grabs her. She wants to tell her son about this child. She gets up and leaves her. And just that quickly, she loses her.

The rest of the dream devolves into an angry encounter with her mother and a scolding of her son. With these distracting emotions, the pathology has reasserted control, and the piano child has been forgotten.

But she can remember her again: her homework is to stick with the little girl and the piano. Once an hour, for just a moment, she sees the child and the piano, and feels what it is like to be with her. It's like one of Colette's imaginal exercises, but pulled directly from the dream.*

The homework has a practical benefit, because the dream is not simply an inquiry into the past; it's talking about how she "loses the child" in her life now, how she strays from feeling and is easily pulled away from her true self by the opposition.

I had a dream where I see a boy and his father arguing. The father wants to give money earned from tobacco stocks to a college. The son says that selling cigarettes is wrong because smoking kills people. He speaks as a boy: straightforward. I intervene, and feel the conflict between them as something

---

*Catherine Shainberg told me that this is precisely how Colette worked with the dream images she brought to her.

I want to resolve. Instead of taking the boy's side, I try to find middle ground, a compromise. I make some complicated argument to justify the father's actions to the son. Clearly in this dream the adult and the child represent two sides of me. When I wake I realize I admire the boy's simple honesty and feel ashamed of my own complicated rhetoric. I'd always been proud of my dexterity with language and argument, but here I see that what's great for the ego is lousy for the soul.

The child shows a face in the dream so that we might be drawn to her (or to him), because the child represents very much who we might be—and once were.

"Generally," Bregman teaches, "children are an invitation. It's like the soul saying, 'It's time to come down here to encounter me. You've learned enough about your predicament. Now it's time to learn about who you really are.'"

Bregman identifies the child with soul, and I can accept that. The soul is my "genesis and origin," the original part of me that's ever young, ever renewing, ever refreshing.

Everyone knows moments of letting loose; it doesn't matter your age. It might be with friends, listening to music, dancing, playing softball or riding a motorcycle, or just taking an early-morning walk in the woods. You feel very alive, fresh, invigorated; you've shaken off the cynicism of the everyday. You say, "I feel like a kid again."

If this capacity exists in us—to be a child—why and how does it go away? Where does it go, in fact? When does it first get compromised? How, sometimes, does it return momentarily in a playful mood, in the intimacies of a love relationship, or in the company of a child?

The term "inner child" has become a cliché, but the experience it points to is powerful. Bregman calls the child in dreams "soul," and that seems to me a wiser name. When soul acquires a voice and body in dreams, it is the body of a child, a little boy or a little girl. There are many basic feelings and attitudes that come with the child: wonder, beauty, simplicity, honesty, directness . . . but now the origin and genesis of these feelings is no longer hidden or inaccessible. Soul emerges and has a face in your dreams. Seeing the pathology leads to a separation. But now, upon your seeing the child, there is a countermovement: the goal is not to separate, but to merge.

In the dreams that followed, I no longer see a boy because I am the boy.

I go to a school meeting without wearing a shirt. Others criticize me, but I feel they have it wrong, that it's okay not to wear a shirt. This seems obvious to me in the dream. I forget adult proprieties and norms; my dream-ego is shifting boy-ward. It's not that I know consciously I am the boy. There is no dream mirror to see my new face in. It's just clear that I'm acting like a boy and responding like one.

In another dream I find myself on a train. This was the first time I actually boarded a train in a series of dreams going back to those faceless train-station clerks.

The train is the "soul's means of transportation," Bregman says, because to board a train meant surrendering control to an unseen conductor. As a strong ego I had lots of trouble getting on board. Driving an automobile in a dream represents autonomy, but can also represent pride and arrogance: "The ego is always at the wheel," as the poet Delmore Schwartz wrote.

My failed train-station dreams formed a long series. There'd been dreams where I search for a ticket counter and fail, dreams where I follow my grandfather and daughter to the tracks. They board a train, but for some reason I'm terrified and refuse.

Now I am sitting in a coach compartment beside my favorite teacher. Looking out the train window, I see huge white clouds billowing in a perfectly blue sky. I think, "These are the clouds of the first day of creation."

Here's the strange part: I am in my underwear. That's just fine with me. As a young boy that feels natural. My homework is to "be the underwear boy," to see myself sitting in my underwear on that train, next to my teacher.

Now I had a new understanding of dreams of being undressed in public like Freud's staircase dream. The issue isn't the nakedness, but the shame. Young children aren't embarrassed about being half dressed or undressed. The way out of the predicament is to learn to feel as a child feels and stop being so uptight.[1]

Children aren't embarrassed by their appetites, either. The boy is open about them; he wants what he wants.

I dreamed I'm in a bakery and my eyes skip over the health bread and go right to the pastries. They are luscious, bulging at the edges with raspberries and cream. I say to the baker, "They look like pastries my grandmother used to bake, folded into a triangle." The baker says, "Naturally, to keep the treasure inside." He is amused as I pick out several large pastries and gobble them on the spot. No money changes hands.

In another dream I follow two other boys as we wade into a river. A fisherman is standing near a giant blueberry "tree." I eat several blueberries the size of plums. Pure fantasy, but something fantastic is going on here that has to do with the expansiveness of the boy consciousness.

The style of the boy dreams shifted. I start off in a realistic-enough setting, a hotel room in a big city. I'm looking out the window at the night sky; I seem to be in a penthouse. Then I get this idea—and here the boy slips in: I crawl out the window. As soon as I think it, I do it. I stroll along the pediment, and now I'm walking on the roof.

The roof is a beauty, I notice—a strange construction of brilliantly fitted, exquisite curves of iridescent copper, like overlapping scales of a fish. I see everything as I look slowly, carefully around. I see the night sky, the glinting of the stars, tall office buildings and hotels with their windows lit up, the skyline against a backdrop of rugged mountains. Now I gaze out at the gleaming lights of the harbor, and the ships spread out in the bay. This is the beginning of a new kind of knowing, a sensual knowing, and along with it an ecstatic slowing down of time. This new quality of time becomes more prominent in my dreams.

I could stay forever on the roof in the night air, high above the unknown city.

But then comes a flicker of adult mind: I'm on a roof. It's dangerous. I might fall. Instantly, three workmen appear at the window.

One calls to me, "How did you get out there?"

I inch back slowly to the workmen, for I'm very afraid. I notice for the first time that the roof is curved and slippery and there are no hand rails. I see how easily I could have fallen off. I'm all about the danger now. There's huge fear. My heart is racing; I'm panicked. One worker in blue coveralls reaches out his hand and guides me back inside the window I crawled out of.

As the dream ends, I'm still shaken. I think: I must have been crazy to crawl out there like that, maybe suicidal. Am I going nuts? Am I secretly wishing to kill myself? The ecstasy has tailed off into fear, and doubt is rushing in as I wake—doubt about the dream, doubt about the work with Bregman. From the point of view of the waking ego there's this fear. From the point of view of the soul, the boy, everything is serene and beautiful. In time I calmed down; my thoughts went back to the ecstasy, the beauty—what came before the fear.

Bregman gave me "homework": once an hour to see myself as the boy on the roof, to stay in that place of wonder and awe, feeling the ecstasy.

By rehearsing the "boy" feelings in homework, I cultivated them and had the opportunity to encounter them again in dreams. I was learning this new consciousness, this new way of being and knowing, as the boy.

I was also learning about this deep layer of fear and panic, and how easily these weapons of the pathology could control me. Just because I was becoming more boylike didn't mean the pathology was done. The fear of death was mixed up with the fear of being the boy. I knew I needed help to overcome the fear. Of all the buttons the opposition has to push, fear is the big red one, the panic button. It can scare the child out of you.

Yet on the other side of the fear, the dreams that followed were visiting and revisiting a whole set of feelings: sensual delight, a lack of shame, courage. The assertiveness, playfulness, ease of the boy became a template for a new ease in life. There was another benefit, too. As I began to feel the boy in me, I felt the child in others. It was a new way of knowing people more deeply, intuitively, heart to heart, child to child.

Generally speaking, Bregman observes that the boy and the girl represent different sides of the soul: "It may be if you're a boy in a dream you're learning how to take on desires because boys are more demanding about their needs. If it's a girl it may be a part of the self that relates to relationship and sensitivity."

Being the child is the way to continue the exploration deeper, but it's also part of a revival of feeling in life. "Just as when you were four," Bregman says, "and saw your daddy you'd run up to him as if it were the most important thing in the world. Can you possibly feel that way again as an adult? Absolutely. You can go home again. It's not easy, but you can. You can feel those feelings that allow you to be open with love."

It is not easy to remain the child in dreams, or out of them. The instability, the flickering of consciousness, feelings of ecstasy followed by fear and panic—the alternation continues in dreams and in life.

What's noticeable in all this is that certain figures—also strangers—seem to know about these fears and they respond to your vulnerability, as the workmen rescued me on the roof.

As I looked back I realized I'd seen friendly figures like this in my dreams all along. Strangers who seemed to be helping me even if I missed who they were. They had been coming at me right from the start, but as long as I was shadowed by pathology, these were missed opportunities. Like the cop who stopped me on my bicycle; he was actually challenging me in a good way, but I didn't get it.

I might take for granted or even be frightened of these very important persons because the opposition doesn't like them and views them negatively.

But as I became the child, I trusted them more, and these allies and friends of the soul became more prominent.

They helped stabilize and support the shift to the boy. They came as a male or a female or both. The closer I came to the consciousness of the boy, the more aware I became of them as they helped take me deeper in the descent into dreams.

Chapter 27

A Very Important
Person

I wasn't alone, then, in the struggle to become the child. Other figures arrived to help. As I went deeper into the boy's consciousness, these very important persons—let's call them VIPs—emerged as strong and distinct personalities.

I glimpsed them as a married couple in the margins of earlier dreams. When I saw the shining boy in the desert, a man and woman stood behind him. I took them for his parents. At the end of another dream, I saw this pair again.

It was an early summer morning; artists and poets walked past me on a wide green lawn.

The actuality of the dream was intense, and the extreme beauty of the faces individual. That is, each face as I gazed at it seemed beautiful in a unique way. The faces were also shining with light. I don't mean supernatural light, but the early-morning sun. It was odd to see so many good-looking people, one after the other, but I kept walking because I had a mission. I'd just heard an extraordinary dialogue I wanted to write down verbatim.

I was like a man carrying an egg on a spoon in a long race. I was afraid I would forget the exact words. So I didn't let the beauty of all those faces I was passing slow me down. I spent the middle part of the dream looking everywhere for a clean sheet of paper. This increasingly desperate search had the emotional flavor of my old lost and wandering dreams: growing frustration, gnawing anxiety.

I saw my wife's knapsack in the grass, and, burrowing inside, I even found a notebook and riffled through the pages. But every last one was written on.

I also found a sketch pad with drawings. The drawings were astounding, and I stopped to admire each one, but I was torn between this beauty and my fear of forgetting the exact words I'd heard at the start of the dream. But I couldn't ruin her drawings by writing on them.

So I went inside a small cottage. In the first room on a round desk were old income-tax forms. I thought I could write in their margins. The whole while I was repeating the words like a mantra because I hoped never to forget them. Just then a man and woman appeared together at the doorway. He stayed back, but she stepped forward.

"What are you doing?" she asked. I looked up and saw a woman of about thirty with a wide forehead, and a simple white dress. Her beauty was beyond that of anyone I'd seen. Her voice was gentle and sweet, and I was completely annoyed. Damn it, she was interrupting me just as I was finally about to write down these precious words I'd been carrying in my head. The battle between word and image was alive and well, and I was a captive of the word.

So I said, as curtly as possible, "I'm trying to write something down."

And she said, again sweetly, "What are you writing?"

Now even more annoyed, I said, "I'm trying to write down my dream." *Trying to.* And she said, "Oh, sorry . . . ," and went away.

Her voice was wistful, gentle, slightly disappointed—how someone very sweet might come into your life, and you, so deeply mired in purpose, would only glance up for a moment and see her as an annoyance. So she had the grace to back away. "Oh, sorry . . . ," and she was gone.

She was trying to call my attention to *how* I was writing. She was trying to slow me down, just as the beauty of the faces, and the beauty of my wife's drawings, were all meant to slow me down. But I was obdurate in my pathological will. In the face of any obstacle, I will press on. There was a driven quality to what I was doing. I was too obsessed to fully take her in. I wasn't enough the boy in this dream to relinquish my obsessiveness even a moment. Later I looked back and understood. This is the neurotic lining of all my writing—a fear of forgetting.

I was too afraid of losing the feeling, which is why I needed to seal it in the container of words. Perhaps at some deep root that is why I first became a writer. But I know now that that fear is a constriction. There is another way to respond to inspiration, the boy's way.

For the soul has faith. The soul knows that the source of inspiration is always there. It's a light that shines equally on everyone, like the early-morning sun on the faces I saw that made them so beautiful. There's no need to fear.

In dreams, I'd known myself as the fearful adult and I'd felt within me the creative boy. But until this particular dream, I had never encountered so distinctly this new very important person.

She came to reassure the boy, for I never would have written a word if he had not been alive somewhere within me. But in my anxiety I saw her only as an interruption, and turned her away.

A missed opportunity.

I didn't see that she was beauty, too. All of it. That in her gentleness and sweetness, her presence and her gesture, she fully embodied exactly what I was trying to squeeze into words. She was the image and living presence of beauty. She was the container who held the feeling of beauty far more compellingly than any words I could ever write. And she was right there in my dream, and I turned her away.

I can understand a skeptic saying, "Big deal, you were writing something and you saw a strange woman. How can you say she is of any great significance in your inner world?" That's a fair question that opens to another, key to the whole descent.

Namely, how can you tell who is who in your dreams? How can you know that this male or this female figure is an ally or friend, and that that one is pathology? The answer is, It's not always easy. Mistakes can be made, but the accumulation of dreams creates a strong pattern.

One way the pattern joins together is that the scent of one dream blends with the scent of another, in an atmosphere of freshness and new beginnings, just as my dream of early-morning light "rhymes" with the sunrise in my desert dream. That one began when I saw I had a new face. And this one began in much the same way.

All that running around, looking for paper—that familiar frustration was my reaction to the initial scene in the dream. I was trying to remember the exact words I heard there; I was desperate to write them down so I wouldn't forget. Before I met all those beautiful people walking on the lawn, I'd seen a poet I know in waking life as Tim. His hair was cut very short, and he looked younger.* He was sitting on the grass with his boss, who told me, "This is the new Tom." He certainly looked new, and if Tim was now Tom, well, his new face deserved a new name. Because it seemed to me full of light.

I asked the boss: "Does the new Tom write the poetry?" And I was told,

---

*Just as I looked younger in the mirror in my desert dream of the boy. See chapter 26, p. 189–191.

"Yes he does." And I said: "What does the old Tom do, the accounting?" And the boss smiled and said, "That part of Tom is dead."

That was the dialogue I had wanted to write down—those exact words. I was anxious never to forget them. The VIP appeared at the other end of the dream. She wanted to reassure me and pull me away from my obsessiveness with words. But I wouldn't let her.

How could I have known she was a VIP?

In other dreams she was sometimes a blonde with a wide forehead, like wide-eyed Athena, but she was also a black woman, a Latina, a Japanese woman. Invariably she was young—in her late twenties, early thirties. Sometimes she was a film star or a popular singer. Invariably she appeared to me as a beauty.

What makes her role convincing is not any one dream, but an accumulation of dreams over months and months. I began to see the pattern and recognize her more readily, and as I did, she became more prominent and distinct. I came to know her by heart. It's an intimacy and a whole way of life deep down in your inner world.

But as with the opposition and also the child, at first I saw her and did not get who she was. I had missed opportunities. When she interrupted my writing, the help offered was not understood or appreciated. Only in later dreams would I come to know her and feel her love.

It may be that for Freud, "Irma" was a premonition of such a figure. He could not recognize her as his doctor self, because she came in the guise of his patient. If "Irma" was a VIP, or her forerunner, he was doomed to overlook her as long as his pathology kept him from being the boy. For "Irma" was clearly calling "Freud" to deeper feeling and trying to separate him from his adult attitudes as a doctor and an authority. That encounter was a missed opportunity.

I believe that in my dream, the woman who interrupted my writing was trying very gently to help. In that sense she was my teacher, and on reflection I recognized that she'd appeared before in other dreams as a teacher. In the sequence of classroom dreams, she appeared as a teacher of poetry. By this time I was knowing myself in the dream as a student.

She was standing before the class entirely naked.

Afterward, as we walked out, another student complained that the teacher had dismissed the class early and hadn't given us notes. So I was concerned and went up to her and asked, "Do you really care about poetry?"

I don't know what more she could have done for me than appear naked in front of the class, but I obviously didn't get the meaning in the dream.

Bregman asked me to talk to her in a gestalt.

Me: Woman, why are you naked if you are serious about poetry?

Woman: *Poetry comes from the naked heart.*

Me: Are you my naked heart?

Woman: *I'm trying to show you there's nothing to be afraid of.*

It wasn't a poetry class. It was a heart class. Her vulnerability and lack of shame were the real lessons. Her beauty is her naked heart. She held open for me the possibility of nakedness—that is, vulnerability without shame. She is an imperishable part of us that knows, deep down, that really we have nothing to hide.

If the boy shows up in underwear or naked, she reassures him by being naked, too, with no shame, no fear—resolute and strong in her beauty and her openness. So these qualities of the heart—emotional openness, faith, beauty—were now embodied, personified in my dreams.

She appeared as an art student in one dream, a painter in another, a poet, a teacher, a singer. She was also, I see now, the black woman who sang on the streets in the orphanage dream: *I left my heart in San Francisco.*

She was black, white, Asian, naked sometimes, clothed in a white robe, or glowing with light; she was gentle ... she was soft-spoken, never harsh ... and by these qualities I came to know her. If asked, "How do you know for sure?" what can I say?

I know her positively as I know the pathology negatively. I know her by her effect in my dreams, which is to open the heart.

I know her by her effect ... and, this is strange to say, I know her by her reality ... There is something deeply convincing about her presence, deeply reassuring.

How is it possible that imaginal figures, dream people, would be more real to us than flesh and blood? The answer is as close as the nearest movie theater. The people we see on the screen become the giant object of our fantasies and projections, more real to us than many people we know. We love them; sometimes we despise them. We become fascinated with them. But their identity is very clear. We know who Julia Roberts is in our consciousness; we know what she represents. It has nothing to do with her life as a human being or what we read in the tabloids. It has to do only with her imaginal life, how she lives in the imagination. The same would apply to Harrison Ford or any other of the iconic stars. They become real to us.

Or the characters they play do. For much the same happens with the great characters of literature in novels or plays. We enter into what Coleridge called "a willing suspension of disbelief." Hamlet may well be a fictional character, but his personality is more firmly engraved and better defined than that of most people we know.

As the boy I entered into a whole new world of relationships with these VIPs, who were teachers more real and intense, wise and aware, than any I've met in the waking world. Their lessons weren't only in words, but in gestures. Instead of giving a lecture on emotional honesty, she appeared naked.

Then I understood something I didn't understand long ago when I first met Tibetan meditators in Dharamsala. One American who'd practiced the higher tantra for years and years told me about visualizing Tibetan deities. They would move off the mandala and into his consciousness, and he would feel himself in connection with them: they were in his head, in three dimensions, like a living, vibrating dream; they spoke to him; they taught him.

And I said, "Weren't they . . . uh . . . just projections?"

And he said, " Yeah . . . they are also projections, except they are a lot more real than anyone I've ever known."

But whatever individual form she takes, the most important thing to feel is who she is to you. This is the beauty of the work. Then you haven't done all this dreaming for nothing. You see her face, and you see what she embodies and what feelings she holds for you. Instead of words, you have a living presence who opens your heart.

It seems very useful when pathology steps out of the shadows and appears in a dream as a personality. Then we see its contours and also come to know its weaknesses, however strong its hold might be on us.

It also feels very powerful not only to see the child but to become the child, to renew a way of being in the world through this child, which we sense within but which only our dreams can show.

But the gains can feel temporary, shaky. Dreams are flimsy in our world. This is the problem the Jacob story dramatizes. We see angels in a dream, but what happens when you wake and the ladder is out of sight? You struggle to hold on to the vision—as I struggled to write mine down because of the fear of losing it. Inspiration flickers like sunlight in and out of clouds. Pathology loses one day but wins another; the child appears, but the child also recedes and gets lost to us.

I think we know ourselves in this flickering, inconstant way as both hopeful and hopeless, alive and dead, soulful and soulless; and we see the same in others. Sometimes, we do sense a part of ourselves that's truly noble and imperishable—when we open our hearts to compassion or are greatly moved by beauty—and in those moments we connect to something within ourselves that feels very real. These moments of inspiration nourish the soul.

Then they evanesce, and at other times—especially when we are dominated by thoughts of pain or trouble, struggling with our predicament, and feeling lost—it seems hard to know this light in ourselves or see it in others.

So that is the great benefit of her appearing in dreams: she stabilizes these beautiful feelings by personifying them.

If pathology is the contamination we struggle with, she is the purity we struggle for.

If there's a darkness within us, she is the light against which we know that the darkness is but a shadow. Her reality is far greater than our predicament, but we cannot know her better until we have moved past the shadows and are ready for a new light.

She is present as a companion: she reassures the child; she draws out the soul.

To know her in dreams is to confirm that all we've ever suspected is beautiful about our own nature is actual and real.

Chapter 28

THE MALE VIP

The Second Gift of the Dream

When I first started working with Bregman, I was a vegetarian. Yet I was approached time after time in dreams by a strange man with helpings of meat.

At first it was hors d'oeuvres. I would be at a party, and a guy offered me a cocktail weenie on a toothpick. I refused. At a wedding, he appeared again at a carving station, slicing a juicy lamb. I turned him down. But this was the key: I knew in the dream what I couldn't admit when awake: the lamb looked good to me; I wanted to eat it. Eventually, in the dream, he showed up with a steak and I ate a bite. It shook me up profoundly. How could I act so differently in a dream from my professed beliefs when awake?

I understood in general that this male VIP was trying to help the boy emerge from any shadows of the opposition. But how could I say that the opposition was on the side of my being a vegetarian? Or that my soul boy was a bloodthirsty meat eater? That seemed all wrong.

But he showed up again and again. As with the female VIP, I could recognize him despite his various guises. He could be any race, but he was inevitably a big guy, forceful and very masculine. The more I became the boy in my dreams, the more he showed up.

He appeared as a big burly chef in a white apron, cooking meats on an enormous double barbecue grill. Big steaks, lamb, a giant sausage. The chef asked me, "What would you like to eat?" His assistant scrambled eggs sloppy in a big pot. I was confused. The chef said, "Sorry, I won't do that again." Then he laughed and heaved up a whole side of beef, and flames jumped through it.

A naked Mexican chef set up a barbecue grill in my motel room. He stalked around and asked me if I wanted five pounds of meat. I held back; I said it was too much.

Another time I woke up in a dorm room with my own private cafeteria. A chef was serving a plate of stew behind a counter next to my bed. I thought, Wow, right in my room, that's nice. A sub on the counter was stuffed with meats. I said, "You're making this just for me?" He pulled out another, even bigger sub with roast beef and gravy dripping down the roll. The chef said, *There's more where that came from.*

In my experience, this is how the male VIP operates in dreams: where she was gentle and supportive of the boy, he was challenging, funny, absurdist—and strongly theatrical in making his points.

In this case, whatever diet I had decided for myself consciously, I'd left the "boy" out of the equation: my "boy" was not a vegetarian. The VIP was building up the boy and separating me from shame, which was the dirty secret underlying my desire to be a pure vegetarian. In that area I was trying to be perfect by restricting my diet, and the secret audience was gravel grandma.

Although I had been raised in a middle-class family, at dinnertime there was a poverty mentality around food. I was shamed if I ate too much meat. I was told to eat bread instead. Vegetarianism may be a good thing, but not if it rests on a neurotic foundation.

The chef was teaching a different lesson. A lesson for the soul. He was using the subs—and the delicious gravy—to illustrate a lesson about generosity. He was saying: The universe is more generous than you know. You don't have to act as if there isn't enough to go around. It was a vivid meditation on a sub dripping with gravy. Imagine living always from generosity, where "*there's more where that came from.*"

None of this would have worked very deeply until the boy came to the forefront. Although the male VIPs approached me from my earliest dreams, I had to work out my predicament first to relate to them properly. As long as I was competitive and uptight around male figures—that is, as long as the opposition was dominant—the encounter with the male VIP would remain a missed opportunity.

So it was in the cop bicycle dream I brought to Bregman my first session. As the reader might recall, I was riding a bicycle when a policeman stopped me: "Can I see your driver's license?" It was just a joke, but I didn't get it and became nervous and edgy. Then the cop raised the ante. Pointing to the bicycle, he said, "Is that your lawn mower?" Again the cop was teasing me like a guy, but I became furious. If I'd laughed or joked back I could have become friendlier with him. Instead I just got angry and felt insulted. In time, I saw through a series of dreams that I was being shown the archetypal pattern of how I failed to relate to men in waking life. And that led in particular to work with my father, described in part two, where I uncovered a whole depth of feeling for him that had long lain dormant under surface levels of annoyance and competitiveness.

This male VIP frees you up, acting as a provocateur, a dramatist, a challenger—often with a grand sense of humor.

It was clear that I could never get closer to him if I had negative feelings about my father. But when those turned around, I was able to relate more deeply to him.

As long as you are in your predicament, the relationship with the male VIP won't work. Because he is very combative and antagonistic to the pathology and the pathology feels the same about him.

But as you are more willing to be the child and the student, the male VIP helps provoke and disarm hidden aspects of the opposition. It's like the old adage: when the student is ready, the teacher will come.

I saw him pretty clearly in a dramatic outsized dream when he appeared as a giant black man dressed in armor.

He lifts a car and drops it on the street, then steps back. A dragon the size of a moving van swings its barbed tail back and forth. I am right there: I feel the tail whoosh over my head. It is pure terror. But the knight steps forward and swings his sword at the dragon, and I jump out of the way.

I told Bregman that at first I thought the battle was just a show, but as I felt the dragon's tail swing overhead and saw its sharp green scales slice an inch from my skin, I felt it was real.

He said, "It is real. Maybe sometimes you look at the dream work as a show. No, this is really the battle. To place yourself that close is the only way you get in that battle directly. Otherwise you just sit on the sidelines and miss the point."

This distinction between sitting on the sidelines and participating in the battle would become more and more relevant as the descent into dreams progressed.

"This dream comes from the knight's efforts to battle and destroy pathology. He is showing off. He's saying, 'Hey, man, don't mess with me.' It's a great way to show you what it means to be in essence, what the experience of being connected to him is like."

He can aggressively probe and provoke and cut away at areas where the pathology hides. When the female had approached me in dreams, she was gentle and sweet, full of light—full of reassurance to bolster the child. But he was more into clarity and distinction. She was unconditional, but he seemed highly conditional.

Like the knight, he brought a sword of discernment: he cut off the dragon tales of the pathology, the false elements of the self, old identifications and aversions: I am this, or I am not that—which is how the beloved ego constructs itself in the worldly way. My established waking identity, how I know myself, is constructed of bits and pieces of external identification and aversions, accumulated political, social, and religious labels.

He will often show up in a provocative form to peel away your old identifications. If you're proud of being a Democrat, he may show up as George Bush; if you have issues with Jews, he'll show up as a bearded rabbi again and again, making his point. If you're homophobic, he may come as a gay man; if you're a Jew who feels superior to Gentiles, he'll be right in your face as Jesus. Whatever race you are, he'll challenge all your hang-ups about race. If you're black, he'll show up white; if you're white, he'll show up black. If you're a woman who cares only for intellectual types, he may show up as a cowboy, a grizzled cabdriver, or a working stiff. He really loves to root out all your snobberies, all your assumptions about who you think you are, because he wants to shake out all the hidden places of pride or shame where pathology still hides.

It can be devastating to discover that long-held political beliefs or religious affiliations have a footing in pathology, but he is merciless at cutting away with his sword.

Every time this happens, you strip off an old identity. You may feel like you are dying a little. And in some dreams, you actually do see yourself die.

To die in your dream is to experience the ultimate fear, and that is also the ultimate alchemy. Here the sword cuts deeply. You wake from such dreams shattered, but knowing you will never be the same. Some old part of you has died completely. It has fallen away from your soul. It can be your most cherished identification that he goes after. It's who you think you are at a much deeper level, and it's a shock to see that one stripped away, and a fear like no other.

Bregman compares the process to a cancer treatment. You have to risk nearly killing the healthy cells to kill off the malignant ones. Of course there's fear. Fear runs through the whole history of dreams, from Dumuzi to now.

Fear gave rise to interpretation as our reflex to the dream; calming fear and anxiety is the purpose of every form of amelioration.

Fear is how pathology controls you at the deepest level, for fear underlies other emotional reactions like anger, or defensiveness or numbness. A lot of people simply feel dead in their lives: "I'm just making doughnuts," one guy in the work told me, because he was afraid to feel very much in his daily life. By overcoming fear in a vivid way, you are now able to reclaim the soul even more completely.

But what proves most important in the descent into depth is your relationship to him. Whereas the female VIP stabilizes the heart, he is the agent for change. He roots out the opposition so you can become the boy or the girl more completely and be closer to him. He can't help you so long as you are in your predicament because you aren't feeling deeply enough. The deep way to connect with him is as the child, and even more deeply from the place of the essential situation of your soul.

In my case, that situation was an orphanage. For there I felt my pain as a boy. I saw that my "boy" was an orphan, just as Joseph the boy saw the essence of his soul in the image of an upright sheaf.

I found this second gift of the dream difficult to accept. Why an orphan? I didn't know what to make of this revelation. There was more to learn from him.

Some dreamers see the child as a cripple, or even dead. Others see a perfectly healthy child full of spunk. It's different for each person. Whatever you see is a deep instruction about where your soul stands and what needs to happen next.

It's important to distinguish the predicament from the situation of the soul.

The predicament is where you begin the descent: the dreams show you a template and hologram of your emotional life. You are chained in the basement, or you are zooming to the moon, or you are lost and wandering. Or other predicaments: you see yourself as a whore among other whores, or you see yourself as a cruel and sadistic sexual exploiter. Bregman associates the predicament with stage one of dreams.

What's important to bring out is that you can't reach out to the VIP from your predicament because the pathology is still interfering. You can reach out only from the vulnerability of the child. You have to feel the child's sadness, aloneness, or hurt.

But once the child emerges in its situation—as an orphan or a cripple, or healthy or otherwise—that isn't the end of the story. There's more to learn.

The dreams can lead you to a change in the situation of your soul. That is the great work of stage two.

In my case, I had to return to the orphanage so I could learn why I belonged there and who was there to help me.

Fortunately, I didn't have only the VIPs: I had my own guide in Bregman, who seemed to know every step of the descent. How he'd gotten this knowledge was something I was curious to learn. But he made it clear that he also had an important predecessor, to whom he owed a lot. He is a modern pioneer who had broken with Freud's dream work to take the descent into dreams deeper. His name is Carl Jung.

Chapter 29

JUNG'S DESCENT
INTO THE WORLD
OF DREAMS

Marc Bregman likes to drive a Chevy Avalanche and wear flannel shirts. He has minimal formal training, is dyslexic, and is a bit of a roughneck. He seems to have little in common with Dr. Carl Gustav Jung, the founder of analytical psychology and an intellectual giant whose collected works run to eighteen volumes.

Yet Bregman picked up the path in dreams that Jung abandoned as too risky to pursue. It's a path Jung first opened nearly a hundred years ago, just after he broke ranks with Sigmund Freud.

The story of Jung and Freud is well known and often told. They first corresponded in 1906, when Jung was a young psychiatrist at a University of Zurich clinic and Freud was already a well-known but controversial figure. At their first face-to-face meeting, in Vienna in March 1907, Freud and Jung spent thirteen hours together in close conversation. Freud came to view Jung, twenty-five years his junior, as a son and heir apparent, the ideal public face for the growing international psychoanalytical movement. Jung clearly viewed Freud as a father figure.

From the start, Jung held back in a filial way from expressing his mental reservations about Freud's work. Yet Freud always suspected Jung of dark unconscious Oedipal motives. On two separate occasions, Freud fainted in Jung's presence and both times attributed the fainting to his fear that the "son" had a death wish for his "father."

Their greatest divergence came in their attitudes toward the importance of religion to the psyche. Freud called himself a "Godless Jew"; atheism, he felt, was the only proper attitude for a scientific psychology. Jung, the son of a pastor, thought the religious factor in the psyche could not be ignored.

Freud insisted that all dreams and also neurotic symptoms could ultimately be traced to conflicts arising from sexual traumas in childhood. Jung recalls a passionate exchange on the subject in Vienna in 1910.

"My dear Jung," [Freud said,] "promise me never to abandon the sexual theory. That is the most essential thing of all. You see we must make a dogma of it, an unshakable bulwark." . . . In some astonishment I asked him: "A bulwark—against what?" To which he replied, "Against the black tide of mud"—and here he hesitated for a moment, then added—"of occultism."[1]

By "occultism" Freud meant religion in general, which he viewed as an infantile illusion. To Jung this passionate dogmatism was itself symptomatic of Freud's unconscious religious feelings.

Jung believed that religious feelings are always a factor in the psyche. If rejected consciously, they reappear unconsciously. He wrote that for Freud the "sexual libido took over the role of a . . . hidden or concealed god."[2]

This core difference carried over into their approach to dreams. Jung always recognized the pioneering contribution Freud had made with *The Interpretation of Dreams*. He wrote after Freud's death, "By evaluating dreams as the most important source of information concerning the unconscious processes, he gave back to mankind a tool that had seemed irretrievably lost."[3] But he chafed at Freud's singular fixation on the "hidden" wishes in dreams, and the interpretations he used to ferret them out.

Jung viewed dreams as "natural" phenomena, and therefore not inherently "tricky" puzzles that required clever interpretation. For Jung the manifest dream is an experience in its own right. As he carved an independent path from Freud, he relied on his own dreams for guidance.

Where Freud always tried to bring the dream back to the daylight of personal memories and events, Jung was moved to go deeper down into an archetypal layer. This pattern of deepening descent was made manifest in a significant dream that also presaged his break with Freud.

On an ocean voyage to America in 1909, the two men passed mornings on deck analyzing the previous night's dreams, a common pastime among the inner circle of the first psychoanalysts. One morning, Jung reported a dream of exploring a two-story town house. The upper story was a European bourgeois home; the lower floor seemed older, with medieval furnishings. Then he "discovered a stone stairway" to the cellar. There he saw vaulted walls from Roman times. On the floor was a stone slab. Pulling on an iron ring, Jung found another stairway "down into the depths" and "entered a low cave cut into the rock" with "remains of a primitive culture." He saw "bones and broken pottery" and "two human skulls . . . very old and half disintegrated."

Freud, in accord with his dream theory, looked for the hidden wish and found it in those skulls. He pressed Jung: Whom did he actually wish dead? Jung named his wife and mother-in-law. Of this exchange, Jung wrote in his memoir, "I did not feel up to quarreling with him, so I told him a lie."

The manifest dream of the house had a symbolic significance for Jung that had nothing to do with hidden death wishes: it was an architectural diagram of consciousness, and it led down into the depths. The dream guided him "for the first time to the concept of the 'collective unconscious.'

"The ground floor stood for the first level of the unconscious. The deeper I went, the more alien and the darker the scene became. In the cave, I discovered remains of a primitive culture, that is the world of the primitive man within myself—a world which can scarcely be reached or illuminated by consciousness."[4]

Jung began to research archaeology and mythology for an objective confirmation of a collective unconscious.*

His own dreams and visions fed the project. He wrote to Freud in 1910, "At present I am pursuing my mythological dreams with almost autoerotic pleasure, . . . I often feel I am wandering alone through a strange country, seeing wonderful things that no one else has seen before and no one needs to see . . . I don't yet know what will come of it. I must just let myself be carried along, trusting to God that in the end I shall make a landfall somewhere."[5]

Jung continued to be Freud's heir apparent, and that spring Freud had him installed as president of the International Psychoanalytical Association. He was still to be the public face of the movement.

But as Jung followed out the implications of his shipboard dream, he developed more and more the distinctive ideas associated with his own form of psychoanalysis, which he called "analytical psychology": the archetypes, the

---

*This search continues among Jungians in the practice of "amplification," in which dreamers are encouraged to research coincidences between their dreams and sometimes obscure myths and symbols. Few scientists are convinced by such researches, and no serious scientist is actively trying to discover biological "proof" of the Jungian archetypes.

collective unconscious, "the sympathy with religious experience, the fascination with myth and alchemy."[6]

By the end of 1913 Jung began to publish his new ideas, which caused a complete rupture, first in the two men's friendship and then in their professional association. Jung resigned his leadership post. "After the parting of the ways with Freud," Jung wrote, "a period of inner uncertainty began for me. It would be no exaggeration to call it a state of disorientation. I felt totally suspended in mid-air for I had not yet found my own footing."[7]

Eventually Jung also resigned his position at the hospital and at the university. It was as if he were stripping away all that he had achieved in the waking world. He developed a new attitude toward his patients' dreams, avoiding "all theoretical points of view" and simply helping "the patients to understand the dream images by themselves without application of rules and theories."[8]

He did the same with his own dreams and visions. From 1913 to 1916, he explored a series of waking dreams, using a form of conscious fantasizing he later called "active imagination."[9] This work is very similar to Desoille's "directed waking dream" and the imaginal exercises of Madame Colette.

He wrote, "I consciously submitted myself to the impulses of the unconscious."[10]

First Jung reviewed his personal memories. He was drawn to his boyhood, when his greatest joy was playing with building blocks. He decided that if he wanted to "reestablish contact with that period I had no choice but to return to it and take up once more that child's life with his childish games. This moment was a turning point in my fate, but I gave in only after endless resistance and with a sense of resignation. For it was a painfully humiliating experience to realize that here was nothing to be done except play childish games."[11] In Bregman's terms, Jung was becoming the boy. This activity released a "stream of fantasies" that often overwhelmed him.

"I knew I had to let myself plummet down into them. . . . I felt not only violent resistance to this, but a distinct fear. For I was afraid of losing command of myself and becoming a prey to the fantasies."

On December 12, 1913, he writes, "I was sitting at my desk once more thinking over my fears. Then I let myself drop. Suddenly it was as though the ground literally gave way beneath my feet and I plunged down into dark depths. I could not fend off a feeling of panic." In this first episode Jung encountered a dwarfish figure he later called "the Shadow," which resembles Bregman's "pathology."

It was the first of many dream descents:

In order to seize hold of the fantasies, I frequently imagined a steep descent. I even made several attempts to get to the very bottom. The first time I reached as it were a depth of about a thousand feet; the next time I found myself at the edge of a cosmic abyss. It was like a voyage to the moon or a descent into empty space.* First came the image of a crater and I had the feeling that I was in the land of the dead. The atmosphere was that of the other world. Near the steep slope of a rock I caught sight of two figures, an old man with a white beard and a beautiful young girl. I summoned up my courage and approached them as though they were real people and listened attentively to what they told me. The old man explained that he was Elijah and that gave me a shock. But the girl staggered me even more, for she called herself Salome![12]

Acting with the openness of the boy, Jung met a pair of figures, male and female. He called them "dominants" in his writing and, later, "archetypes"—literally, "primal impressions." I've been calling them VIPs. Jung called the female VIP "anima" and the male VIP "animus."

In later fantasies, Elijah was replaced by Philemon, who "represented a force which was not myself. . . . I held conversations with him and he said things which I had not consciously thought." Philemon and other figures "brought home to me the crucial insight that there are things in the psyche which I do not produce, but which produce themselves and have their own life."[13]

He understood that others would view his plunge into fantasy as "a risky experiment," that it was "a questionable adventure to entrust oneself to the uncertain path that leads into the depths of the unconscious."

Yet, looking back on the experience, he wrote, "The years when I was pursuing my inner images were the most important in my life—in them everything essential was decided. It all began then; the later details are only supplements and clarifications of the material that burst forth from the unconscious and at first swamped me. It was the *prima materia* for a lifetime's work."[14]

Near the end of his life Jung refers to this three-year period with a sense of an exploration started but curtailed, for he never again plunged with this

---

*The parallels to the "descent to the chariot" are clear; the voyage up to the heavens was figured as a voyage down into the depths.

degree of intensity into the depths. Nor did he recommend this sort of experiment to others. He writes, "I tried it out on myself and others thirty years ago and must admit that although it is feasible and leads to satisfactory results it is also very difficult." It can lead to a "dangerous impasse."

That's because in order to enter this imaginal journey, it is necessary to take the images seen in dreams as real. In his last major attempt to theorize his own experience, *Mysterium Coniunctionis* ("The mystery of the conjunction"), Jung describes this necessary step as a shift in basic attitude toward dreams from "aesthetic" to "judgment."

By "aesthetic" Jung means that the dreamer "simply continues to observe his images without considering what they mean to him."[15]

The dreamer refuses the charge of the dream and doesn't believe that the images really apply to his or her life. This aesthetic attitude underlies dream amelioration.

The dreamer stands apart from the dream and interprets: the dream becomes an aesthetic object for the interpreter, something perhaps entertaining, amusing, or stimulating. But the images in the dream aren't taken with ultimate seriousness. This is what I went through in my work with Bregman. It was clear, for instance, that I had an "aesthetic attitude" toward my dream of K de G. This soft attitude—the dream as entertainment or gentle instruction—persists today in many popular approaches to the dream.

But Marc Bregman is made of tougher stuff. He understood that the aesthetic attitude is an obstacle to going deeper.

In dealing with the tenacious opposition, you have to feel that the dream refers to your own personal struggle and angst. "Without the angst," Bregman said, "you are doing nothing.

"The aesthetic in Jung's terms—that's often the attitude of a client who is still in a predicament. If you simply view your dreams as beautiful or terrifying, or weird, they can't change you."

By contrast, what Jung called "judgment" means taking the judgment of the dream as personally and ethically "binding."

"[T]he transition from a merely perceptive, i.e. aesthetic, attitude to one of judgment is far from easy," Jung warned. "It is not a matter that can be taken lightly."[16]

Jung continued, "One naturally asks oneself what fear if fear it is prevents him from taking the next step, the transition to an attitude of judgment (the judgment of course should be morally and intellectually binding)."

The fear and uncertainty arise because "voluntary participation in the fantasy is alarming to a naïve mind. . . . The danger . . . is that in a psychopathically disposed patient, it will unleash a psychosis."[17]

Bregman commented, "We call it 'controlled psychosis' in the dream work. We take this fear and use it as part of the alchemy. To move from point A to point B, the fear of psychosis or psychosis itself is actually the way through."

In my dream of knight and dragon I could sit on the sidelines thinking, This is just a show, or I could taste the fear by participating in a life-and-death moment. If you take the position of "judgment," the dragon is real, the animus is real, the sword is real. Then the fear in the dream is real, too, and so is the potential for change.

I saw that operate in Freud's dreams: his refusal to take seriously the "staircase maid" kept the dream at a certain aesthetic distance. He didn't feel the full "judgment" of the dream. His interpretation led him only to other maids and other staircases, not inward to participating in the reality of the dream, the anguish of being paralyzed.

In my case, seeing gravel grandma or the dictionary lady as a present threat to my happiness helped me recover the feelings and energies of "the boy." I accepted the "judgment" of the dream—that this figure was a real threat to me that had to be taken seriously. Then the dreams could become an arena for struggle and change.

Jung writes, "In myths the hero is the one who conquers the dragon. . . . [But] he is no hero who never met the dragon or who once he saw it, declared afterwards that he saw nothing. Equally only one who has risked the fight with the dragon and is not overcome by it wins the hoard, the 'Treasure hard to attain.' He alone has a genuine claim to self confidence for he has faced the dark ground of his self and thereby has gained himself."[18]

To Bregman, "the dragon" Jung speaks of is pathology. "Our sense of normalcy is wrapped up with the old deal we've made to accommodate pathology, and if this deal is threatened it feels like a threat to sanity."

But *sanity* means "wholeness," while a commitment to pathology is living on half shares, with whole parts of ourselves, including the feelings of the child, unknown and unexplored.

Only by making the effort to face the dragon can the dreamer attain "what the alchemists called 'the *unio mentalis*,'" unified consciousness.

"*Unio mentalis*" means that the world of the unconscious and the world of the conscious mind have become one reality for the person, not two separate domains. To move from "the aesthetic" to "judgment" would mean we can no longer characterize dream and reality as opposites. The dreams become as real and significant as waking reality.

Jung experimented with "judgment" in his early years, but backed away from it. Bregman felt that he would have needed a "cadre of enlightened clients" to proceed and that this would have been difficult at a time when psychotherapy was on a medical model, promising cures of neurosis and a path to normalcy.

But after thirty-five years, Bregman has developed a group of longtime clients who view the dream path primarily in a spiritual framework. They aren't looking to be adjusted to normalcy if *normal* means "pathological," which it often does.

Although most people working with Bregman use the terms "animus" and "anima" for the VIPs in dreams, it became clear to me that Bregman and Jung use these words entirely differently. That is why although Bregman acknowledges his debt to Jung, he would never call himself a Jungian.

To Jung, the anima represents the "personification of the feminine nature of a man's unconscious." The animus represents "the masculine nature of a woman's."[19] Thus for Jung, the soul of a woman is personified in dreams as a male; the soul of a man is personified in dreams as a female.

But in Bregman's work, the soul of a person, the inner or unconscious personality, is represented by a child, not by the anima or animus. This child can be a boy or a girl or both for any given client.

Jung's spoke of other archetypes. The "Shadow" is similar to the opposition, or what Bregman calls pathology—or similar enough not to dwell on here.

The "Self" archetype for Jung represents the union of conscious and unconscious—and appears in a dream as a holy or numinous or religious figure—for many dreamers, Jesus or the Buddha. Jung was circumspect about the religious implications:

> In the West the archetype is filled out with the dogmatic figure of Christ;
> in the East, with . . . the Buddha and so on. The religious point of view,
> understandably enough, puts the accent on the imprinter, whereas scientific
> psychology emphasizes the typos, the imprint, the only thing it can under-
> stand. The religious point of view understands the imprint as the working
> of an imprinter; the scientific point of view understands it as the symbol of
> an unknown and incomprehensible content. Since the typos is less definite

and more variegated than any of the figures postulated by religion, psychology is compelled by its empirical material to express the typos *by means of a terminology not bound by time, place, or milieu.*[20]

Many people in the work have also seen numinous figures, and some have seen Jesus or the Buddha. But Bregman does not speak of a "Self" archetype. For him, the "animus" and "anima" themselves have a numinous quality. They represent the "unknown and incomprehensible content," though Bregman calls it simply "the divine." For some dreamers, a third figure, "the father" also comes into play, and all three—animus, anima, and "the father"—can appear as numinous or holy figures.

For Bregman, the key point is that the dreamer becomes the child and as such can feel the love of the animus, the anima, or the father. This he calls "the soul under the tutelage of the divine."

Freud felt that any recognition of religious feelings in psychology was unscientific. Jung felt that Freud was failing to act as a scientist precisely because he refused to recognize the evidence of religious feeling in the psyche.

Bregman for his part is not claiming to be a scientist at all. He frames the descent into dreams as a discovery of the realm of the soul.

Freud and Jung were caught up in the project of early modernism—which is very far along today—to reduce all truth to the truth of objective science. But this is not the way of dreams.

Rather, the descent is a powerful way to open up an inward subjective space, to discover the inner landscape of depth. The parallels between Jung's earliest explorations and Bregman's work are remarkable. Jung, through childlike play with blocks, became the boy and, through waking visions much like Colette's, encountered pathology and his very important persons. But since the archetypes as Jung defined them are ultimately "unknown and incomprehensible," it's not a problem that Bregman conceives them differently.

He earned his own vision, through years of direct experience and the transformation of his own pain.

Chapter 30

MARC BREGMAN
MEETS THE ANIMUS

The first time I heard about Marc Bregman I was told he was a postman. In a certain way that intrigued me. I don't think I ever would have gone to a regular psychotherapist to learn about dreams, but in a perversely ironic way I thought a postman had a better chance of being for real.

When we met, Bregman hadn't worked at the post office in ten years, but there was an extensive period where he delivered dreams and mail. How Bregman wound up in the post office in the first place is tied up with his conflict with his father, for Bregman, like me, had father problems.

He was born in 1947 into a Jewish household in Philadelphia.

His father worked as a machinist and encountered raw anti-Semitism at his job. Yet he moved the family into a working-class suburb of Philadelphia where Jews were a target for abuse.

Bregman describes his father as a very angry man, a "tyrant" who "terrorized" him as a young boy. That led to rebellion. Hating his father, Bregman associated with kids who hated theirs. Because his father had made a particular point of stressing Judaism, he avoided Jewish friends and sought out non-Jews. Now he looks at that time in wonder: "How can you live your life if you hate someone who is your own bone?"

After an indifferent high school career, where he was hampered by a reading disability, Bregman joined the army in 1965. He lived in Germany and grew attracted to radical politics. After his discharge, he returned to the United States and roamed around the country.

He joined various communes that were heavily political. He would get close to the man in charge, the organizer, and become the second banana.

But the story always ended the same way: he would figure out the leader's failing and go after him, undermining him with the rest of the group. The more he ran away from his father, the more he was locked into the role of a "bastard son."

Bregman was living his predicament. His life had the plot of a stage-one dream: he was running in circles, from situation to situation, commune to commune. He was caught in a labyrinth: looking for a father to be close to, then trying to destroy him, then feeling destroyed in turn. He spent three months here, four months there, doing outreach for a church and social work of various kinds. Feeling desperate, he looked for a way to change his life. He thought a trip to mystical Nepal would do the trick.

The trip was a complete disaster. He got sick with dysentery in India, and his traveling companions, a pair of hippies, dumped him off in a remote village. Fortunately, the tribal people there nursed him back to health. He'd nearly died, and instead of finding God, he'd found nothing.

He felt suicidal. At this low point his life began to turn.

He decided to go back to college in Burlington, Vermont, where he became the protégé of a Jungian therapist and psychology professor. They did projects together where Bregman was valued for his street smarts. He also discovered he had intuitive gifts in astrology and tarot, and took on clients. When he added Jung and dreams to the mix, his clients liked what he did.

By the time he graduated with a B.A. in the late 1970s, he was in his early thirties, married to Dianne Guyette, and supporting five children from her previous marriage. He needed a well-paying job and found one at the Burlington post office. By day he delivered mail; in the evenings he saw dream clients.

In the postal service he encountered anti-Semitism. He was persecuted by redneck Vermonters as a Jew and a "granola head."

Now he felt himself thrown back into the torments of his childhood. He saw the bosses as tyrants like his father. He was in post office hell, struggling every hour, and even if he was able to help his dream clients, he saw no way to help himself out of his predicament. This went on for years.

One day at work he forgot a receipt for a registered letter. His supervisor smashed a Styrofoam cup of coffee and raged at him. Bregman reacted with fear, just as he had as a boy, but as the supervisor yelled at him, Bregman looked carefully into his eyes and realized the man was laughing inside. It was all just a show.

Bregman realized he'd been projecting. The supervisor wasn't his father; he was "just doing his stupid job."

Suddenly his shame was gone. He didn't have to play the role of his father's bastard son at work. With that his fear also went away. As surely as in a dream, he had seen through his own dark father pathology—and having seen through it, he had a new way to be in the world.

He consciously decided to use his job at the post office to do inner work. He would break the pattern with his father by breaking the projection on the supervisors. Where his clients worked these issues out in dreams, Bregman did it consciously in his waking life.

"I had a lot of growing to do, a lot of undoing. I didn't want to be my father's bastard son anymore."

When two supervisors persecuted him for being a Jew, he responded by bringing them bagels and cream cheese and teaching them Yiddish.

"As a child I hid my Jewishness, so now I would do the opposite. I had to stand up and face the shame of hating myself." He felt that God was directing him to do these things. If a guy hated him for whatever reason, he'd hang by the case where he sorted mail.

"He'd call me names and I would be pleasant. I was radicalized from a place of love. At some point I was healed."

When that change happened, clients started raining down on Bregman. He felt that by opening up to this change in himself—separating from his pathology—he learned better what the dream work was all about.

"I needed to be healed first. You can't have knowledge unless you are healed."

In order to separate from the dark father pathology, he had to be healed of his rage against his father.

There was something else: he felt that God had done this for him. This is where he first learned about obedience.

"I learned that if I just do what I'm asked as the son, the student, then things happen. If I don't, I know the wheel. I've been through it a million times."

Bregman told me once that he has a "meat and potatoes" spirituality. I knew that this was completely different from the approach I'd always taken. By "meat and potatoes" he meant understanding how God acted in his life.

He told me, "I believe in a one-to-one relationship with the maker, and rituals are not important to me."

He saw the same spiritual struggle in his clients' dreams that he'd lived out for himself. For as his work with them deepened, their dreams were leading him beyond the parameters of normal psychotherapy into a religious domain.

"Any psychologist would tell you, 'The goal is to give people a better, well-adjusted life.' I was still living in that parameter. I had no idea that the dream work was really real. I understood it at the symbolic level; I was very Jungian. I could talk with the rest of them, but it was all talk.

"But people were experiencing things beyond the psychological parameters I had learned. Something else was going on, and I became afraid of it. When a person started having spiritual encounters, that's where I said, 'You graduated. You go off with that guy in your dream . . .'"

But then he decided he was being cowardly. Because of his experiences in the post office, he was growing. So he stopped dismissing his clients when they entered this more advanced stage of work beyond the pathology even if he didn't always understand it.

He made a commitment to follow them: "I knew going with their work was a way to learn about my work. My ignorance didn't seem to get in the way."

In his early days with clients, he'd figure their dreams out mentally, through pure stubbornness and pathological will. This worked, but it was also grueling.

He suffered from severe migraine headaches during the sessions. Sometimes, afterward he would pull over to the side of the road and vomit.

But then the animus appeared to him in a waking vision, put his hands on his forehead, and rubbed away the pain. The animus said, "Stop thinking and let go."

"I realized I could hear him if I stopped thinking."

The vision confirmed for him that he needed to rely on intuition.

"I'd be with a client, and instead of trying to figure him out, I'd just go back to that place the animus opened up in me. I could hear him, and he would tell me what to say. He'd whisper, 'Do a gestalt with . . .' and I would do it. Or I would hear, 'Ask about his mother.' I would ask about his mother."

This shift took years to fully understand. Instead of seeing his work as psychotherapy, he understood the dream work process as something the animus was doing through him.

"Instead of my being out here, I would 'back in' to the animus. I would have a client and I'd pray; I'd wait for 'him' to talk. I'd listen incessantly."

I'd noticed that often in our work there would be long silences. That was Bregman "listening," because if he didn't know what to say, he would just say nothing and wait.

"There was a whole underneath world coming up that wasn't there before."

Bregman put all his bets on the animus. "Most people don't want to do what they're told. Even if they were given that opportunity they wouldn't do it. Obedience means to be. And to be what? To be other than your ego. To have died."

The animus taught him, client to client, word for word. "Say this." "Do that." He would just obey. "Like a dummy, I would do it and then later I would understand. It made sense. It was hard, but I was willing to be obedient."

Bregman has a firm persuasion of the reality of the animus that I have felt only in fits and starts. I admire his faith even if I must struggle to find it in myself. I admire it because it seems to work. I feel he's the most brilliant therapist on the planet, but Bregman insists his only gift is obeying what he hears.

"Everybody's experience is different," Bregman said. "But at a certain point people begin to know something you have to be a madman to know, and that's when they look at me and I know that they know. That changes everything for me and the client. I am not the one because you know it, too. And what you do about it is your business."

Bregman spoke of "a depth of the absorption in the archetypal world."

"People in the work become conscious of its presence and its reality. Which dissolves the reality of 'this world.' It's not just conceptual; it's a reality. When going through that transition you feel like you are dying. You feel psychotic. But if you get through it, you become a different person."

Nevertheless, while this was happening, he had to wake every morning and drive to the post office. He had five kids to support.

When I first heard that Bregman was a postman, I thought it was cute, because the Talmud says, "A dream uninterpreted is like a letter unopened."

But as I knew him better, I felt how deep the wounds with his father were that had led him to the post office in the first place, and how much courage it took for him to devote himself full-time to dream work.

I now felt a certain kinship with Bregman because so much of my own personal work was about my father even though our fathers were so very different.

One way it worked out differently is that I seemed to have a "father" who appeared in my dreams. This was definitely not my father, but a male archetype that Bregman distinguishes from the animus.

The "father" helped me solve the mystery of the orphanage.

Chapter 31

RETURN OF THE ORPHANAGE DREAM

The Father Archetype

I could not understand why I was in an orphanage. My logic was: I come from a family of five children, so how could an orphanage be my true home? (This is truly an example of interpretation from waking to dream, which is backward.) I did not realize the gift of the dream. "Orphan" is an essential image of my soul's situation.

I needed to learn how to be the orphan boy, to feel his feelings of pain and abandonment. Because only from that place could I get the help I needed.

Another dream around that time carried the same disturbing hint. Again I wandered the streets; again I found myself in a large institutional building, maybe the same orphanage building, only this time I was in the basement. It was full of homeless people milling around. I was trying to figure out what I was doing there when a strange man in shabby clothes touched me on the shoulder and said, "I have a disease." I recoiled at that touch: This is not me, I thought, this is not my life. I woke and still did not understand. Living in a nice home, and in good health, how could I see the "homeless man" as my twin or that I, too, have a strange disease.

We recoil from other's pain because we don't want to feel our own. In my case, I go into my head, into abstractions, complex ideas, even theology. But as a theologian once said to me, God is too important for theologians.

As I became the vulnerable boy, and the student, I was able to learn about pain, which runs through everyone and is all around us.

I had a whole series of encounters with the anima that helped me feel this universal pain, for her role is to deepen the feeling of the child.

One time she took me high above the known world.

We were flying in the clouds together and looking down below. She showed me scenes of disaster: people's homes were broken; they were living without shelter. The man who touched my shoulder in the basement was part of that homeless world. But so was I, only I didn't know it yet.

In another dream, I saw a tall, beautiful woman with a wide forehead and straight hair, dressed in white. The anima again. I noticed that her ears were perfectly formed. I said, "You have beautiful ears." She said, "I know." I said, "I am sure you are beautiful inside. I would like to know you better."

Then, as if to answer my request, the anima and I were walking together through a culvert, a large concrete pipe as high as a house. We passed families huddled together on the concrete. It was getting harder and harder for me to pass by these people; it hurt to see their suffering. Children sat on the hard ground; mothers and fathers sat side-by-side; little babies crawled on the concrete, which was also wet in places. The people didn't say a word as we passed by.

The scene in the culvert seemed horrifying—but the anima led me through. She was showing me the world as she saw it. The culvert world is our world. The anima was opening my eyes and heart: for the way people ignore suffering of others is the way they ignore the suffering in themselves.

I didn't see yet that I also lived in the culvert. It's how our second-degree hiding looks to the anima.

I learned more directly how that separation from God feels in another dream. In a library a professor lectured on a painter. I left my seat and wandered off to gaze at a painting on the wall. It was chalky blue—an expansive sky, like the sky in one of Constable's cloud paintings, but even stranger and bolder. The sky was gorgeous, and I could have just fallen into it. My heart opened, and then I noticed a woman crying at the back of the room.

I came to her. She said, "I am the widow of the painter."

I took her hand to comfort her. She was wild with grief; tears were shaking out of her eyes, and she was shuddering. I said, "Did he leave you at least one of his paintings?" She said, "Not even one." I was trying to console her. I was reacting with concern, but concern isn't deep enough. I still saw it as *her* pain.

I didn't know how to respond to her wild, uncontrolled grief without saying something, so I said something silly: "Did he leave you at least one of his paintings?" She felt the grief of the widow separated from her husband, which is the grief of the lost princess in Nachman's tale. It was a grief I felt often whenever I sank out of awareness and back into pathology, whenever it overwhelmed me, as at times it did, so that I found myself again cut off, living in the dark culvert as if it were the only reality.

The truth is: I am an orphan. She was holding for me the immense sadness that I couldn't fully accept yet myself, which was why in the dream I tried to quiet her down. Her loss was her separation from "the painter." It was my loss, too, but I didn't know who "the painter" was.

My homework was to be with her—without trying to do anything for her. That was key: just let her be wild with grief.

The goal of the dream work is finally a special kind of knowing, a gnosis. It is the knowing that the VIPs, the archetypes, bring you. It is Jung's "*unio mentalis.*"

This gnosis comes through what Nachman of Bratzlav calls a "purified imagination," an imagination free of blind spots and pathology.[1]

Gnosis is the child's way of knowing—not educated or intellectual or mental, but knowing from the heart.

In this knowing from the heart, time slows down and you enter a new world. It is an extended, indelible, vivid experience in dreams where you feel the power of the archetypes. I'd come to know the anima and the animus, the pathology had been battled, I'd seen the boy and become him, and now, after so much work, I met the figure Bregman calls, simply, the father.

I'd always wondered about the father Bregman talked about, and how he differed from the animus. Now I was standing before him for the first time.

Not my father. The work with him had made this moment possible. But the father didn't look like mine. He looked like Gregory Peck in *To Kill a Mockingbird.* I brought him a metal canoe and asked if it was all right to put it in the water.

The father examined the boat carefully, turned it upside down to look at the hull.

He pointed to a small hole and said, "Nope." We weren't ready to go. I felt very bad. Now a woman appeared and said, "You sure it isn't okay? Why can't you . . . ?" But I could see that the father was right. I could see the holes. The father told me, "A bad plan is worse than no plan at all."

These words as I repeat them sound totally banal. I know they do. But in the dream, they came in with a great depth. This felt different from the animus. The animus is dramatic, theatrical. This was low-key but very solid. The father represents an entirely different order of experience. He connects you to a reality that comes from the soul's way of knowing.

I felt very sober when I woke knowing that my "boat has holes in it." I understood he knew my impatience. I was so eager to get somewhere, to push ahead, to make progress. I wanted so much to be with the father, but it wasn't up to me. I was rushing things, pushing. I was coming to him with this boat as if I were the one in charge of the journey. But I'm not. I was being impatient. He would come to me when I was ready.

So I felt disappointed, but I knew that it wasn't the right time, or, as he said, "a bad plan is worse than no plan at all." I had to give up any plan of my own. My homework was to feel the orphan's sadness, just be with it, wanting the father to help, and then, perhaps, it would be time.

To have no plan at all is excellent as a program for the soul. Because all that's left is to feel the pain of being separate from God. The main thing is to feel the pain. Otherwise there is nothing to work with. You have to understand your essential situation, who you are in relation to the archetypes— as they'd been trying to show me ever since the dream of Miguel and the orphanage.

I did my homework, and in time I saw the father again.

At first, though, I did not see myself. I saw a boy in a dream who had been living in an orphanage for many years.

One day this boy's father came to see him. It was a surprise. The orphan didn't even know he had a father. The boy liked this father, all right, but didn't let himself feel too much about it, because after all he'd lived so many years without him.

But as he was about to leave the boy, the father pointed to his hand and said, "We have the same hand."

The son looked at his own hand and saw. Yes, it was the same as his father's. He had his father's hand. He walked slowly into the bathroom and cried violently, heaving sobs for not knowing his father for so many years.

I looked up and saw my face in the mirror. At that moment I realized I was the one crying those big tears.

The last time I'd heard such wild weeping in a dream, it was the painter's widow in the library. She was crying because she was separated from "the painter," creator of the blue, blue sky. I'd felt pity for her widowhood, her separation from her husband.

But now I felt that separation for myself. She didn't have to hold it for me anymore. I had the feeling now.

The hundred times I'd read about second-degree hiding I'd never burst into tears knowing the grief and sadness of being orphaned from the father. Now, finally, the feeling was real.

Maybe I had wanted to find God by reading about him, or by speculating about religion as I had been ever since Dharamsala, or by praying or meditating, but I couldn't do it with my intellect. I couldn't do it with all my adaptations and compromises and all my irony and fancy words, and all the complications and reservations and doubts that still fly around in my head, translated back and forth between religions, Judaism and Buddhism and Christianity and Sufism and Gnosticism, and the old stories and everything else. I had to do it from the heart of the boy.

You can't bring your conditioned, compromised self to the father. He doesn't want that one.

He wants the boy who is vulnerable and sad, looking at his hand, weeping, who knows the truth: I miss you, I miss you, father.

And who suspects, looking at his own hand, that yes, it is true: God's hand is my hand. My hand is God's hand.

If God is going to have a hand in this world, it's going to have to be my hand and yours.

Chapter 32

NORTH OF EDEN

Religion talks about soul, but where can we look to find it? Is it in a book or a sermon, or is *soul* just a word without a meaning, another abstraction to puzzle the mind with interpretations? What's the point of hearing doctrines about the fate of the soul after death if we have no experience of soul in this life?

I believe there is an answer in dreams. The experience of soul is imaginal but not imaginary. I can feel it for myself. And I can feel it in others when I see, behind the adult, the little boy, the little girl.

Each dreamer gets a unique image of the soul, and everyone who dreams has this path of knowing the hidden life of the soul.

Here is an outline of the path as I understand it. First you must encounter your predicament, and see your opposition; this is the first gift of the dream. Then you can find the essential image of the soul; this is the second gift. Finally, as the child you explore this imaginal space and learn from the archetypes; this is the third gift.

These are the three gifts of the dream: to discover your pain, to see your soul, and to explore its realm.

I come back to the beginning. I did not follow a conscious plan; for long periods I had no plan at all. But now I see that it all began in the summer of 1995 when I was curious about images and their role in religions of the word. I learned visualization with my teacher Colette Aboulker-Muscat in Jerusalem. She led me to appreciate how images are sovereign in the mind.

Then I looked into the case of the disappearing revelation dream and examined the history of interpretation, from the rabbis to the Church Fathers to Freud.

I also learned in Genesis three forms of revelation dream: Abimelech's warning, Joseph's sheaf, and Jacob's ladder.

In the summer of 2001, I met Marc Bregman, and my work turned radically inward to the world of my own dreams.

I became a student of Bregman and his dream work, and am now an apprentice teacher with clients of my own.

There are many others further along: his fellow teachers and former students have joined together in a lively community. Marc Bregman had mixed feelings about this development as it has unfolded over the past ten years. He'd been quite content seeing clients one-on-one. But that's not what the animus wants, he said.

Bregman's relationship with the animus has changed over the years.

"For me," he said, "the anima has been a predominant teacher. For 80 percent of my work it was anima anima anima. Only in the latter stages of the work has the animus been my bosom buddy. It took me a long time to heal enough to have an understanding of the male the way the animus wanted it.

"Personally I've been very blessed to now be in relationship with the animus."

"How did it change?"

"One day in a dream the anima said, 'Hey, look. Your boss. He's waving to you.' I looked and he was waving and he said, 'Come in.' I said no. I don't want to go with him. Nah. I woke up."

It was a missed opportunity.

"About three months after that, doing my assignment of being open to meeting him, as I came out of a building in a dream, he picked me up in his car and whisked me to an unbelievable church—twelve-by-twelve beams with carvings. He said, 'Look around.' In a little alcove I saw a grouping of pictures, and they were all of me. They were me in the most flattering way, me in ways I didn't even know me. I cried. I began my relationship with him then.

"It culminated a year ago. In a dream I was in a food co-op. Tim Robbins the actor—he's a potent man, sweet and big. He was the animus, and with him is a little guy, about five-foot-four in farmer's jeans, running around with a clipboard working his ass off. Robbins is sitting around. I want to be part of what's going on. I say, 'Great, what can I do?'

"I found some spoiled food and ran after the little guy with the clipboard and said, 'Hey, let me take this spoiled food back.'

"I chased him from room to room. Suddenly he turned around and came right to my face. He got closer and closer. I got scared and said, 'Who are you?' 'I am yo-o-o-o-u,' he said, and went right through my body and filled me up. I realized I am this guy. I am the guy from the pictures a year ago. A little guy.

"And I didn't want to be him. That's not my image of myself. I'm more of a bear, a Marlboro man. But to the animus, that's not who I am. That's not who he was seeing.

"So I've been working on that for over a year. I'm the little guy. I feel him in me. I do everything in service to the animus as this guy with a clipboard.

"So this wasn't a big death. I've died so many times I couldn't tell you. This is just the latest death. A small one: beep—and my Marlboro man is gone. I'm a little guy running around working. And I hate clipboards. I hate those things and now I've got one in my truck."

Whoever Bregman thought he was, he took to heart the picture of him that the animus showed him. He was best off being a lowly assistant, for that is the situation of his soul.

The animus wasn't communicating just with Bregman, but with other people in the community.

At first they used a small lodge on mountaintop property Bregman owned for men's and women's retreats. This property is in a township north of Eden, Vermont. They began to call themselves "North of Eden."

Then someone had a dream of building a big barn to use as a retreat center. She donated money, and a sparkling new barn was built for classes, with a kitchen, and sleeping areas for overnight accommodations. Now a regular series of weekend workshops are being held there. Other people have dreamed about playing specific roles, from groundskeeper to webmistress to workshop organizer. During the construction phase, Bregman found himself one cold winter morning with a clipboard in his hand, just like in his dream.

He was waiting for a plumbing contractor, wondering why the hell he was doing this. But then he recalled, "Because he—the animus—told me to."

He has become the little guy in his Tim Robbins dream, the clipboard guy.

But he was also intensely guiding the dream teachers behind the scenes. (Though he would say it's not him, but the animus.)

They are building a community of dream teachers and figuring out how to bring this work out into the world. The core group at North of Eden, or NOE, as they call themselves for short, are discovering the joy but also the difficulties of taking dreams and bringing them into the social space. They struggle with outing their pathology, keeping themselves honest, sharing the uncomfortable dreams. It is an intense experiment in shared dream life, and the boundaries between "real" and "dream" are fluid, for the NOE people dream of one another, and of the process they are in, and sometimes new words and new concepts come straight out of their dreams. So they live in and out of each other's dreams.

I find the prospect of a community of interactive dreamers—interdreamers—inspiring and scary. Will it survive and grow, or fall apart? Can a path of individual dreams merge into a social path?

This is a creative bunch. The group's Web site—www.northofeden.com—is full of contributions. Bregman has coauthored a book about "the work," titled *The Deep Well Tapes*. Others are writing their own books, or exploring their individual dream journey in poems, essays, diaries, paintings, drawings, and songs.

An important new form of teaching came when several members of NOE had similar dreams of people tied together with strings. Over time they developed workshops in which they act out dreams, playing the parts of anima and animus, pathology and dream-ego. The strings are used to show that a person is tied to pathology—or to the archetype. These string workshops, or "strings," are powerful dramas. I won't forget soon the despair in the eyes of one man, tied up, with his pathology yapping at him while the animus walked away, out of reach. And in another "string" I witnessed a man break through and drive out the shame that had troubled him ever since he was sexually abused as a boy. It was a haunting exorcism, and everyone in the room broke into tears with the force of it.

The string work is the most powerful way I've seen of bringing this dream work out into the world. And then there are words.

Certainly the images of dreams are producing lots of words, and many are published on the NOE Web site. Just as Jung tells us he spent forty-five years trying to come to terms with his three-year plunge into waking visions, so now the NOE group is producing a huge volume of writing to give words to the images they are seeing on their individual journeys.

The history of the disappearing dream showed me how every religion inspired by the dream becomes a prisoner of its own sacred books, and how new insight, new energy, and new connection are blocked by the very words and teachings and rituals that were once meant to free them. Martin Buber called this process "ossification." He saw an inevitable tension between "religiosity," the immediate experience, and "religion," the rituals and concepts built around it: for Buber it is a perpetual struggle between the unconditional and the conditioned, between "forces" and "forms."

I have been calling it the struggle between the dream and the interpretation, the image and the word.

Moment to moment in my life it's much more simple. It's about how I react to the pain of the person before me, by being willing to go into my own pain. In that place I find the sad orphan boy. And as him I find my connection and can be the father's son.

It's knowing as a child knows, in the immediacy of the heart. The image is simple. I look at my hand, and see I have the same hand as my father.

The whole journey ends—for now—with the simple image of a boy looking at his hand and seeing that it looks like his father's hand. And that is how I can come to feel deeply that a human being is created in the image of God.

It is the old dream of seeing God's face, the promise of religion to provide some direct and immediate experience; but all the theology and abstraction, all the books and commentaries, can remove us from it.

The promise is found in Genesis 1:26: "God created the human being in his image." This verse raises all the struggles and contradiction of the image and the word, for how can any person look like an invisible God?

The first great Jewish philosopher, Maimonides, tried to solve this problem long ago, in *The Guide of the Perplexed*. We, too, are perplexed by the contradiction between the perfect, abstract, invisible God of philosophy and the very humanlike God of the Bible. Verse by verse, phrase by phrase, the philosopher systematically reinterprets every biblical expression that suggests a humanlike God, a God who sits, stands, rises, sees, hears, speaks; who is sorrowed, angered, pleased; and who has eyes, nostrils, a face, and a hand. He argues that all such expressions are mere metaphors—human language meant to describe divine abstractions.

So when he came to the verse in Genesis about man being made in the image of God, the philosopher interpreted *image* to mean "intellect." That humans and God have intellect in common. This interpretation suggests so much about how I and many others have always approached religious experience: for, until doing this dream work, I was much more comfortable reading and writing, thinking abstractly, conceptualizing, than directly experiencing.

The simple yearning to know God in the heart got lost along the way. But the journey in dreams took me back to a child's way of knowing.

I still love the old books, and always will. These days it delights me to find confirmation of places my dreams have taken me. A century before Maimonides, another commentator on the Torah read the verse in Genesis very differently. His name was Rabbi Shlomo Isaac, and he lived in Troyes, France. Tradition calls him Rashi, and he is considered the greatest of all the commentators.

God, Rashi says, created man "*with*" his image.* All the rest of creation was by fiat. But human beings are uniquely handmade. Man is "made by a seal as a coin that is made by a die."

In a very deep way, this says that our essential human nature is shaped by an image.

The word Rashi uses for "image" is the Hebrew equivalent of *typos,* the Greek word for "type."[1] Jung's *archetype* came from the same root. It also means a "primal stamp" or aboriginal impression.

We are stamped like a coin with a certain face of God, a face that can appear as many faces, like the many faces of the archetypes we see in dreams.

In one rabbinic teaching it's said that when an ordinary king stamps a coin with his face, each coin looks the same. But when the King of kings stamps the human face with his Image, each looks uniquely different, yet all are indeed faces of the King.[2]

In the end we are talking about a mystery of creation, and our participation in that mystery as human beings. Different religious languages express this mystery in different ways.

Yet in dreams it's simple: the anima and animus appear as a pair, as in my first glimpse of the married couple standing behind the boy in my desert dream.

In *Mysterium Coniunctionis,* Jung used alchemical language to speak of this same pairing as "Sun" and "Moon," essential male and female forces in a mating or "*coniunctio*" that represents "unified consciousness."[3]

---

*In Hebrew, the particle "b" in *b'tzalmo* can mean "in" or "with"; thus Rashi reads "*b'tzalmo*" as "with his image."

That is the same daring image that the Tibetans imagine. In the very inner throne room of the *kalachakra* mandala, when the practitioner has arrived at last, one sees again a pair of deities, male and female, conjoined, in that primordial area of consciousness the Tibetans call the "pristine consciousness zone."

Mystical Judaism speaks of male and female faces of God as the Holy One, Blessed is He and His Shekhinah, and it is said that each Sabbath these two participate in a divine union in the heavenly realm, which produces souls in the world below.

It's lovely and strange to contemplate these mysteries of divine union coming from so many distinct traditions; they seem to confirm that these images have been seen again and again as they are in our dreams. This is what led Jung to look for a collective unconscious.

Rabbi Isaac Luria, the last of the great kabbalists, elaborated the kabbalah of the visages of God, the *partzufim*.[4] He envisioned five faces, which he called grandfather, father, mother, son, and daughter. Luria specifically stated that the image of God with which man was created was two of these *partzufim* working together—the "son" and the "daughter." So Luria explained the text in Genesis: "God created the human being with his image, male and female created He Them."[5]

Did Luria dream up the *partzufim*? We know he was a prodigious dreamer who nightly visited the heavenly academies to learn there. In my own dreams, animus and anima appear together as husband and wife, father and daughter, brother and sister, just as Luria conceives of them.

The insight from Luria is that the mystery and lure of the conjoined Image "Male and Female" is stamped into us from the start. They come into our dreams from a timeless place to bring us news of our genesis and origin. They are the parents and teachers of the soul.

That we are made by image is a very surprising affirmation from a tradition conventionally seen as devoted exclusively to the word.

The experience of the dream work takes me in the end to union, not separation. The old battles between word and image and between reality and dream are misunderstandings, limitations of consciousness, or constrictions of soul.

They have led to all the confusions and bitter schisms in religion between devotees of the word and the image—including my own confusions.

Instead of a struggle between word and image, it's time to look for a conjunction—where the word and the image embrace as one.

The mind runs and returns between the image and the ineffable, between the invisible God and a God who has a face. One meditates on the absolutely infinite. Then swiftly one returns to an image: the face of the sweet anima, with her broad forehead and beautiful ears. One runs to the infinite and returns to the fierce animus, with his rough humor and strong interventions. One runs to the awesome and infinite and returns to the face of the father—calm and wise. The image reaches a hand out to us and increases our love; the ineffable humbles us and reminds us of the awesomeness of God.

Though it is impossible not to return to duality, for that is how the mind works, ultimately there is no division between the visible and the invisible, the image and the word. The whole struggle between word and image that defines religious and human history is in the end a limitation of our minds.

In dreams I feel I've rediscovered the roots of a natural religion. That door has been closed for a long time; it began closing in Genesis. But it can be reopened, and that is what Bregman is doing.

This dream practice has no fixed ceremonies, no creeds or beliefs—just dreaming and waking, and learning what is in the heart.

I'd rather have the simplest experience of the soul than all the words surrounding it. To my thinking now, religious beliefs without experiences of soul are like a house without a foundation.

What of those two famous antonyms, dream and reality? Can I really say that dreams are necessary to live a complete life? Can I say that dreams are real and that reality as we know it has its root in dreams?

This, too, asks for a meditation, a long and slow one over months and months, as I do the work every day on this dream path, as my dreams give me images for my homework, as my homework deepens those images so they reappear in my dreams. I dream of the boy and then awake; I meditate on the boy, and the boy grows stronger in my dreams, and in my life.

Day follows night; the waking images follow the images in the dreams. The dream-mind and the conceptual mind alternate and play. We see the world we imagine, and we imagine the world we see; there is no end to this sort of running and returning. Is the dream real, or is real real? There is no single answer as I keep moving between them. This is the path of dreams and of poetry. It is a path between reality and soul.

"Folks expect the poet to indicate the path between reality and their souls." I read those words of Walt Whitman one day,[6] and that night I fell into a dream, and in the dream I saw a giant poet, eight feet tall—another guise of "the father."

This was a lucid dream: I was aware of all that was going on, and especially how calm and joyful I felt.

There was a strange miracle in the dream: whatever the giant father-poet said, I immediately saw before us. His words became images as he spoke them.

We were climbing a shaded path, and he said, "You can see the light even better out of the shadow." Before my eyes appeared a bright patch of sunlight on the grass.

I knew he meant also the dream path I am on, with its dark doubts and torments and its bright revelations. Yet he also meant the path we were walking: the grass was simply grass, the hill a hill.

In certain dreams the visual effects are painterly, with outrageous colors and wild brush strokes, but this lucid dream had the vivid photographic clarity of real life.

That is the way of the father in my dreams, anyway. That is the atmosphere he brings with him; he is deeply real. He is, as I heard long ago about "Rabbi K de G," entirely human and warm.

We came to the top of the hill he had indicated, looking down from an awesome height into a valley below. I saw a meadow circled by surrounding hills, like a green eye. It was the color of my eyes.

I understood: the field of the grass and the field of my eye are the same field.

This was a dream of correspondences: it said the images of the outer world correspond to the images of the inner.

So I learned from the father. Any lingering bitter taste of pathology was assuaged: I saw on our path that we need the darkness in our lives to better see the light.

As for dream and reality, inner and outer: we need the eye to see the field and the field to know the eye. We need the inner world to see the outer, and the outer to see the inner. It's all one, though when we live in the culvert of separation, it seems two.

I felt exquisitely happy when I woke. I felt grateful to the father, and I knew his powerful love.

I felt joy in the dream and out. I knew what Jacob felt when he opened his eyes and saw that this world is awesome. I had walked with the father, and his teaching comforted me. I knew he was pointing me onward with love. I know I have a far way to go.

When I am in a place of longing and vulnerability, I can be the son and student in my dreams. And in my life.

When I forget, I fall back into my intellectual pride and arrogant ways, and I'm separated and lost once again.

The work goes on in an ever-deepening spiral, but the movement is never smooth. Part of me, even now, still waits in the orphanage, and feels hurt because he thinks the father left him.

But in my homework I see he comes back for me and takes me by the hand.

While I was writing this book, two of my teachers passed away: Colette Aboulker-Muscat of Jerusalem and Tarab Tulku of Copenhagen. I hope what I've written about their work honors their memory.

Marc Bregman continues to inspire me and teaches me how to know the world of dreams. In the generous spirit of the gift he has received, Marc has made a gift to this book of his teachings, and to me of his time, patience, and love. I believe he has renewed the dream journey of the ancients and brought into the world a profound and practicable way to use dreams for insight and discovery of the soul. I feel grateful to be his student and friend.

I want to thank Rabbi Zalman Schachter-Shalomi, who told me if I wished to be a storyteller (a *maggid*) I needed to learn how to interpret dreams. Reb Zalman's teachings in the summer of 1999 first woke me to the idea of the importance of the "faces" of God in prayer, but sparks of his generative soul can be found all over this work.

I also want to thank Rabbi Meir Fund for sharing his view of the dream and Rabbi Yitzhok Adlerstein for giving me insight into dream practices in the yeshiva world. Rabbi Ozer Bregman gave me invaluable references to the work of his rebbe, Nachman of Bratzlav. Rabbi Aryeh Wineman spoke with me about dreams and Nachman. None of these rabbis should be held responsible for any errors I've made in discussing Jewish beliefs and ideas, nor should anyone assume that they necessarily endorse anything I've written here.

I want to thank the dreamers who have let me tell or retell their dreams as part of this book. I also want to acknowledge a wonderful writer, my student and friend, the late Matt Clark, who appeared in a dream and told me to "write a book and illustrate it." I've tried to do that, Matt.

My daughter Kezia first got me into this subject by asking me about dreams. My daughter Anya has stimulated my thoughts with her own questions and ideas. My conversations and exchanges with the painter Archie Rand and the poet David Shapiro have been inspiring and invaluable. My dear friend, the poet and anthologist Howard Schwartz, has been supportive throughout and has directed me to many Jewish texts and sources.

In the course of writing this book I've drawn on the ideas and concepts of many scholars and experts from a variety of fields, and I want to acknowledge my debt to their work: Joel Covitz, Antonio Damasio, Diane Eck, Arthur Green, James Hillman, Elaine Pagels, and Elliot Wolfson. This book touches on a wide range of knowledge, from the ancient history of Sumer to contemporary PET scans of the dreaming brain. No one person can be expert in these areas. As a generalist writing for a general audience, I have used the work of many scholars and thinkers, living and dead, who are much more knowledgeable than I am. It's customary to say that one is standing on the shoulders of giants; unfortunately, I'm fairly sure that from time to time I accidentally kick some of these giants in the ear.

I can only apologize and say I hope to open a reconsideration of the seriousness of dreams that others will continue. I invite interested readers to do their own research and go to the important work of these scholars and authors to verify and refine what I offer here.

I thank the students of Colette, including Carol Rose, Eve Ilsen, and Tirzah Moussaief, both for their help in understanding her work and for their conversation and friendship at the time I studied with Colette in Jerusalem. I thank Laurel Chiten for bringing me to Morrie Schwartz. I thank Lene Handberg, who now leads the Unity in Duality organization and who helped arrange my visit in Copenhagen with her teacher, the late Tarab Tulku. I thank many of my friends in NOE, students of Bregman's work: among those in particular I'd like to mention are Christa Lancaster, Ellen Keene, Peter Burmeister, Laura Ruth, and especially Sue Scavo, who have helped in many different ways. I thank also Jon Gregg and Louise von Wiese of the Vermont Studio Center, who not only inadvertently led me to the dream work but who gave me space and time during my many visits to Vermont. I thank the late artist Lou Albert, who first told me about Bregman and his work.

I am also grateful to the IASD, The International Association for the Study of Dreams, for the opportunity both to attend their annual conference and to hear directly the work of experts I mention here, including Dr. William Domhoff, Dr. Paul Lippmann, Dr. David Kahn, Dr. Houston Smith, and Dr. William Dement. These scholars and the IASD in general, keep the dream alive.

I thank the Louisiana State University Department of English, which provided me with a DEFE grant that gave me valuable release time in the summer of 2004 and again in the fall of 2005 to complete this book. I am very grateful for the support of the Vermont Studio Center over a number of years. It is a place of refuge for poets and artists, and I have been privileged to live in their company. During part of my stay there I received a grant from the Nathan Cummings Foundation to serve as director of the Art Spirit program at VSC, and I am grateful for that grant as well. I want to thank Richard Katrovas and the Prague Summer Program for inviting me to make a public lecture at Charles University on dreams in the summer of 2005. I want to acknowledge *Natural Bridge,* which published a version of my chapters on Freud in issue 15 (Spring 2006).

To my clients, especially to William T. and DC, thank you. I have learned so much from working with you and thank you for permission to tell your story in dreams. I want to thank all those other dreamers who gave permission to use their dreams. I thank my longtime agent, Katinka Matson, and my editor at Harper San Francisco, Gideon Weil, for their advice, encouragement, and critiques. I also thank Carl Walesa for his astute copyediting and Carolyn Allison-Holland for supervising the production with aplomb.

Finally I want to thank my companion in dreams, my wife and my beloved, Moira, most of all for being Moira but also for sharing with me her thoughts and feelings and ideas about this work every step of the way. We've lived through many storms, including Katrina, and we're still going strong.

—New Orleans, 2007

Notes

Chapter 1: The Descent into Dreams

1. James Bissett Pratt, *The Religious Consciousness: A Psychological Study* (New York: Macmillan, 1920), 200. Pratt (1875–1944) studied philosophy under William James at Harvard and was a pioneer in the study of psychology and religion.

2. Deut. 31:16–18. The theme of God's hiding his face is associated with forgetting. "God has forsaken me, and God has forgotten me" (Isa. 49:14); "God has forgotten, He hides His face" (Ps. 10:11). God's forgetting corresponds to the withdrawal of *hashgacha,* or divine providence, which is the curse in Deuteronomy: "I will hide My face from them, and they shall be devoured, and many evils and troubles shall befall them" (Deut. 31:17).

3. Nachman of Bratzlav, *Likutey Moharan,* ed. Moshe Mykoff and Ozer Bergman (Jerusalem and New York: Breslov Research Institute, 1999), vol. 6 (lessons 49–57): 301–5 and ff.

4. Nachman writes: "There are two concealments. When God is hidden in a single concealment, it is very difficult to find Him. Yet when He is hidden in a single concealment, it is still possible for an individual to toil and strive until he finds Him, since he is aware that God is hidden from him. But when God is concealed in a concealment-within-a-concealment—in other words, the concealment itself is concealed from him so that he is completely oblivious to the fact that God is hidden from him—it is entirely impossible to find Him, since he is not at all aware that God is hidden there. This is analogous to 'I will *haster astir* [thoroughly hide]' (Deut. 31:18)—that is, 'I will conceal the concealment'—so that they will be completely oblivious to the fact that God is hidden." Nachman of Bratzlav, *Likutey Moharan,* 6:301.

Chapter 2: The Gate of Heaven in Newton, Massachusetts

1. Gershom Scholem, *Major Trends in Jewish Mysticism,* 3d rev. ed. (New York: Schocken Books, 1961), 41.

2. James Charlesworth, *The Old Testament Pseudepigrapha,* vol. 1 (Garden City, NY: Doubleday, 1983), 223.

3. Scholem, *Major Trends in Jewish Mysticism,* 41.

4. Ibid., 63, quoting *hekhalot zvtrti.*

5. Aryeh Wineman, *Mystic Tales from the Zohar* (Philadelphia: Jewish Publication Society, 1997), 19–20.

6. Louis Jacobs, ed., *The Schocken Book of Jewish Mystical Testimonies* (New York : Schocken Books, 1997), 185–86.

7. Scholem, *Major Trends in Jewish Mysticism,* 47.

8. Franz Kafka, *The Trial* (New York: Schocken Books, 1998), 215–17. This famous passage is known as the parable "Before the Law."

Chapter 3: Collette and the Waking Dream

1. Cf. Gitta Amipaz-Silber, *The Role of the Jewish Underground in the American Landing in Algiers, 1940–1942* (Jerusalem: Gefen Publishing House, 1992).

2. Catherine Shainberg, *Kabbalah and the Power of Dreaming: Awakening the Visionary Life* (Rochester, VT: Inner Traditions, 2005).

3. Robert Desoille, *Entretiens sur le rêve éveillé dirigé en psychothérapie* (Paris: Payot, 1973), 111–12 (my translation).

4. Gaston Bachelard, *Air and Dreams: An Essay on the Imagination of Movement* (Dallas: Dallas Institute Publications, 1988), 114.

5. Bachelard, *Air and Dreams*, 115.

6. Herbert Benson, *The Relaxation Response* (New York: Harper Collins, 2000), xxxix–xl.

7. Augustine *De Genesis* 12.24.51.

8. Cf. Henry Corbin, "Mundus Imaginalis, or the Imaginary and the Imaginal," *Spring*, 1972, 1–9.

9. Gerald Epstein, *Healing Visualizations: Creating Health Through Imagery* (New York: Bantam, 1989).

Chapter 4: Kitchen Kabbalah and the Vault of Images

1. See http://www.schoolofimages.com/. See also Shainberg, *Kabbalah and the Power of Dreaming*.

Chapter 6: The Case of the Disappearing Dream

1. Arthur Green, *Seek My Face, Speak My Name: A Contemporary Jewish Theology* (Northvale, NJ: Jason Aronson, 1992), 36–37.

2. Arthur Green, *Tormented Master: The Life and Spiritual Quest of Rabbi Nachman of Bratslav* (Woodstock, VT: Jewish Lights, 1992).

3. For a complete translation of Vital's dream from Sefer ha-Hezyonot 2:5, see *Jewish Mystical Autobiographies: Book of Visions and Book of Secrets,* trans. Morris Faierstein (New York: Paulist Press, 1999), 78–82. I have quoted here from an unpublished translation by Howard Schwartz.

4. Joel Covitz, *Visions of the Night: A Study of Jewish Dream Interpretation* (Boston: Shambhala, 1990), 2–5.

Chapter 7: A Convention of Dreamers

1. Encarta, s.v. "sleep," http://encarta.msn.com/encyclopedia_761570982/Sleep.html.

2. J. M. Siegel, "Brainstem Mechanisms Generating REM Sleep," http://jsiegel.bol.ucla.edu/rem_sleep.htm.

3. F. Crick and G. Mitchison, "The Function of Dream Sleep," *Nature* 304 (1983): 111.

4. "A Brief Biography of Calvin S. Hall," http://psych.ucsc.edu/dreams/About/calvin.html.

5. To help other researchers, Domhoff has on file, available to any researcher who wishes to use them, the dreams of Barb Sanders ("now over 4000 in number"), as well as a normative sample of 250 dreams coded with the Hall/Van de Castle coding system; this material is available at http://www.dreambank.net/.

6. G. William Domhoff, "The Purpose of Dreams," http://psych.ucsc.edu/dreams/Library/purpose.html. A version of the lecture was published in the ASD journal.

7. Paul Lippmann, "The Canary in the Mind," pt. 1, *Dreamtime* 20, no. 2 (Summer 2003): 4–7; pt. 2, *Dreamtime* 20, no. 3 (Winter 2003): 4–7, 41.

8. Lippmann, "The Canary in the Mind," pt. 1, 5.

9. G. W. Domhoff, "Moving Dream Theory Beyond Freud and Jung" (paper presented at the symposium "Beyond Freud and Jung?" Graduate Theological Union, Berkeley, CA, September 23, 2000), http://psych.ucsc.edu/dreams/Library/domhoff_2000d.html.

Chapter 8: Marc Bregman and a Punch in the Gut

1. Rodger Kamenetz, *The Jew in the Lotus* (San Francisco: HarperSanFrancisco, 1994), 196.

2. Mark Epstein, *Thoughts Without a Thinker: Psychotherapy from a Buddhist Perspective* (New York: Basic Books, 1995), 135.

3. James Hillman, *Insearch: Psychology and Religion* (Dallas: Spring Books, 1994), 125.

4. G. William Domhoff, "The Purpose of Dreams," http://psych.ucsc.edu/dreams/Library/purpose.html.

Chapter 9: The Book of K de G

1. Avivah Zornberg, *Genesis: The Beginning of Desire* (Philadelphia: Jewish Publication Society, 1995).

2. "In the ages of crude primeval culture man believed that in dreams he got to know another real world; here is the origin of all metaphysics. Without the dream one would have found no occasion for a division of the world." Friedrich Nietzsche, *The Portable Nietzsche*, ed. Walter Kaufmann (New York: Viking Press, 1954), 52.

Chapter 10: You Are a Dead Man

1. Electronic Text Corpus of Sumerian Literature (ETCSL), http://www-etcsl.orient.ox.ac.uk/section1/tr143.htm.

2. Curtiss Hoffman, "Dumuzi's Dream: Dream Analysis in Ancient Mesopotamia," *Dreaming: Journal of the Association for the Study of Dream* 14, no. 4 (December 2004): 240–51.

3. I explored these dreams in *Terra Infirma: A Memoir of My Mother's Life in Mine* (New York: Schocken Books, 1999).

Chapter 11: Jacob, the Hero of the Revelation Dream

1. Sigmund Freud, *The Interpretation of Dreams* (New York: Avon Books, 1965), 660.

2. Midrash Rabbah Genesis 70:3.

3. Kalonymus Kalman Shapira, *Conscious Community: A Guide to Inner Work* (Northvale, NJ: Jason Aronson, 1996), 25.

4. Shapira, *Conscious Community*, 25.

5. Shapira, *Conscious Community*, 17–18.

Chapter 12: Joseph the Dreamer and Joseph the Interpreter

1. "His father rebuked him, and said to him, What is this dream that you have dreamed? Shall I and your mother and your brothers indeed come to bow down ourselves to you to the earth?

"And his brothers envied him; but his father kept the matter in mind." Gen. 37:10–11.

2. "AND JOSEPH DREAMED A DREAM, AND HE TOLD IT TO HIS BRETHREN. AND THEY HATED HIM THE MORE FOR HIS DREAMS. From this we learn that a man should not tell his dream save to a friend, otherwise the listener may pervert the significance of the dream and cause delay in its fulfilment. Joseph communicated his dream to his brethren, and they caused its fulfilment to be delayed for twenty-two years. Thus we find it written: AND HE SAID UNTO THEM, HEAR, I PRAY YOU, THIS DREAM WHICH I HAVE DREAMED. We see here how he begged his brethren to listen to him, and insisted on telling them his dream, which, had they given it another meaning, would have been fulfilled accordingly. But they said to him: 'Shalt thou indeed reign over us? or shalt thou have dominion over us?' and with these words they sealed their own doom." Soncino Zohar, Bereshith, sec. 1, 183b.

3. Midrash Lamentations 1:18; Berachot 55b.

4. Soncino Zohar, Bereshith, sec. 1, 199b.

Chapter 13: The Untimely Disappearance of the Dream

1. Very technically, ten dreams (*chalom*) and one "vision of the night." The count: Abimelech, one; Jacob, three; Laban, one; Joseph, two; baker, one; cupbearer, one; Pharaoh, two. It's worth noting that Maimonides does not agree with this count. He states that all the prophecies in the Torah come through dreams or visions, except for Moses'. (See *The Guide of the Perplexed*, vol. 2, chaps. 41 and 42.)

2. Daniel dreams, but this late figure is not counted among the true Hebrew prophets.

3. "Raba said: All that Ezekiel saw Isaiah saw. What does Ezekiel resemble? A villager who saw the king. And what does Isaiah resemble? A townsman who saw the king." Mas. Chagigah 13b.

Raba explains that Ezekiel went into great elaborate detail because he wasn't accustomed to seeing the King; whereas Isaiah's vision is terse and matter of fact because he's like a city sophisticate who sees the King most every day.

Chapter 14: The Rabbis Ameliorate the Dream

1. "The Lord stood above [the ladder], and said, I am the Lord God of Abraham your father, and the God of Isaac; the land on which you lie, to you will I give it, and to your seed;

"Your seed shall be as the dust of the earth, and you shall spread abroad to the west, and to the east, and to the north, and to the south; and in you and in your seed shall all the families of the earth be blessed. Behold, I am with you, and will keep you in all places where you go, and will bring you back to this land; for I will not leave you, until I have done that about which I have spoken to you" (Gen. 28: 13–15).

2. Babylonian Talmud Berachot 55a.

3. Babylonian Talmud Berachot 55a.

4. Babylonian Talmud Berachot 55b.

5. For instance, Rabbi Samuel B. Nahmani follows Freud when he says, "A man is shown in a dream only what is suggested by his own thoughts." Babylonian Talmud Berachot 55b.

6. Midrash Lamentations 1:18. Eleazar cites Gen. 41:13.

7. Babylonian Talmud Berachot 56b.

8. Ibid, 55b.

9. Certain of the rabbis seem aware of this, for they note that a bad dream comes to good people and a good dream to bad. "R. Huna said: A good man is not shown a good dream, and a bad man is not shown a bad dream." Berachot 55b.

10. "Just as wheat cannot be without straw, so there cannot be a dream without some nonsense." Berachot 55a.

11. He is sometimes referred to as "Rava." The name "Raba" is an abbreviation of Rabbi Abba. His full name was Rabbi Abba ben Joseph ben Hama. He lived in Mahoza in Babylonia.

12. Chaim Potok gives a sense of Raba's enduring influence:

"I remember the hours I used to spend as a child marveling at Abbaye and Rava, the agility of their minds, the nimble way they responded to insuperable problems of law, contradictions between various texts of a Mishnah, conflicting traditions attributed to the same individual. 'Abbaye said . . . Rava said . . . Abbaye said . . . Rava said . . .': How many thousands of times I must have spoken those words during my years in the yeshivas I attended." Chaim Potok, *Wanderings: Chaim Potok's History of the Jews* (New York: Fawcett Books, 1983), 238.

13. Chagigah 5b.

Chapter 15: Peter Sees a Dream, and Jews and Christians Part Ways

1. See chap. 13, p. 99–100.

2. B. Bat. Metz. 59d, as retold by Howard Schwartz in *Reimagining the Bible: The Storytelling of the Rabbis* (New York: Oxford Univ. Press, 1998), 32.

3. See Peter Schafer, "New Testament and Hekhalot Literature: The Journey into Heaven in Paul and in Merkavah Mysticism," *Journal of Jewish Studies* 35 (1984): 19–35. See also Moshe Idel, *Kabbalah: New Perspectives* (New Haven, CT: Yale Univ. Press, 1990), 74–96.

Chapter 16: The Gnostic Heresy and the Mystical Dream Journey

1. This recalls the story in Numbers 12 where both the dream and Miriam are "demoted." Mary Magdalene and Miriam are female authorities whose source of spiritual authority is the imaginal. Cf. chap. 13, p. 99–100.

2. Elaine Pagels, *The Gnostic Gospels* (New York: Random House, 1979), 9.

3. Pagels, *The Gnostic Gospels,* 11.

4. Tertullian *De anima* 42.7, cited in Patricia Cox Miller, *Dreams in Late Antiquity: Studies in the Imagination of a Culture* (Princeton, NJ: Princeton Univ. Press, 1994), 67.

5. Augustine *De Genesi ad Litteram* 12.13.28, cited in Steven Kruger, *Dreaming in the Middle Ages* (Cambridge: Cambridge Univ. Press, 1992), 49.

6. Covitz, *Visions of the Night,* 57–58. The rabbi is citing Raba, Berachot 55b.

7. Kruger, *Dreaming in the Middle Ages,* 51–52.

8. Pagels, *The Gnostic Gospels,* 21.

9. Jean-Claude Schmitt, "The Liminality and Centrality of Dreams in the Medieval West," in *Dream Cultures: Explorations in the Comparative History of Dreaming,* ed. David Shulman and Guy G. Stroumsa (New York: Oxford Univ. Press, 1999), 279.

10. Gershom Scholem, *Origins of the Kabbalah* (Princeton, NJ: Princeton Univ. Press, 1991), 17.

11. Scholem, *Origins of the Kabbalah,* 21.

12. Zohar Bereshith 1:183.

13. Elliot Wolfson's *Through a Speculum That Shines: Vision and Imagination in Medieval Jewish Mysticism* (Princeton, NJ: Princeton Univ. Press, 1997) is a very important study of this idea and the role of vision and image in Judaism.

14. Daniel Matt is a scholar producing a new translation into English of the Zohar, a monumental undertaking. So far three volumes have been published by Stanford University Press in the Pritzker Zohar series.

15. David Bakan, *Sigmund Freud and the Jewish Mystical Tradition* (Princeton, NJ: D. Van Nostrand Company, 1958).

Chapter 17: Sigmund and Irma

1. Freud to Fliess, June 12, 1900, in Freud, *The Interpretation of Dreams,* 154n1.

2. Freud to Fliess, August 6, 1899, in Freud, *The Interpretation of Dreams,* 155.

3. Freud, *The Interpretation of Dreams,* 155n.

4. Freud, *The Interpretation of Dreams,* 155.

5. Freud, *The Interpretation of Dreams,* 138.

6. Freud, *The Interpretation of Dreams,* 139–40.

7. The notion that manifest dream content is bizarre and therefore needs explication is a premise of his theory and later theories, such as Hobson's. As Domhoff points out, based on evidence, most dreams are not in fact bizarre or inexplicable in content. Domhoff's succinct summary of the refutation of Freud's theories can be found in Domhoff, "Moving Dream Theory Beyond Freud and Jung." See http://psych.ucsc.edu/dreams/Library/domhoff_2000d.html.

8. Freud, *The Interpretation of Dreams,* 140.

9. Susan Sontag, *Against Interpretation and Other Essays* (New York: Picador, 2001), 6. Sontag clarifies that she does not mean "interpretation in the broadest sense, the sense in which Nietzsche (rightly) says, 'there are no facts only interpretations.' By interpretation, I mean here a conscious act of the mind which illustrates a certain code, certain 'rules' of interpretation" (5). She specifically critiques Freud (and Marx's) "aggressive and impious theories of interpretation" (7).

10. Rosemarie Sand, "Manifestly Fallacious," in *Unauthorized Freud: Doubters Confront a Legend,* ed. Frederick C. Crews (New York: Viking, 1998), 87.

11. The rabbis evidently believed the same, and used it to good advantage. "King Shapor [I] once said to Samuel: You [Jews] profess to be very clever. Tell me what I shall see in my dream. He said to him: You will see the Romans coming and taking you captive and making you grind date-stones in a golden mill. He thought about it the whole day and in the night saw it in a dream." Berachot 56a.

12. Freud, *The Interpretation of Dreams,* 197. Domhoff notes the research that contradicts this premise. See note chap. 7, note 9.

13. Freud, *The Interpretation of Dreams,* 660.

14. Ken Frieden, *Freud's Dream of Interpretation* (Albany: State Univ. of New York Press, 1990), 73–74. Frieden writes, "Rabbinic voices in the Talmud and Midrash anticipate several aspects of Freud's work on dreams. First in their underlying assumptions: rabbinic tradition emphasizes the importance and complexity of interpretation. Second in their skepticism: rabbis occasionally express disbelief and antagonism towards dream interpreters who claim to make prophetic pronouncements. Third, in their techniques: rabbinic commentators frequently arrive at their results by resorting to puns and verbal associations. Finally in their content: some rabbis insinuate the sexual significance of dreams. Such resonances do not however imply a direct influence on Freud who labored incessantly to avoid coming to terms with his precursors" (74).

15. Freud, *The Interpretation of Dreams*, 136.

16. Freud, *The Interpretation of Dreams*, 141.

17. Freud, *The Interpretation of Dreams*, 154.

Chapter 18: The Two Belly Buttons

1. Freud, *The Interpretation of Dreams*, 143n2.

2. Freud, *The Interpretation of Dreams*, 564.

3. Freud, *The Interpretation of Dreams*, 143n1.

4. Again, certain of the rabbis understood this and said that a bad man would receive good dreams and a good man bad; however, others, like Samuel, chose rather to dismiss the bad dreams and mind only the good.

5. Freud, *The Interpretation of Dreams*, 141.

6. Harold Bloom compares him to Montaigne; both delight in the ironic confession.

7. Freud, *The Interpretation of Dreams*, 301.

8. Freud, *The Interpretation of Dreams*, 658–59.

9. See the discussion in chap. 29, p. 216ff, and in C. G. Jung, *Mysterium Coniunctionis: An Inquiry into the Separation and Synthesis of Psychic Opposites in Alchemy*, Bollingen Series 20 (Princeton, NJ: Princeton Univ. Press, 1963), 529ff.

10. Freud, *The Interpretation of Dreams*, 301. Again, as Domhoff and others argue, the regularity of dreams in the sleep cycle argues against Freud's premise. See Domhoff, "Moving Dream Theory Beyond Freud and Jung."

11. C. G. Jung, *Memories, Dreams, Reflections* (New York: Vintage Books, 1989), 161–62.

12. Sand, "Manifestly Fallacious," 92.

13. Freud, *The Interpretation of Dreams*, 129, 369, 522n.

Chapter 19: Blind Spots Removed While You Wait, and the Book of K de G Speaks

1. Frederick Perls, *Gestalt Therapy Verbatim* (Lafayette, CA: Real People Press, 1969), 66–67.

Chapter 20: How Dreams Abolish Time, and the Secret of K de G at Last

1. B.T. Mo'ed Qatan 28a.

Chapter 24: The Opposition: Freud's Staircase Dream

1. Freud, *The Interpretation of Dreams*, 272.

2. James Hillman, *Re-Visioning Psychology* (New York: Harper Perennial, 1992), 71. Hillman writes, "Discovery of the unconscious has meant the widespread and overwhelming recognition of the psyche's autonomous activity of pathologizing. That discovery and that recognition have led to one even more significant: the rediscovery of soul. . . . Out of *psyché-pathos-logos* came the meaning of the suffering of the soul, or the soul's suffering of meaning" (71).

Chapter 25: The Orphanage Dream

1. Freud, *The Interpretation of Dreams*, 477–78. I use here the translation by A. A. Brill (1911).

Chapter 26: Becoming the Boy

1. Freud's interpretation of dreams of nakedness goes in an entirely different direction. The dreamer's wish is to expose himself or herself; the lack of reaction of other characters in the dream expresses the wish that the dreamer could expose himself to another without being censured. Freud makes the dreamer guilty of a forbidden wish. See *The Interpretation of Dreams*, 275–80. "Dreams of being naked are dreams of exhibiting" (278).

Chapter 29: Jung's Descent into the World of Dreams

1. Jung, *Memories, Dreams, Reflections*, 151.

2. Jung, *Memories, Dreams, Reflections*, 151.

3. Jung, *Memories, Dreams, Reflections*, 169.

4. Jung, *Memories, Dreams, Reflections,* 158–60.

5. Jung to Freud, April 17, 1910, in Richard Noll, *The Jung Cult: Origins of a Charismatic Movement* (Princeton, NJ: Princeton Univ. Press, 1994), 189.

6. Peter Gay, *Freud: A Life for Our Time* (New York: W. W. Norton. 1988), 237.

7. Jung, *Memories, Dreams, Reflections,* 170.

8. Jung, *Memories, Dreams, Reflections,* 170.

9. See Noll, *The Jung Cult,* 209.

10. Jung, *Memories, Dreams, Reflections,* 173.

11. Jung, *Memories, Dreams, Reflections,* 174.

12. Jung, *Memories, Dreams, Reflections,* 181.

13. Jung, *Memories, Dreams, Reflections,* 183.

14. Jung, *Memories, Dreams, Reflections,* 199.

15. Jung, *Mysterium Coniunctionis,* 529.

16. Jung, *Mysterium Coniunctionis,* 530.

17. Jung, *Mysterium Coniunctionis,* 530–31.

18. Jung, *Mysterium Coniunctionis,* 531. The phrase "Treasure hard to attain" is used by Jung to signify the goal of individuation.

19. Jung, *Mysterium Coniunctionis,* 391.

20. C. G. Jung, *The Essential Jung: Selected Writings,* ed. Anthony Storr (Princeton, NJ: Princeton Univ. Press, 1983), 267.

Chapter 31: Return of the Orphanage Dream

1. Arthur Green writes, "In his earlier days Nachman had felt that what man needed was liberation from fantasy. In the tales, and in . . . his last public discourse, Nachman began to propose a liberation within fantasy: the imagination itself had to be purified so that it could become a vehicle that would lead man back to God." Green, *Tormented Master,* 342.

Nachman believed that "[a]s prophecy spreads forth, the imaginative faculty is purified and restored."

Chapter 32: North of Eden

1. *Pentateuch with Targum Onkelos, Hapthtaroth and Rashi's Commentary: Genesis,* trans. M. Rosenbaum and A. M. Silbermann (Jerusalem: Silbermann Family/Routledge & Kegan Paul, 5733 [Jewish calendar year]), 7.

2. Mishnah Sanhedrin 4:5.

3. Psychologist Sanford Drob argues that "Jung, in the last decades of his life, had taken a deep interest in the psychological aspects of a number of Kabbalistic symbols and ideas; ideas which he had been exposed to primarily through his reading of 16th and 17th century alchemical texts, and, especially, through the writings of the Christian Kabbalist and alchemist, Christian Knorr Von Rosenroth (1636–89). As a result, Jung's last great work, *Mysterium Coniunctionis,* completed in his 80th year in 1954, though ostensibly a treatise on alchemy, is filled with discussions of such Kabbalistic symbols as Adam Kadmon (Primordial Man), the Sefirot, and the union of the 'Holy One' and his bride. These symbols became important pivots around which Jung constructed his final interpretations of such notions as the archetypes and the collective unconscious, and his theory of the ultimate psychological purpose of humankind." Sanford Drob, "Jung and Kabbalah," *History of Psychology* 2, no. 2 (May 1999): 102–18. The paper is available online at http://www.newkabbalah.com/index3.html.

4. See the discussion of the *partzufim* in Aryeh Kaplan, *Innerspace: Introduction to Kabbalah, Meditation and Prophecy* (Jerusalem: Moznaim, 1990), 92–109. Kaplan writes: "The terms used for the Partzufim are found in three of the most opaque books of the Zohar. . . . It is here as well that the Partzufim are spoken of as constituting a kind of archetypal family matrix, Arikh Anpin is the grandfather, Abba and Ima are the father and mother, and Zer Anpin and Nukva are the children. . . . These partzufim constantly interact with each other in an anthropomorphic manner, combining and separating, expanding and diminishing. . . . In particular, the twin Partzufim Zer Anpin [the son] and Nukva [the daughter] are represented in various states of gestation, birth, nursing and finally maturity depending

on their capacity to transmit Divine sustenance to the universes that lie below them. Ultimately the Sefirot and Partzufim represent different aspects of God's relationship with man and creation. Since this relationship is a dynamic one, it is best described in anthropomorphic terms which allow us to relate to God in a very human way. The truth is, however, that these anthropomorphisms are in no way meant to refer to God himself" (93).

5. For a discussion, see Kaplan, *Inner Space*, 94. Kaplan refers to Rashi's interpretation, "God made man with his image": "Rashi's understanding of this verse points to this conclusion. Since God cannot be described in terms of any image, 'His' has the function of a possessive adjective and the verse is referring to an image God created. If you understand this Rashi correctly, he is saying that the *Tzelem*-Image is the blueprint or the prototype that God created, according to which He made man" (94).

Kaplan goes on to explain that this prototype (or archetype) is the *partzuf* Zer Anpin, also known as the "son." In Bregman's terms, the animus. And further, this archetype of creation requires a partner—none other than Malchut, also known as "the daughter"—to bring creation to completion.

Kaplan writes, "Specifically the Tzelem-Image of Zer Anpin was used in the creation of man." However, the "son" does not act alone but works "with a mirror-image feedback mechanism"—namely, "the daughter." This male-female pair together constitute the working "Image" with which the human being is created. Their relationship is imagined in various combinations—brother-sister, husband-wife—depending on the situation. Thus man is created in God's image; "Male and Female created he Them" has the meaning of referring to this twinned male-female combination of *partzufim* that together form the spiritual blueprint of the complete human being.

In his paper "The Lurianic Kabbalah: An Archetypal Interpretation," psychologist Sanford L. Drob outlines the correlations between Luria's system and Jung's. The paper is available online at http://www.newkabbalah.com/index3.html. Drob develops his ideas more completely in two books: *Kabbalistic Metaphors: Jewish Mystical Themes in Ancient and Modern Thought* (Northvale, NJ: Jason Aronson, 2000) and *Symbols of the Kabbalah: Philosophical and Psychological Perspectives* (Northvale, NJ: Jason Aronson, 2000).

6. Or so I remembered them. See Walt Whitman, *Leaves of Grass: The First (1855) Edition* (New York: Penguin Books, 2005), 10–11. The full and correct quote is: "The land and sea, the animals fishes and birds, the sky of heaven and the orbs, the forests mountains and rivers, are not small themes . . . but folks expect of the poet to indicate more than the beauty and dignity which always attach to dumb real objects . . . they expect him to indicate the path between reality and their souls." The whole statement is remarkably resonant with my dream, or vice versa.

A Brief Annotated Bibliography

Marc Bregman and North of Eden

The Deep Well Tapes, by Marc Bregman with Sue Scavo and Ellen Keene, is available. To order a copy, contact North of Eden at info@northofeden.com. The book provides a detailed and comprehensive introduction to Bregman's approach to working with dreams.

The Web site for North of Eden is http://www.northofeden.com/. The site features ongoing theoretical work by Bregman and poems, stories, and accounts of the dream work. For those interested in doing the dream work with trained teachers, contact information can also be found on the site.

Colette Aboulker-Muscat

Works by Colette Aboulker-Muscat

Alone with the One. New York: ACMI Press, 1995. Colette's poetry collection.

Mea Culpa: Tales of Resurrection. New York: ACMI Press, 1997. Fascinating stories of how Colette used imagery to heal the mind and soul.

Works about Colette Aboulker-Muscat

Amipaz-Silber, Gitta. *The Role of the Jewish Underground in the American Landing in Algiers, 1940–1942.* Woodmere NY: Gefen Books, 1992. An account of the heroic role of Colette's family in the liberation of Algiers.

Works by others based on Colette Aboulker-Muscat's healing visualization teachings

Epstein, Gerald. *Healing into Immortality: A New Spiritual Medicine of Healing Stories and Imagery.* New York: Bantam Books, 1994.

———. *Healing Visualizations: Creating Health Through Imagery.* New York: Bantam Books, 1989. Includes many specific visualizations for various medical conditions.

———. *Waking Dream Therapy: Unlocking the Secrets of Self Through Dreams and Imagination.* New York: ACMI Press, 1992.

Shainberg, Catherine. *Kabbalah and the Power of Dreaming: Awakening the Visionary Life.* Rochester, VT: Inner Traditions, 2005. Guides the reader through the possibility of inner growth through dream work; it opens with an account of how the author met and worked with Colette.

Web sites about Colette Aboulker-Muscat and Healing Visualizations

http://www.geocities.com/colette_aboulker_muscat/. Images, voice, and memories of Colette.
http://www.schoolofimages.com/ (Catherine Shainberg).
http://www.drjerryepstein.org/ (Gerald Epstein).

Robert Desoille

Bachelard, Gaston. *Air and Dreams.* Dallas: Dallas Institute Publications, Dallas Institute of Humanities and Culture, 1988. The philosopher of imagery touches on the significance of Desoille's work.

Desoille, Robert. *Entretiens sur le rêve éveillé dirigé en psychothérapie.* Paris: Payot, 1973.

Tarab Tulku and Tibetan Dream Yoga

The official Web site for information about the late Tarab Tulku's work, including conferences, courses, and publications, is http://www.tarab-institute.org/.

H.H. The Dalai Lama. *Sleeping, Dreaming, and Dying: An Exploration of Consciousness with the Dalai Lama.* Boston: Wisdom Publications, 1997. Narrated and edited by Francisco Varela, this account of the fourth Mind and Life conference of 1992 gives the Dalai Lama's response to Freud and Jung.

Rinpoche, Tenzin Wangyal. *The Tibetan Yogas of Dream and Sleep.* Ithaca, NY: Snow Lion Publications, 1998. A very lucid and helpful account of the Tibetan system of dream yoga, by a lama who lives and teaches in Charlottesville, Virginia. His organization's Web site is http://www.ligmincha.org/.

Young, Serenity. *Dreaming in the Lotus: Buddhist Dream Narrative, Imagery and Practice.* Somerville, MA: Wisdom Publications, 1999. The role of dreams in the religions of India and Tibet. The title has a real ring to it.

International Association for the Study of Dreams

The Web site of the International Association for the Study of Dreams (IASD) is http://www.asdreams.org/.

The IASD publishes two journals, *Dreaming* and *Dream Time,* and holds annual conferences.

The History of Dreams and Interpretation

Gnuse, Robert. *Dreams and Dream Reports in the Writings of Josephus : A Traditio-Historical Analysis.* Leiden, New York, and Cologne: Brill, 1996. As preparation for an analysis of dreams in Josephus, the book offers a careful and concise account of dreams in the ancient world, including the Near East, the biblical tradition, Greece, and Rome.

Kruger, Steven. *Dreaming in the Middle Ages.* Cambridge: Cambridge Univ. Press, 1992. The focus here is on the Church Fathers and later medieval dream stories and theories from the fourth to twelfth century.

Miller, Patricia. *Dreams in Late Antiquity: Studies in the Imagination of a Culture.* Princeton, NJ: Princeton Univ. Press, 1994. Miller provides a history of early Christian dream interpretation and its classical background, as well as analysis of several dream texts from late antiquity.

Shulman, David, and Guy Stroumsa, eds. *Dream Cultures: Explorations in the Comparative History of Dreaming.* New York: Oxford Univ. Press, 1999. A comparative cross-cultural history of dreams, from China and India to the West, and from ancient to modern times.

Dreams and Jewish Mysticism

Covitz, Joel. *Visions of the Night: A Study of Jewish Dream Interpretation.* Boston: Shambhala, 1990. An abridged translation and study of Almoli's *The Interpretation of Dreams* by a Jungian therapist and rabbi.

Green, Arthur. *Tormented Master: The Life and Spiritual Quest of Rabbi Nachman of Bratslav.* Woodstock, VT: Jewish Lights, 1992. A landmark psychological biography of the great Hasidic master. Green includes accounts of several of Rabbi Nachman's significant dreams.

Jacobs, Louis, ed. *The Schocken Book of Jewish Mystical Testimonies*. New York : Schocken Books, 1997. An anthology of source material, from Ezekiel's vision and the chariot riders to the account of the Baal Shem Tov's mystical ascent.

Jewish Mystical Autobiographies: Book of Visions and Book of Secrets. Translated by Morris Faierstein. New York: Paulist Press, 1999. The dream accounts of the kabbalist Hayim Vital and the Hasidic master Rabbi Isaac Safrin of Komarno.

Kaplan, Aryeh. *Innerspace: Introduction to Kabbalah, Meditation and Prophecy*. Jerusalem: Moznaim, 1990. The best concise introduction to kabbalah by an acknowledged nonscholarly authority.

Wolfson, Elliot. *Through a Speculum That Shines: Vision and Imagination in Medieval Jewish Mysticism*. Princeton, NJ: Princeton Univ. Press, 1997. A very important study of vision and image in Judaism, focused primarily on Jewish texts from late antiquity to thirteenth-century kabbalistic literature.

The Merkabah, Gnosticism, and the Kabbalah

Idel, Moshe. *Kabbalah: New Perspectives*. New Haven, CT: Yale Univ. Press, 1990. An authoritative critique and extension of Scholem's work on Jewish mysticism.

Pagels, Elaine. *The Gnostic Gospels*. New York: Random House, 1979. A readable and influential account of Gnosticism by a respected scholar.

Schafer, Peter. "New Testament and Hekhalot Literature: The Journey into Heaven in Paul and in Merkavah Mysticism." *Journal of Jewish Studies* 35 (1984): 19–35.

Scholem, Gershom. *Major Trends in Jewish Mysticism*. 3d rev. ed. New York: Schocken Books, 1961. A magisterial history of Jewish mysticism, from the chariot riders to Hasidism.

Sigmund Freud

Bakan, David. *Sigmund Freud and the Jewish Mystical Tradition*. Princeton, NJ: D. Van Nostrand Company, 1958. An attempt to link Freud to kabbalah and Jewish mysticism.

Freud, Sigmund. *The Interpretation of Dreams*. New York: Avon Books, 1965. The most important twentieth-century book on dreams.

Frieden, Ken. *Freud's Dream of Interpretation*. Albany: State Univ. of New York Press, 1990. Uncovers Freud's hidden debt to the rabbinic sages.

Carl Jung

Jung, C. G. *The Essential Jung: Selected Writings*. Edited by Anthony Storr. Princeton, NJ: Princeton Univ. Press, 1983. A usable sampling of Jung's major ideas and concerns.

———. *Memories, Dreams, Reflections*. New York: Vintage Books, 1989. Jung's late-in-life reflections include an account of his break with Freud and his first ventures into the imaginal world.

———. *Mysterium Coniunctionis: An Inquiry into the Separation and Synthesis of Psychic Opposites in Alchemy*. Bollingen Series 20. Princeton, NJ: Princeton Univ. Press, 1963. Jung's last major theoretical work focuses on alchemy and returns to the spirit of his earliest imaginal explorations.

James Hillman

Hillman, James. *The Dream and the Underworld*. New York: Harper & Row, 1979. In his reliably brilliant and erudite fashion, Hillman demonstrates the importance and reality of dreams.

———. *Insearch: Psychology and Religion*. Dallas: Spring Books, 1994. Though he has nearly repudiated the ideas in this book, Hillman here makes a strong case for the imagination as the locus of religious experience.

———. *Re-Visioning Psychology*. New York: Harper Perennial, 1992. In his 1972 series of Terry Lectures at Yale University, Hillman brought psychology back to soul.

Frederick Perls

Perls, Frederick. *Gestalt Therapy Verbatim*. Lafayette, CA: Real People Press, 1969. Live-action transcriptions of Perls doing gestalt therapy.

Dreams and Science

Crick, F., and G. Mitchison. "The Function of Dream Sleep." *Nature* 304 (1983): 111. A brief paper that outlines Crick's contention that dreams are better off forgotten.

Domhoff, G. W. "Moving Dream Theory Beyond Freud and Jung." Paper presented at the symposium "Beyond Freud and Jung?" Graduate Theological Union, Berkeley, CA, September 23, 2000. http://psych.ucsc.edu/dreams/Library/domhoff_2000d.html. A very helpful summary of scientific evidence that refutes basic ideas of Freud and Jung.

———. *The Mystique of Dreams: A Search for Utopia Through Senoi Dream Theory*. Berkeley: Univ. of California Press, 1985. A debunking of a persistent New Age myth.

Hobson, J. Allan. *The Dreaming Brain: How the Brain Creates Both the Sense and the Nonsense of Dreams*. New York: Basic Books, 1989. An MIT researcher's theory of the brain mechanisms behind dreams.

Lippmann, Paul. "The Canary in the Mind." Pts. 1 and 2. *Dream Time* 20 (Summer 2003): 4–7; (Winter 2003): 4–7, 41. A presentation at the 2003 International Association for the Study of Dreams conference. Details the current relationship between psychoanalysis and the dream.

Index

Page references followed by *fig* indicate an illustration.

Aaron, 99
Abimelech's dream, 83, 84, 85, 134, 137, 160
Aboulker, Henri, 30, 45
Aboulker, José, 30
Aboulker-Muscat, Colette. *See* Colette
Abraham's story, 83, 98, 234n.57
activation-synthesis theory of dreams, 55
active imagination technique, 214
Adlerstein, Rav Yitzhok, 105–6
aesthetic attitude, 216
aesthetic vs. judgment approach (Jung), 134, 216–18, 220–22
Air and Dreams (Bachelard), 31–32
Akiba, 19
Albert, Lou, 67
Albom, Mitch, 15
Almoli, Rabbi Shlomo, 53, 79, 122, 123
Alone with the One (Aboulker-Muscat), 28, 47
amelioration, 58, 111, 112, 113, 139, 142, 143, 152, 161, 164, 213, 220. See also *hatavat chalom*
amplification, 105–7, 133, 135, 136–37, 146, 160, 209, 213
angels: in Jacob's gate of heaven dream, 24–25; as THEY, 77; visualization and images of, 19, 22, 23
anima, 215, 218–19, 226, 227, 231, 233, 236–37
animus: Bregman on learning from the, 224, 231–33; encountered in orphanage dream, 226; the father compared to, 227–29; of VIP dreams, 218
archetypal dreams, 185, 213. *See also* VIP dream characters
archetypes: gnosis knowing through, 227; "image" as, 235; "the Self," 218–19; "the Shadow," 214, 218; as the third gift of dreams, 230
Aristotle, 7
Artemidorus, 122, 123
Association for the Study of Dreams (ASD) conference, 54, 57–58
authority: Christian lineage of, 109–13; Gnostic Christians on, 114–15; Jewish lineage of, 109, 111–12; papal, 114

Babylonian Talmud "Blessings," 103–4
Bachelard, Gaston, 31–32, 39, 241n.16, 248n.5, 256n.4
baker's dream, 94, 97
Baal Shem Tov, 21, 109, 120
Bana'ah, 103
becoming the boy dreams, 189–97
blind spots: described, 144; gestalt therapy for getting past, 144–45; *K de G* dream, 145–47
Bogomils, 117
The Book of Dreams and Visions, 52
Bregman, Marc: arriving at home of, 68–69; on children appearing in dreams, 184, 193; comparing Jung's approach with, 217–18; dream facilitation approach taken by, 13, 70–72, 85, 90, 92; on dreams cast by the divine, 83; on emotions and feelings as dream signposts, 143–44, 186–87; Freud's dream interpretation using approach of, 129–38; introduction to, 4–5, 6, 67; on learning from the animus, 224, 231–33; "meat and potatoes" spirituality of, 222–23; on overcoming fears to interpret dreams, 208–9; on pathology of dream opposition, 172, 177–78, 218; personal background of, 12, 60, 211, 220–22; as teacher of dreams, 4; teaching approach taken by, 69; THEY questions asked by, 76, 77, 78–79; on tracing dreams, 132; on understanding VIP dreams, 205, 206–7; unlocking *K de G* dream secret with, 151–53
Buber, Martin, 120–21, 233–34
Buddhism: Dalai Lama on visualization and, 28; on reality as open space, 17; Tibetan, 17, 30, 34, 38, 203
butler's dream, 94, 97, 137
Byzantine Church, 9

Cathars, 117–18
Charlemagne, 117
chashmal (electrum or amber), 100
children: becoming the boy dreams on, 189–97; Bregman's identification of soul with, 193;

children (*continued*)
  dream meaning of, 184; Freudian approach to
  dream, 185–87; separation from dream, 188
Chiten, Laurel, 16, 17, 21–23, 25–26
Christian images, 39
Christianity: Gnostic, 114–21; Jewish origins
  of, 110; on sources of dreams, 117; split
  from Jewish tradition by, 110–13; tracing the
  authority in, 109–13
Chuang Tzu, 78
Church Fathers. *See* Christianity
circumcision, 110
Colette: *Alone with the One* by, 28, 46; connections between kabbalah and work of, 48–49;
  on freedom through choosing one's images,
  38–40; introduction to, 3–4, 14; *morphologie*
  or *physiognomie* teachings of, 43; personality and family background of, 27–30, 42–43;
  "petits chocs" (little shocks) technique used by,
  42–47; rejection of "spirituality" term by, 28,
  29, 47; on "reversing" trauma, 149; on secret
  of Jewish spiritual survival, 37–38; *stratégie*
  approach used by, 45–46; teaching approach of,
  69; teaching to overcome word-image struggle,
  9; visualization teaching of, 18, 21, 23–24, 26,
  30–36, 45–49, 230; walking dream work by, 47
conceptual mind, 38
Conscious Community (Shapira), 89
cop bicycle dream, 206–7
Corbin, Henry, 34
Cornelius's dream, 111
Covitz, Joel, 53, 79, 85, 94, 115–16
Crick, Sir Francis, 57, 83, 85, 104

Dalai Lama, 28, 37
David's dream, 6–8, 50, 84, 187, 191
Dement, William, 54–55, 59
DeMille, Cecil B., 8
Desoille, Robert, 31, 32, 39, 43
Deuteronomy: animosity to prophet-dreamers
  in, 99–100;
on God's anger, 10; on recitation of prayer, 40
"directed waking dream" (*rêve évellée dirigé*), 31
discernio (or discernment), 116
DLPFC (dorsal-lateral prefrontal cortex), 55
Domhoff, William, 57–59, 70, 127, 243nn.30,
  35, 39, 244n.94, 245n.99, 248n.7, 251nn.7, 10,
  252n.10, 253
dreamers: amplification practice by, 213; death
  promised to, 99; Freud's assumptions about,
  127; Joseph as interpreter and, 92–97; North
  of Eden (NOE) community of, 231–33
dream, gifts of, 3, 13, 82, 93, 96, 136–38, 157–65,
  170, 172, 177, 181, 184, 208–9, 231; dream
  journey, 53, 82, 233; dream journey and

Zohar, 119; essential image or situation of
  the soul—orphanage dream, 225; essential image or situation of the soul (see also
  Joesph's dream of the sheaf), 82, 93, 96, 137,
  230; warning dream or predicament (see also
  Abimelech's dream) and Freud, 132, 134. *See*
  also Jacob's ladder dream
The Dreaming Brain (Hobson), 55
dream interpretation: direct revelation overshadowed by, 11–12; by Joseph, 92–97; Freud's
  approach to, 12, 122–28, 129–38; Gnostic
  Christianity approach to, 115–21; Jungian approach to, 12, 135, 213–18; kabbalistic Jewish
  approach to, 53; Marc Bregman's approach
  to, 13, 70–72, 85, 90, 92, 129–38; overcoming
  obstacles to learning, 4; in Roman and Greek
  world, 103; Talmud on, 51, 79, 102–7; THEY
  questions to ask during, 76, 77, 78–79
dream labyrinths, 161–65
"dream mind" functions, 38
dream/REM sleep study (1950s), 54–55
dreams: activation-synthesis theory of, 55;
  archetypal, 185, 213; caution about sharing
  your, 247n.2; distinction between waking
  vision and, 117; earliest written records on,
  11; emotions and feelings as signposts of,
  143–44, 186–87; Freud on egoistic lining
  of, 133–34; Greeks on nature of, 77; Hasidic
  take on, 51–53; images manifested by, 136;
  lost and wandering, 161–65; pauper's dream
  parable on, 90; psychoanalytical approach
  to, 57–58; reality versus, 237–39; recorded in
  Genesis, 82–85; REM sleep and process of,
  55–57; repression of, 10–11; special language
  of, 159–60; spiritual teaching-personal
  psychology gap revealed by, 64–66; Tertullian
  on nature of, 115; three gifts of, 157–60, 230;
  time abolished by, 148–53; trivializing our, 85;
  as visionary experience, 50. *See also* manifest
  dreams; visualizations
dream shaman concept, 58
dream stories: ancient near east: Dumuzi's
  dream, 11, 80–81, 84–85, 105, 208; Ziusudra's
  dream, 81
dream stories: Hebrew Bible: Genesis: Abimelech's
  dream, 83–85, 90, 93, 96, 129, 133–34, 172, 177,
  181, 231, 243n.54; Jacob's ladder dream, 11–12,
  20, 49, 51, 52, 53, 64, 85–90, 106, 121, 203,
  231; Jacob's ladder dream and Freud, 136–37;
  Jacob's ladder dream (text of dream), 243n.57;
  Joseph's sheaf dream, 93–96, 98, 139, 160,
  231; Joseph's sheaf dream as essential image,
  136–37, 209; Joseph's star dream, 94
dream stories: Hebrew Bible: Numbers, Moses,
  Miriam and Aaron, 10, 99, 106, 224n.73

dream stories: Hebrew Bible: Deuteronomy, dreamers of dreams, 99, 111
dream stories: Hebrew Bible: Isaiah, 100, 243n.56
dream stories: Hebrew Bible: Daniel, 243n.55
dream stories: Talmudic: Rabbi Eliezer's "split beam," 104, 243n.62
dream stories: New Testament: Cornelius's dream, 111; Peter's waking vision, 110–13
dream stories: Freud: fleeing children dream, 185–87; Irma dream, 123–24, 127, 129–33; staircase dream, 174–76, 217
dream stories: Jung: house dream, 212–13
dream stories: Bregman: clipboard dream, 231–32
dream stories: Kamenetz: "anima" dreams: beautiful faces, 198–201; naked poetry teacher, 201–2; book dreams, 150–51; boy dreams, cop bicycle dream, 70–72, 76, 84, 132, 152, 167, 172, 196, 206–7; dictionary lady, 180, 190, 217; gravel grandma dream, 166–73, 178, 180, 187, 206, 217; K de G dream, 73–97, 126, 145–47, 149–53; orphanage dream, 182–85, 225–29; train station dream, 70–71; VIP dreams, 198–210, 218, 224, 226, 227–29, 231–33
dream stories: clients: Olivia's "man tied up" dream, 142, 143, 145; William T's "girl on beach" dream, 140–41, 143, 145, 188
dream theories: activation-synthesis, 55; aesthetic vs. judgment, 220–22; archetypal, 185, 213, 214, 218–19, 227, 230, 235; Frederick Perls, 144, 145; Greeks, 83, 93, 109, 128; latent vs. manifest, 140–45, 188; rabbinic, 11–12, 125–26; Sigmund Freud, 12, 122–38, 169, 250n.1; Sir Francis Crick, 57, 83, 85, 104; Sumerian, 80–81; Tertullian, 11, 115
dream warnings: baker and butler's, 94, 97, 137; learning to take to heart, 153; Pharaoh's, 94–95; sent by God, 83
Dumuzi's dream, 80–82, 84, 85, 208

Eleazar, 103, 104
Eliezer, 111
Elijah, 19, 112
emotions: as dream signposts, 143–44, 186–87; fear, 196, 208–9
Enlightenment, 10
Enoch, 18–19
Epstein, Gerald, 30, 35
Epstein, Mark, 66
Exodus, 8, 99
Ezekiel, 52, 80, 100–101, 137, 243n.56, 251

father, the (archetype): 219, 227–29, 234, 237–39, 251n.4
fear: opposition through, 196; overcoming, 208–9

feelings: as dream signposts, 143–44, 186–87; fear, 196, 208–9
first gift. See opposition
Fliess, Wilhelm, 122, 123
free association, 75, 126–27
Freud, Sigmund: attitude toward women by, 131; on children appearing in dreams, 185–87; clinical model proposed by, 169; dream interpretation approach by, 12, 122–28, 129–38; on dreams of nakedness, 250n.1; dream work by, 58, 59–60, 82; on egoistic lining of dreams, 133–34; fleeing children dream, 185–87; free association technique of, 75, 126–27; "mesmerism" studied by, 43; professional relationship with Jung, 211–13, 219; repression concept of, 10–11; "specimen dream" of Irma, 123–24, 127, 129–33; staircase dream of, 174–76, 217; "the uncanny" notion of, 77. See also The Interpretation of Dreams (Freud)
Frieden, Ken, 125, 245n.101, 251
Fund, Rabbi Meir, 51

gate of heaven dream, 24–25. See also Jacob's ladder dream
Genesis 1:26, 234
Genesis: on creation of male and female in image of God, 236; on dreamers of dreams, 99; dream revelation in, 137; dream stories of, 11, 82–85, 137; on Jacob's gate of heaven dream, 24–25, 88–91; on Joseph the interpreter, 92–97; K de G book dream pointing toward, 79, 82; struggle between word and image in, 9; three gifts corresponding to three dreams in, 160
Geshtin-anna, 80, 81, 84
gestalt therapy: to get past the blind spots, 144–45; K de G book dream understood through, 145–47
Gilgamesh, 83
gnosis (knowledge), 87–88
The Gnostic Gospels (Pagels), 114
Gnostic Christianity: authority doctrine of, 114–15; on dreams and visions, 115–21
Gnosticism: Church Father's resistance to, 115–21; influencing Judaism, 118
God: David's dream about seeing, 6–8, 50, 84, 187, 191; dream warnings sent by, 83, 94–95, 97, 137, 153; face versus invisible, 237; found through the father, 227–29; hidden face of, 10, 102, 118, 120, 245n.4; ideas about, 7; male and female in image of, 236, 252n.5; the partzufim visages of, 236, 251n.4-52n.4; seeing face of, 6–9, 50; significance of losing images of, 10
Golden Calf, 8
gravel grandma dream, 166–73, 178, 180, 187, 206, 217

Greeks, 83, 93, 109, 128
Green, Arthur, 50, 52, 242nn. 23, 24, 246n.144, 250
"green leaf" exercise, 47
Gregg, Jon, 67
Gregory the Great, 116
The Guide of the Perplexed (Maimonides), 234
Guyette, Dianne, 221

Hall, Calvin, 58
Hasidic tradition, 21, 108–9, 120–21
hatavat chalom, 105. *See also* amelioration
Healing Visualizations (Epstein), 30, 35
hidden God, 10, 102, 118, 245n.4
Hildegard of Bingen, 117
Hillman, James, 12, 66, 177
Hisda, Rabbi, 103, 125
Hiyya, Rabbi, 20
Hobson, Alan, 55, 125
Hoffman, Curtiss, 81
Holocaust, 51
Homer, 83

Ilsen, Eve, 30, 38, 53
images: using "anonymous," 32; Christian, 39;
    Desoille's approach to visualizing, 31; of
    Ezekiel and Isaiah's visions, 100–101; freedom
    through choosing one's, 38–40; Golden Calf,
    8; of Jacob's dream, 88; "kitchen kabbalah"
    use of, 40–41; learning the true power of, 3;
    Maimonides on intellect as, 234; male and
    female in God's, 236, 252n.5; message of dream
    through, 136; as sovereign in the mind, 4;
    stratégie approach to creating, 45–46; as *typos*
    or archetype, 235. *See also* word-image struggle
imaginal, 32, 34, 38–39, 46–50, 90, 107, 112–15,
    120–21, 147–49, 159, 182, 202–3, 214, 216,
    230, 242n.20, 244n.73, 251
imaginal exercise, 149
Insearch: Psychology and Religion (Hillman), 66
The Interpretation of Dreams (Freud): dream
    analysis in 127, 130, 132, 249n.14; ethical sig-
    nificance issue discussed in, 134; Freud as new
    "Joseph" in, 12; Joseph's dreams discussion
    in, 137; as pioneering contribution, 122, 212;
    staircase dream discussion in, 174–76. *See also*
    Freud, Sigmund
Irenaeus, 117
Irma dream: using Bregman's approach to in-
    terpreting, 129–38; Freud's interpretation of,
    123–24, 127; Jung's approach to, 135
Isaiah, 100

Jacob's ladder dream, 24–25, 86–91, 160. *See also*
    gate of heaven dream
Jerusalem Temple, 24

The Jew in the Lotus (Kamenetz), 16, 17
Jewish dietary law, 110
Jewish mysticism: dream accounts in, 51–53; Ha-
    sidic tradition of, 21, 108–9, 120–21; history
    of, 18; on male and female faces of God, 236.
    See also Judaism; kabbalistic tradition
Joseph the dreamer: family jealousy of, 92–93;
    sharing dream with others, 247n.2; sheaf and
    star dreams of, 93–94, 136, 160; transition to
    interpreter by, 95–97
Joseph the interpreter: on baker and butler's
    dreams, 94, 97, 137; images returned to words
    by, 136–37; on Pharaoh's dream, 94–95; tran-
    sition from dreamer to, 95–97
Joseph's sheaf dream, 93, 136, 160
Joseph's star dream, 94
Judaism: Christian origins and move away from,
    110–13; dietary law of, 110; dream interpre-
    tation in context of, 102–7; Gnostic ideas
    influencing, 118; lineage of authority in, 109,
    111–12; resistance to dream material in, 53.
    See also Jewish mysticism; rabbinic sages
Jung, Carl: aesthetic vs. judgment approach of,
    134, 216–18, 220–22; comparing Bregman's
    approach with, 217–18; dream interpreta-
    tion approach by, 12, 135, 213–18; interest in
    kabbalistic symbols by, 251n.3; *Mysterium
    coniunctionis* by, 216, 235; on pathology, 177;
    professional relationship with Freud, 211–13,
    219; séances investigated by, 43; on *unio men-
    talis* to conquer "the dragon," 217–18, 227

"kabbalah" (that which is received), 20–21
kabbalistic tradition: Colette's use of, 30–31;
    connections between Collette's work and,
    48–49; on dream interpretation, 53; Gnostic
    influences on, 118; Hasidic influence on, 21,
    108–9, 120–21; Jung's interest in, 251n.3;
    kitchen, 40–41; on meditations, 21; origins of,
    120; Zohar ("Book of Splendor") of, 20, 95,
    118, 119. *See also* Jewish mysticism
Kafka, 24
Kahn, David, 55–56, 125
K de G book dream: discovering the secret mes-
    sage of, 149–53; Freudian approach applied
    to interpreting, 126; images of, 97; initial
    interpretation of, 73–79; pointing toward
    book of Genesis, 79, 82; using gestalt therapy
    to understand, 145–47
"kitchen kabbalah," 40–41
kosher food, 110

Leonardo da Vinci, 43
Library of Tibetan Works and Archives, 32
Lippmann, Paul, 59

"little shocks" (petits chocs), 42–47
lost dreams, 161–65
Luria, Rabbi Isaac, 30, 52–53, 120, 236
Lurianic kabbalah, 43, 120, 252n.5

Machir, Rabbi, 30
Maimondies, 22, 234–35, 243n.34
Major Trends in Jewish Mysticism (Scholem), 18
manifest dreams: getting past the blind spots,
   144–45; how they become revelation, 142;
   Olivia's dream as example of, 142, 143, 145;
   William T's dream as example of, 140–41, 143,
   145, 188. *See also* dreams
Mary Magdalene, 114, 115
meditation: calm produced through, 29; failings
   of Buddhist, 66; merkabah, 18–20, 31, 39;
   Tibetan Buddhism approach to, 17, 30, 34;
   tum mo (inner heat), 34
merkabah meditation, 18–20, 31, 39
Michelangelo, 39
Miguel (dream child), 183–85, 187, 188
Miriam, 99
Mishnah, 109
morphologie (or *physiognomie*) teachings, 43
Morrisville (Vermont), 67–68
Moses, 8, 19, 99–100
Moses de Leon, 119
Moussaief, Tirzah, 30
Muhammad, 9
Mysterium Coniunctionis (Jung), 216, 235
mystics: definition of, 40; merkabah, 18–20, 31,
   39; *Mystic Tales from the Zohar* (Wineman), 20

Nachman of Bratzlav, 10, 52, 120, 148, 227,
   251n.1
Nag Hammadi, 115
Nathan (Babylonian sage), 112
Nechama, 26
North of Eden (NOE) community, 231–33
North of Eden (NOE) Web site, 233
Numbers, 99–100

Olivia's dream, 142, 143, 145
Oneirocriticon (Artemidorus), 122
opposition: different manifestations of, 176–81;
   as first gift of dream, 230; force of, 157–58;
   pathology of, 172–73, 176, 177–81, 216; predicament of lost dreams and, 161–65; process
   of breaking down, 166–73; through fear, 196
Oral Torah, 109, 112
orphanage dream, 182–85, 225–29
ossification, 234

Pagels, Elaine, 114–15, 116
papal authority, 114

partzufim (visages of God), 120, 236, 251n.4-
   52n.4, 252n.5
pathology: Bregman on dream interpretation,
   172, 177–78, 216; dream interpretation opposition as, 172–73; exploring prevalence
   of dream opposition, 176; impact of dream
   opposition, 177–81; Jung's "dragon" as, 217;
   struggle between purity and, 203–4
Paul (Saul), 112–13
pauper's dream parable, 90
Peck, Gregory, 227
Perls, Frederick, 144, 145
Peter's waking vision, 110–11, 112
"petits chocs" (little shocks), 42–47
physiognomie (or *morphologie*) teachings, 43
Pirke Avot, 109
Pitron Chalomot (Almoli), 122
The Poetics of Space (Bachelard), 31
Potiphar's wife, 94
Pratt, J. B., 7
The Psychoanalysis of Fire (Bachelard), 31
psychology: definition of, 66; gap between soul
   healing and, 65–66

Raba (Babylonian sage), 19, 106–7, 118, 148,
   243n.56, 243n.67, 243n.68, 244n.78
rabbinic sages: on fall of the Second Temple, 10,
   106; influence on Freud's interpretation by,
   125–26; on interpretation versus direct revelation, 11–12; on Jewish lineage of authority,
   109, 111–12. *See also* Judaism
Rashba (Rabbi Shlomo ben Aderet), 29
Rashi, 235
Rebbe, Kotzker, 52
religious consciousness, 5
REM sleep: Dement's study on, 54–55; dreaming
   brain during, 55–57
repair (*tikkun*) principle, 35, 43, 45, 47
revelation: dreams as source of, 108; Genesis
   record on dream, 137; how manifest dreams
   become, 142; marginalization of dream,
   121; overshadowed by dream interpretation,
   11–12; wakeful vision as highest form of, 117
"reversing" trauma, 149
Re-Visioning Psychology (Hillman), 177
Ribash (Rabbi Isaac Ben Sheshet Barfat), 29
Ribera, José de, 86, 88
Rinchen, Geshe Sonam, 32
Robbins, Tim, 231, 232
Rose, Carol, 30

Sachachter, Rabbi Zalma, 28, 32, 51, 52, 108
Samuel, 104
Sand, Rosemarie, 136
Sarah, 83

Saul (Paul), 112–13
The Sayings of the Fathers According to Rabbi Nathan, 109
Schachter, Rabbi Zalman (Reb Zalman), 28, 30, 32, 51–53
Schmitt, Jean-Claude, 117
Scholem, Gershom, 18, 118
Schwartz, Charlotte, 16
Schwartz, Morrie: facing death, 15–16; initial meeting with, 16–18; last visit with and death of, 25–26; practicing visualization with, 21–23, 47; second gift. *See* soul
Second Temple, 10, 106
sefirot (hidden God), 118, 119, 120
"the Self" archetype, 218–19
Sephardic kabbalah tradition, 40–41
Shabbatai Zvi, 120
Shainberg, Catherine, 30, 47
Shapira, Rabbi Kalonymus, 89
Shapur II, King, 107
"the Shadow" archetype, 214, 218
Sheshet, Rabbi Jacob ben, 49
silence experience, 46
Simeon bar Yohai, 20, 119
Sistine Chapel, 39
soul: Bregman's identification of children with, 193; dream ability to change your, 210; dream interpretations of the, 194; essential image of, 230; *psyche* as meaning, 177;
soul healing-psychology gap, 65–66
spirituality: Bregman's "meat and potatoes," 222–23; Colette on regarding, 28, 29, 47
Star Wars (film series), 7
stratégie approach, 45–46
Sumerians, 80–81

Talmud: dream discussion in the, 79, 102–7, 115; *sefirot* (hidden God) mentioned in,118
The Ten Commandments (film), 8
Tertullian, 11, 115
THEY questions, 76, 77, 78–79
third gift. *See* archetypes
Thirty Years' War (16th century), 9
Thomas Aquinas, St., 7
Thoughts Without a Thinker (Epstein), 66
Tibetan Buddhism: on "conceptual mind," 38; meditation approach used in, 17, 30; *tum mo* (inner heat) technique used in, 34; visualizing Tibetan deities, 20

tikkun (repair) principle, 35, 43, 45, 47
time and space: dreams allowing "reversing" of, 149; dreams without boundaries of, 148–49
To Kill a Mockingbird (film), 227
Torah, 50, 51, 98, 99, 102
Tormented Master (Green), 52

The Trial (Kafka), 24
Tuesdays with Morrie (Albom), 15
Tulku, Tarab, 38, 67, 148
tum mo (inner heat) meditation, 34

"the uncanny" notion, 77
UNESCO study, 39
unio mentalis concept, 217–18, 227

Vermont Studio Center, 66–67, 78
VIP dream characters: Bregman's "animus" and "anima" for, 218, 224, 226, 227–29, 231–33; examples of, 198–201; gnosis knowing through, 227; identifying the female VIP in, 201–3; second gift of dream through male VIP, 205–10. *See also* archetypal dreams
Visions of the Night (Covitz), 53, 79
visualizations: Colette's teachings on, 18, 21, 23–24, 26, 30–36, 45–49, 230; Dalai Lama on power of, 28; kabbalistic meditations for, 20–21; merkabah mystics approach to, 18–20, 31; with Morrie Schwartz, 21–23, 47; *stratégie* approach to, 45–46; Tibetan Buddhism use of, 17; of Tibetan deities, 203; Zohar ("Book of Splendor") accounts of, 20. *See also* dreams
Vital, Chaim, 52
Vitruvian drawing (Leonardo da Vinci), 43, 44*fig*
von Wiese, Louise, 67

waking visions: "active imagination" for understanding, 214; Christian interest in, 117; Colette's work with, 47; Desoille's theory on, 34; distinction between dreams and, 117; marginalization of, 121; Peter's, 110–11, 112; warnings. *See* dream warnings
Wetti of Reichenau, 117
William T.'s dream, 140–41, 143, 145, 188
Wineman, Aryeh, 20
"wingspan" concept, 43–45
The Wizard of Oz (film), 173
word-image struggle: as beginning in Genesis, 9; described, 9–10; Freud's strategies for, 136–37; Joseph the interpreter's approach to, 136–37; ossification process of, 234; religious significance of, 9–10; sources of, 236–37. *See also* images

Yehoshua, 111
Yermiyahu, 111–12
yordei merkabah (descenders to the chariot), 18–20

Ziusudra, 81
Zohar ("Book of Splendor"), 20, 95, 118, 119
Zornberg, Avivah, 75

Plus:

History of Last Night's Dream
Reader's Guide   264

Dreams of the Father   268

Plus: **Insights, Interviews, and More**

History Of Last Night's Dream
Reader 's Guide

1. In chapter one, Kamenetz speaks of Western "religions of the struggle between the image and the word "(p. 9). What does that mean to you? What role if any have dreams played in your own religious experience? Have you ever seen the face of God in a dream?

2. Kamenetz teaches Morrie Schwartz (*Tuesdays with Morrie*) a visualization that takes him to "heaven." He links it to Jacob's ladder dream and the early mystics known as "chariot riders"? (pp. 22–23) Do you see the same connections? What do you make of the new names that Morrie and Laurel receive (pp. 25–26)

3. Colette Aboulker-Muscatt teaches that "images are sovereign in the mind." What does that mean? What is the difference between the "imaginal" and the "imaginary"? (p. 34) Do you experience images as powerful in daydreams or dreams?

4. In chapter 8 Kamenetz first meets his dream teacher, Marc Bregman, a former Vermont postman. What is your impression of Bregman as a teacher and how would you compare him to Colette (Chapters 3–5) or to other teachers you have known? Bregman approaches the "cop dream" (p. 71) "as if the cop in the dream had a motive, as if I had a choice in responding." What do you think?

5. The first "gift of the dream" in Genesis is the warning dream (chapter 10). Have you ever had a

warning dream? Did you change your behavior as a result of the dream?

6. The second gift of the dream relates to the dream of Jacob's ladder. Kamenetz points out that this dream is direct revelation, without interpretation. But "the promise of a dream is difficult to realize" (p. 88) Why is it so hard for Jacob to accept the reality of his dream? Discuss the parable of the beggar who dreamed he was a king. (p. 89) Have you ever had a big dream that shook you up and changed your life?

7. Kamenetz relates the third gift, "the essential image" to the story of Joseph the dreamer. According to Kamenetz, who are the first interpreters of the dream in the Bible? (p. xx) Discuss the difference between Joseph the dreamer and Joseph the interpreter. Why is this a turning point in the history of dreams and interpretation?

8. Kamenetz traces the struggle between dream and interpretation in the rabbinic sages and the church fathers (chapters 14–15). Discuss "dream amelioration" (p. xx) Why did the rabbis emphasize it. Do you practice your own form of amelioration?

9. In chapters 17 and 18, Kamenetz overturns Freud's theory that dreams are riddles to be interpreted. Instead he applies Marc Bregman's approach to Freud's dream of Irma. Which approach to Irma's dream seems more powerful?

10. In Chapter 4 Kamenetz refers to "the case of the disappearing dream" by which he means the loss of the revelation dream as a possibility in our own time. In chapter 18, (pp. 136–137) he brings the

case to a close, concluding that "the butler did it". What does this mean?

11. In chapter 9, Kamenetz introduces the dream of K de G, and in chapter 20 (pp. 146–147) he returns to that dream. Compare his first understanding (p. 79) to what he comes to at the end. What does the book of K de G mean by saying, "It's your genesis. It's your origin." (p. 146) How did his new understanding of the dream bring him closer to his father? Has a dream ever changed any of your close relationships?

12. Part three of the book describes a journey into dreams as a way of realizing the "three gifts of the dream" Kamenetz discusses in part two. In chapter 21, Kamenetz indicates that interpretation and amelioration cannot take us on this journey. What do you think?

13. In chapters 23–24, Kamenetz shows his own experience of "the opposition" in his dreams, as well as in Freud's and in his clients. Have you ever dreamed of the "opposition"? Have you ever seen yourself acting in dreams in ways that reminded you of your own worst traits or behaviors? What would it mean to take the warning in such dreams seriously?

14. Chapters 25 and 26 discuss the "situation of the soul", and how dreams can show us how the soul stands in relation to the divine. Discuss the "orphanage dream"(pp. 182–185) and the appearance of "the boy"(pp. 189–191) Bregman says, "Generally, children are an invitation. It's like the soul saying, "It's time to come down here to encounter me." (p. 193). What do you think? Have you ever

dreamed of children? What reaction did you have to children in your dreams?

15. Chapters 27 and 28 describes the male and female archetypes that Kamenetz nicknames the "VIP's". Have you ever encountered mysterious strangers in your own dreams? How did you react to them?

16. In chapter 31, Kamenetz describes yet another archetype, the "father", and he brings to a conclusion a sequence of dreams that begins with the lost and wandering dreams (chapter 22), and the orphanage dream in chapter 25. Discuss the "return to the orphanage dream" (pp. 228–229) The concept of the "hiding of God's face " (chapter 1) is no longer just an idea, Kamenetz writes, "now I felt that separation (from God) for myself." (p. 229) Why is this important? What does it mean emotionally—and theologically—that the father says to the orphan, "We have the same hand"? (p. 229)

17. In chapter 32, Kamenetz returns to the discussion of dreams vs. reality that began in Chapter 1. He asks, 'Can I really say that dreams are necessary to live a complete life? Can I say that dreams are real and that reality as we know it has its root in dreams?" (p. 237). Based on your experiences, how would you answer those questions?

Dreams of the Father

Rodger Kamenetz's latest spiritual trip is into the subconscious

by Jascha Hoffman

In 1990, Rodger Kamenetz traveled to Tibet with a group of American Jews to meet the Dalai Lama. On that trip, which he describes in *The Jew in the Lotus,* he happened to learn that some Buddhists meditate within their dreams. He began to wonder how dreams had been understood in Jewish texts and found that, while they had once been considered a source of revelation, dreams had been all but exiled from the tradition because they were deemed too disturbing or difficult to understand. As Kamenetz went deeper into his own dreams, which he calls "the oldest spiritual technology on the planet," he found that they did not have any explicitly Jewish content. But in their own strange way—as he recounts in his new book *A History of Last Night's Dream*—they did, over the years, begin to lead him back to something like God.

You say that dreams have been exiled from Judaism since Genesis.
There is a twin tradition. One is of the dream as direct revelation that requires no interpretation. That's embodied in the dreams of Joseph as a boy, and in Jacob's dream of a ladder between earth and heaven. And then there is the whole tradition of interpretation which actually begins with Joseph's brothers, who have been quite correctly identified as the first dream interpreters. Their interpretation is full of anxiety and rage.

And you see that same mistrust reflected in the Talmud.

To give them credit, I think the rabbis were concerned for the average person who may not want to take a mystical venture into dreams, or who may not be equipped, or who may be fearful. They also wanted to assert that the Torah is the primary spiritual guide. They limit the scope of the dream very severely based on a passage in Deuteronomy essentially saying that no dream can contradict the Torah.

How has this affected the way we understand dreams now?

Our own response to dreams is often that they're painful or that they are difficult. They bring up feelings we don't want to face and we call out for an interpreter who will remove the sting of the dream and soothe us. One can find this not only in the rabbinic project but in the Freudian project, which says that the real meaning of the dream is hidden. But in my view the real meaning of the dream is right on the surface.

You once dreamed of an enormous book that was keeping you from writing.

I walk into my study and I have this feeling I'm going to write something. But in front of the computer monitor is this very large blue book with the letters "K de G" on the cover. The author is the Rabbi K de G, which seems to stand for "Kamenetz on Genesis." The book reads from back to front and it appears to be a commentary on Genesis. As the dream ends, I'm thumbing through the pages from back to front and have completely missed the fact that behind the book, at a distance, was my father who had given it to me.

So the problem wasn't so much that this holy book was keeping you from writing, but that it was standing between you and your father?

The book was a gift from my father that could have brought me closer to him. A few years ago I had a dream where my house is falling down and I just call my dad and ask for help. And he comes with a bunch of painters and carpenters and suddenly the house is repaired. It was just the first in a series of dreams that helped to lead me closer to him. One of the great gifts for me was to have this different relationship with my father in the last years of his life.

And what was coming between you and your father in waking life?

My pride. There's another dream where we're sitting at a kind of Talmud study. My father knows what a certain word means and I don't. But I don't ask him; I think I can figure it all out for myself. I don't want to be the vulnerable son who needs help. But at a deeper level, this was not just about my relationship to my father, but about my relationship to the Father.

You hear people talk that way in church, but not as often in synagogue.

My answer would be two words: *Avinu Malkeinu*. Our Father, our King. Obviously Jesus said stuff like that because he also went to Rosh Hashanah services. There's a whole Yiddish tradition of referring to God as tateynu, as "dear Father." Our ancestors were very comfortable with the idea that God was a father and a king and a shepherd. But now if we have an emotional relationship to God, that's immediately seen as goyish. We have drained the feeling level out of our liturgy and then we wonder why people can't connect. They're not just words. If God is a father, then I must be like a child.

So how does God appear to you in your dreams?

At the end of the book, I describe a dream where an orphan boy is being visited by his father. The father shows him his hand and says, "My hand is the same as yours." Then the father leaves and the boy starts sobbing and looks in the mirror. And he's me: I see my face. That sadness of having lost the Father, in this case not my father but the Father, that yearning to reconnect, not to be an orphan but to be his son—that's the quest. It's rather like what Rabbi Nachman said: You have to connect to God from your broken heart. The dream reawakened the feeling of loss, the pain of the separation from God. It's a tremendous gift to feel that.

You've been studying under Marc Bregman, a self-styled "dreamworker" in Vermont.

Marc Bregman grew up as a Jewish kid in Philadelphia in a kind of anti-Semitic environment. He had a strict Jewish father and he rebelled in the 1960s. After he moved to Vermont he was working in the post office by day and seeing clients about their dreams at night. He's certainly not a traditional Jew or even a nontraditional one. But I know that he is a man of God.

And you have your own clients now. How do you work with their dreams?

We meet once a week for an hour. We try to find the feelings in the dream, the belly button, as Marc calls it. Then we have homework, which is to visualize a moment from one of the dreams that needs change. There's a rhythm back and forth from night dream to daydream and from daydream to actual life. Usually people come with a problem they're trying to wrestle with but the dreams often point to some underlying predicament. It could be other people's expectations. It could be family obligations, guilt, or a sense of duty. We just keep going

271

deeper and over time there's a shift. The dream becomes a live rehearsal. The changes you make in dreams can change how you behave.

In what sense is this approach to dreams Jewish?

When you're taking a dream seriously it becomes a spiritual practice. How does that connect to what's offered by this tradition we belong to where we have Torah and commentary and rabbinic authority and services and holidays and all of that? We struggle with a feeling of loss of connection to God. Religion tries to give us intellectual or ritual answers. People often outsource their spiritual struggles to the experts. Hence the tremendous pressure on rabbinic figures in our community. If we don't have a personal feeling of a quest, at least if some of us don't, then it makes the rabbi's job very, very hard.

Could you have understood your dreams without coming to them from a Jewish angle?

It seemed necessary for me to go through the books, to go through Genesis, to go through the rabbis. And yet it's true that having done that, it no longer seems quite as relevant. You can find the gift of the dream without Genesis. But it's promised there.

You had a series of dreams in which men kept trying to feed you meat.

I had alternated between various dietary restrictions from semi-kosher to vegetarian and wasn't too faithful to any of them. And all of a sudden these guys are showing up in my dreams serving meat. It started as hors d'oeuvres and ended with giant hunks of beef thrown on a grill by bare-chested Mexican chefs. It was obvious that these were good guys and that they were challenging me with a kind of a male generosity of spirit.

What did you dream last night?

Recently I dreamed I woke up and went to the window. I looked outside and the ground was covered with snow and I felt such joy. It took me back to being a kid in Baltimore thinking, I'm going to spend the whole day playing and I won't have to go to school. You worry and you plan, you try to make yourself happy, you try to make other people happy and then the snow just falls, you know? It falls on its own.

Jascha Hoffman is on the editorial staff of *The New York Review of Books.* This article originally appeared on nextbook.org on December 14, 2007

Plus: **Insights, Interviews, and More**

CPSIA information can be obtained
at www.ICGtesting.com
Printed in the USA
LVHW032017050819
626290LV00013B/85/P